The Media and Body Image

If Looks Could Kill

Maggie Wykes and Barrie Gunter

SAGE Publications

London • Thousand Oaks • New Delhi

First published 2005
Reprinted 2006

 SAGE Publications Ltd
1 Oliver's Yard
55 City Road
London EC1Y 1SP

SAGE Publications Inc.
2455 Teller Road
Thousand Oaks, California 91320

SAGE Publications India Pvt Ltd
B-42, Panchsheel Enclave
Post Box 4109
New Delhi 110 017

British Library Cataloguing in Publication data

A catalogue record for this book is available
from the British Library

ISBN-10 0 7619 4247 5
ISBN-10 0 7619 4248 3 (pbk)
ISBN-13 978 0 7619 4247 4 (hbk)
ISBN-13 978 0 7619 4248 1 (pbk)

Library of Congress Control Number available

Typeset by C&M Digitals (P) Ltd., Chennai, India
Printed in Great Britain by Athenaeum Press, Gateshead

Contents

1 Could Looks Kill?

Despite normal hunger, slender shape and a successful social life, many young women deprive themselves of nutrition to the extent that they risk serious illness and even death.' Epidemiological research has indicated that women's preoccupation with food and body shape is widespread, while the incidence of eating disorders such as anorexia and bulimia is on the increase. In the United States, a survey of over 2,500 schoolgirls aged between 13 and 18 found that more than three-quarters said they wanted to lose weight and two-thirds had dieted in the past year to lose weight (Whitaker et al., 1989). Even more poignantly, 8 per cent of this sample reported that they had vomited during the past year to lose weight, 2 per cent had used diuretics and 17 per cent, diet pills. The researchers concluded that between 0.2 per cent and 7.6 per cent of their sample could be considered as anorexic. In another American survey, it was reported that 20 per cent of young college females had claimed to self-starve (Pyle et al., 1990). Eating disorders can include anorexic or bulimic behaviour; the first involves the rejection of food and the second purging after eating.

Long-term studies have indicated a 20 per cent mortality rate after 30 years (Theander, 1985), and anorexia is very much like committing slow suicide. In the UK, recent research on 37,500 schoolchildren found 60 per cent of 14- and 15-year-olds felt overweight even though they were actually average and below weight. Dr Regis of Exeter's Health Education Unit commented that 'more effort was needed to stop teenage girls becoming obsessed with trying to emulate waif-like models' (*Daily Mail*, 27 October 1998).

The likelihood is that diagnosed eating disorders may only be the visible tip of a contemporary obsession with body shape that engenders addictive and/or destructive behaviours as a means of weight and shape control. Smoking, drug use, over-exercise, cosmetic surgery (Wolf, 1992) and self-harm may well also be part of the profound subjective dissatisfaction with their body image that is evident and prevalent among, young women in particular. Extreme weight control tactics are not unknown amongst young men but it has long been established that it is women who tend to exhibit more dissatisfaction with their bodies (Heunemann et al., 1966).

Body obsession has historical precedents, particularly in relation to religious ascetism and associated fasting (Bordo, 1993), but is arguably both different from earlier examples and more pervasive than ever before in contemporary Western culture (Counihan, 1999). The modernity of the apparent expansion of 'fasting' and its focus on the body rather than on the soul appears to parallel the explosion of the mass media over the past 40 years. Consequently, causal or probable relationships between media representations and body image have been regularly, theoretically posed since Orbach (1978), who briefly noted the tendency for the media to produce a picture of ideal femininity as 'thin, free of unwanted hair, deodorised, perfumed and clothed ... They produce a picture that is far removed from the reality of everyday lives' (1978: 20–21).

Body shape ideals

Anorexia and bulimia are behavioural syndromes. Body image is a psychological construct. While they represent distinct phenomena, however, they are frequently closely interrelated. In fact, body image concerns and a preoccupation with dieting among teenagers often emerge together (Byely et al., 2000). The 'body image' construct tends to comprise a mixture of self-perceptions, ideas and feelings about one's physical attributes. It is linked to self-esteem and to the individual's emotional stability (Cash and Szymanski, 1995; Thompson, 1990).

Clinical statistics based on medical treatment rates can be referred to in relation to anorexia and bulimia. Normative statistics of body image disturbance, however, are less easy to find. Most of the research on body image perceptions has been conducted with college student samples that are not representative of the general population. Such studies have been primarily concerned with investigating the antecedents of body image dissatisfaction rather than with establishing its national prevalence. In the United States, attempts have been made to produce statistics beyond college samples to indicate how widespread a problem negative body image might be.

During the 1970s and 1980s, the magazine *Psychology Today* conducted large-scale surveys of body image among adult men and women aged 18 to 70 years (Berscheid et al., 1973; Cash et al., 1986). A further nationwide US survey was conducted among adult women only (18–70 years) in the early 1990s (Cash and Henry, 1995). These surveys indicated that both men's and women's body image perceptions have become more negative over time (Cash and Henry, 1995; Cash et al., 1986). In 1985, three in ten (30%) American women said that they were unhappy with their overall physical appearance, a figure that increased to nearly one in two (48%) by 1993 (Cash and Henry, 1995).

In the UK, much of the evidence about the prevalence of body image satisfaction or dissatisfaction has derived from readership surveys run by glossy magazines. One survey conducted in 2000 by *Top Santé* was reported in a national daily newspaper as having found that half of a sample of 5,000 women with an average age of 37 years classified themselves as overweight. More than eight in ten (83%) said that they felt inhibited by their body and that their life would be considerably improved if they were happy with their body (Stevenson, 2000).

The same magazine conducted a further survey in 2001, and on this occasion 3,000 women with an average age of 38 replied. Once again, the great majority (85%) were unhappy with their shape and nine in ten (90%) said that their appearance depressed them. There was further evidence that women think a lot about their bodies. Whatever their size, over seven in ten (73%) reportedly thought about their size and shape every day and eight in ten (80%) felt that their lives would be considerably enhanced if they felt totally happy with their body (*Daily Mail*, 9 August 2001). The central concern of women as revealed by these surveys was that they felt they were too big. In the 2001 survey, the average respondent claimed she had tried to diet at least six times, with more than eight in ten (86%) saying they had dieted at some point, and around three in ten saying they had fasted (32%), displayed bulimic tendencies (31%) or anorexic tendencies (28%).

Yet not all the evidence from these surveys has been consistent. A survey of 3,000 women aged between 18 and 40 who were interviewed on behalf of Garnier cosmetics in Britain, the United States and Australia reportedly found that most said they thought about their bodies a lot. While many dreamed of improved physical attributes such as a flatter stomach (46%), firmer buttocks (20%) and shapelier legs (14%), when asked to name a celebrity whom they most admired for her body shape, the most popular choices (Kylie Minogue, 23%; Catherine Zeta-Jones, 15%; Jennifer Lopez, 12%) were preferred because of their shapely figures rather than for their slenderness (Lockett, 2002).

Locating a source of blame

Blaming the media for reproducing and extolling representations of unrealistic female bodies that influence young women to starve themselves has almost become a popular truism. Just as the mass media have been frequently accused of causing perceived increases in sexual and violent crime so they are now subject to a barrage of criticism for persuading young girls that thin is beautiful. Even medical opinion notes the media as a possible causal factor. Crisp argued that anorexia 'meets the psychosocial concerns of the person concerned' (1992: 5). He highlighted two major socio-cultural developments as contributing to its relative contemporary prevalence: the fundamentally altered nature of sexual relationships and mass media and communication.

Contemporaneously, within psychology, a growing volume of research since the 1960s has explored body image perception. The importance of the subject has stemmed, to a significant degree, from the association of certain idealized body images with disordered eating habits, the increased prevalence of which in some societies is recognized as a major health problem (Streigel-Moore et al., 1986). The core of body image dissatisfaction has been located within a discrepancy between the perceived self and ideal self. The ideal self-image may be considered as either an 'internal ideal' or a 'societal ideal' resulting from the dictates of the surrounding cultural and societal environment as to what constitutes the perfect body. Perceived-ideal discrepancies that cause dissatisfaction in relation to aspects of the body that are regarded as malleable, such as weight and the distribution of fat, are believed often to provoke attempts to narrow this discrepancy through such methods as dieting and exercise (Silverstein et al., 1988).

Explorations of eating disorders and related body shape perceptions have indicated that there are biological, psychological, social and cultural factors linked to symptoms of disordered eating. Any number of these factors may individually or collectively set the stage for the development of disordered eating (White, 1992). While such symptoms can occur among a wide variety of people (men as well as women), most of the research attention has centred on their more commonplace occurrence among young women (see Dolan, 1989; Schwartz et al., 1982; Stoutjesdyk and Jevne, 1993).

The appearance of body image dissatisfaction has been observed to emerge among young girls at the very beginning of their teenage years. Certainly, 13-year-olds have been found to report concerns with their body size and appearance that are in turn linked to lowered self-esteem. However, girls as young as 11 years have been found to exhibit similar perceptions in those cases of early arrival of puberty (Williams and Currie, 2000).

The emergence of body image concerns is important because it is frequently associated with the appearance of disordered eating patterns too. This is worrying when it occurs in the early teen years that are important physical growth years. The more dissatisfied young girls are with their bodies, the more likely it is that they will under-eat at this vital period of physical development (Griffiths and McCabe, 2000). Both parents and peer groups play a significant role in relation to onset of body image disturbance and disordered eating. Any suggestion of a concern on the part of a parent with their own body or the display of dieting on their part can create a psychological climate in which such behaviours are encouraged in impressionable teenagers (Vincent and McCabe, 2000).

Gender and body image

In academic and wider public discussions about media and body image, most of the attention is focused on the impact that media representations of body shape have upon women. This emphasis often disguises the fact that men, too, are increasingly defined by their bodies. According to Henwood, Gill and McLean (2002: 183), 'Patterns of consumption, lifestyle choices and media representations of men now often focus upon men's appearance and the male body. … Media advertising routinely depicts in positive ways youthful toned muscular male bodies or focuses on style in men's clothing and physical appearance'. What effects do these representations have?

Some writers have argued that media images can present ideals in terms of physique for men just as much as for women (Henwood et al., 1999). There is a need to consider the extent to which men's bodies are treated as commodities or objects to be gazed upon in the same way as had previously been claimed about the representation of women's bodies. The nature of any media impact in the realm of masculinity, however, must take into account the typical benchmark self-perception for men. While research has shown that women tend to regard themselves as bigger than they really are, for men the opposite is true. Men tend to perceive themselves as underweight and as thinner than they actually are and report a desire to be larger (Harmatz et al., 1985; Miller et al., 1980; Mintz and Betz, 1986). Men also overestimate both women's and other men's preferences for a large, muscular physique for men (Cohn and Adler, 1992).

As with women, society's view of men may have been shaped and reinforced by media images. The use and display of men in advertising could have served as a particularly potent social conditioning force in this context. It is pertinent to ask whether a muscular, toned, fit and hard-bodied ideal is being promulgated in respect of men in the same way as a thinness ideal is being projected for women. In comparing themselves to such an ideal, how are men affected? Does it leave them feeling anxious and less confident or less secure about themselves (Mort, 1988; Nixon, 1996)?

It has been suggested that men seek to embrace physical strength, hardness and power to reinforce the traditional masculine ideal – and at the same time to distinguish itself from ideas about femininity. The female form is traditionally conceived as soft and rounded, while the masculine form, in contrast, is taut and lean. The male preoccupation with abdominal stomach muscles in the face of a decline in physical labour and increased girth, embodies an attempt to hold on to this traditional masculine ideal of muscular strength and condition (Baker, 1997; Henwood et al., 2002).

Body image studies among men have begun to demonstrate that men can display as much dissatisfaction with their bodies as do women. Furthermore, this finding has occurred in a number of different countries.

One study of college-age men in Austria, France and the United States found that, across all three countries, young men chose an ideal body shape that was considerably heavier and more muscular than the shape they judged they currently had. They also believed that women preferred a male body that was heavier and more muscular (Pope et al., 2000). With women, lower body self-esteem and higher body dissatisfaction have been found to motivate a drive for thinness. A comparable drive for muscularity has been hypothesized to occur among men who are unhappy with their body image. Boys and young men who are dissatisfied with their current body shape have been found to display a drive to put on weight in the form of more muscle (McCreary and Sasse, 2000). Anecdotally, this tendency has been linked with male magazines' emphasis on muscular physiques for men (and the 'six-pack' stomach) which, in turn, is believed to have created a climate in which young men are encouraged to take drugs such as anabolic steroids to achieve the body they want. Abuse of such drugs can lead to serious health problems, including impotence, heart disease, cancer and violent mood swings (Chapman, 2000).

Given changes in gendered roles and the growing socio-cultural emphasis on looks and grooming, it may well be that men feature more and more frequently with poor body image, low self-esteem and consequent self-harming or mental health problems but there is no doubt that currently it is overwhelmingly a problem of and for young women. So this book focuses first and foremost on femininity and the representation of female bodies. It also focuses on Western cultures, particularly the United States and Britain, where eating disorders appear to be pandemic. We again acknowledge, however, that this may well not be a static situation and the future may see a more universal incidence of self-starvation.

Cultural standards of beauty

In Western societies especially, a general preference for a thin body shape has become established as the norm. Culturally, however, this is not yet a universal phenomenon, nor indeed has it been consistent even within Western nations. Many societies have associated a plump physique for women with attractiveness and in some cultures obesity has been admired (Ford and Beach, 1952; Rudofsky, 1972). For over 30 years in Western societies, however, young females have reported more positive attitudes towards a small body size and thin physique, with the exception that a well-developed bust is often preferred (Calden et al., 1959; Nylander, 1971).

Large-scale surveys have produced consistent evidence that the desire to lose weight is prevalent among many national populations, especially among women (Button et al., 1997; Davis and Katzman, 1997; Serdula et al., 1993; Streigel-Moore et al., 1996). However, the positive connotations of a slender body shape occur very frequently in Western cultures. A thin body shape is associated with success personally, professionally and socially (Bruch, 1978). At the same time, food – perceived as a cause of loss of thinness – can take on a negative hue for many women (Chernin, 1983; Orbach, 1978). The pleasures of food represent a temptation that must be brought under control through rigid and restrictive eating patterns for the greater good of attaining some socially sanctioned beauty ideal.

Despite the early observations of cross-cultural differences in body shape ideals, evidence has begun to emerge that Western-style concerns about body shape occur in non-Western populations, particularly among individuals who have had frequent contact with Western people and their culture. One study of young white and Asian women living in London and young Asian women living in Lahore in Pakistan who were English-speaking found similar associations between body dissatisfaction and attitudes to eating throughout all three groups. All the women who participated were recruited from slimming and fitness gyms in both cities. The youngest women in each case exhibited the greatest body image dissatisfaction (Bardwell and Choudry, 2000). A further study conducted among young women in South Africa found that eating disorders linked to body self-esteem were prevalent across black, white and Asian women (Wassenaar et al., 2000).

Other research has confirmed that similarities in judgements about physical appearance and attractiveness can occur across cultural groups, but some subtle differences also prevail. An American study presented figure drawings to Caucasian, African American and Hispanic college students who were asked to choose figures that most closely matched their current body shape, the body shape they would most like to have, the shape they felt would be found most attractive by the opposite sex, and the opposite-sex figures they found most attractive. Dissatisfaction with body shape was greatest among women regardless of ethnicity. However, both men and women misjudged which shapes the opposite sex would rate as most attractive. The women guessed that the men preferred shapes thinner than those they actually reported. African American women, however, had the most accurate views about what men would find attractive, and Caucasian women held the most distorted views in this respect. The men, throughout, guessed that women preferred shapes bigger and bulkier than those actually indicated by the women (Demarest and Allen, 2000).

Norms of feminine beauty in Western culture, however, have varied considerably over time (Goodman, 1995; Seid, 1989; Wolf, 1992). Although female attractiveness was once epitomized by a plump body shape, the contemporary ideal, at the close of the twentieth century, emphasized a slender body. As we will see in more detail in later chapters, researchers have documented this cultural shift by showing that female magazine centrefolds, beauty pageant contestants and female models have become thinner over time (Garner et al., 1980; Seid, 1989; Wolf, 1992).

The impact of this changing ideal for feminine beauty is further exemplified by the increasing pervasiveness of dieting among women, especially young women. Polls conducted in the early 1960s (Wyden, 1965) on a nationwide sample of adults in the United States found that over 30 per cent were especially concerned about their weight. Only 10 per cent of overweight adults were dieting, another 20 per cent were trying not to gain weight and another 40 per cent were concerned but not doing anything about it. A separate poll by the same author showed that such concern rarely led to corrective measures (Wyden, 1965). In contrast, other research reported that as many as 70 per cent of high school girls were dissatisfied with their bodies and wanted to lose weight (Heunemann et al., 1966). Over subsequent years, further polls of American youth revealed that 30 per cent of high school girls and 6 per cent of boys were dieting on the day they were interviewed, although only 15 per cent of the girls, but 19 per cent of the boys were overweight. Furthermore, over 80 per cent of girls, but fewer than 20 per cent of boys expressed a desire to weigh less and over 40 per cent of girls had been on a diet by their senior year in high school, whereas only 24 per cent of their male cohorts had ever dieted (Dwyer et al., 1967, 1969, 1970). By 1977, the percentage of college women either on diets or consciously trying to control their eating in order to keep their weight down was up to 82 per cent (Jacobovits et al., 1977).

Coincident with this increasing norm of thinness, rates of body dissatisfaction and eating disorders among women have risen (Silverstein, Peterson et al., 1986). Research on body image has indicated that women consistently perceive themselves as overweight (and as heavier than they actually are) and report a desire to be thinner (Cohn and Adler, 1992; Mintz and Betz, 1986). Women also tend to report an ideal body size that is significantly thinner than their perceived actual body size (Cohn and Adler, 1992). Finally, women overestimate both men's and other women's preferences for female thinness (Cohn and Adler, 1992). Explanations for these different perceptions have increasingly pointed to the media and to claims that an idealized, slender female form is over-represented with possible harmful consequences for the self-perception of women who do not see themselves as complying with the stereotype of acceptable feminine beauty.

Certainly, the cultural standard of beauty in relation to body shape is promulgated, to a significant degree, via the major mass media. Modern institutions of advertising, retailing and entertainment produce vivid notions of beauty that change over time. These mediated 'ideal' images place pressure upon women in particular to conform to the body image currently in vogue. During the 1950s and early 1960s, the major media of the day focused upon the upper torso of women, placing emphasis upon the aesthetics and sexual allure of a large bosom. Subsequently, this body fashion was replaced by an emphasis upon being slender and, concurrently, many young women, not clinically diagnosed as anorexic or bulimic, nevertheless expressed dissatisfaction with their bodies. Their main concern is the avoidance of becoming overweight (Cash, 1990). Some writers have harshly criticized the mass media for playing a powerful role in conditioning women to adopt the thin standard as the ideal body shape (Mazur, 1986).

Yet, despite the criticisms levelled at the media in this context, surprisingly little work has actually addressed either the nature of media representations of the body or the ways in which audiences may interpret and use such images. During the 1990s, this position began to change. A few studies, mostly in the United States, of the antecedents of body image perceptions and disordered eating propensities place special emphasis on the mass media as potential causal agents (for example, Botta, 1999, 2000; Champion and Furnham, 1999; Grogan et al., 1996; Harrison, 1999, 2000a, b; Harrison and Cantor, 1997). In the UK, in 2000, the British Medical Association (BMA) agreed with academics Levine and Smolak that there 'is a great deal of theorizing and media criticism, available but far too little systematic research' (BMA, 2000: 31). A summit meeting held at 10 Downing Street (the British Prime Minister's office) in June 2000 confirmed both general concern about self-starvation and the need for more research into the role of the media.

About the book

This book starts to address the lack of research on the media, body image and eating disorders by bringing together new empirical work on both media representations and audience responses, within a broad discussion of socio-cultural change, gender politics and self-identity. It is joint-authored in two parts, to investigate textual work (see Wykes, 1998, 1999, 2001, 2003) and audience research (see Gunter, 2000) as rigorously and informatively as possible. The introduction and conclusion compare and contrast the two theoretical paradigms and analyse the differing methodological approaches and findings critically and creatively.

Part One, entitled Media Representations focuses closely on textual theory and analysis. It overviews theories of eating disorders, subjective identity, history of representation and the role of socio-cultural discourses. It investigates the contemporary 'moral panic' over the media and the body and the lack of detailed analysis of the mediated material blamed for the current health crisis by theorizing the role of the mass media in gendered discourses and analysing textual examples from print and screen. Part One concludes by integrating the findings of detailed analysis within the broader debates of the role of the media, gender norms and values, health, sexual politics and commerce.

Part One comprises Chapters 2–5. Chapter 2, Dying to be Thin, focuses closely on the history of eating disorders and reviews medical, psychoanalytic, sociological and feminist research. It argues that any proper understanding of behaviours and concepts, which are suicidal at worst, frequently socially disabling and even at the level of least harm, inhibiting and damaging to self-esteem for many young women, must look beyond the tip of the iceberg that presents as diagnosed anorexia or bulimia. It argues that the media works on the body in much more subtle and broad ways than simply the promotion of a thin aesthetics and that the pursuit and promotion of slenderness is in many ways a metaphor and sometimes a disguise for a whole range of perceived gender norms within the agenda of sexual politics. The chapter argues that thin is a feminist issue because it is symptomatic of a context within which power works to construct very particular models of acceptable femininity in a range of discourses such as the family, the law, religion and, most systematically, covertly and invasively, the media.

Chapter 3, Body Matters, explores the history of the representation of the body and reviews theoretical work on the body as a cultural construct. It places self-starvation in the context of other body dysfunctional and displacement activities such as self-mutilation, drug abuse, over-exercise, fashion and cosmetic surgery in order to better understand how women are so subject to seeing themselves as 'deviant' bodies. The chapter considers what are desirable, normal, acceptable looks in our culture and how such norms are disseminated and by implication what is considered abnormal and other than desirable.

Chapter 4, Print: Selling Sex and Slenderness, argues that glossy magazines, although not innocent of promoting a thin aesthetics, are not solely responsible for constructing gender norms and values and that the slender-is-sexy norm would only be 'saleable' if it fitted into wider mediated concepts of gender and identity. The chapter uses the press as a case study for identifying those concepts and their prevalence, because newspapers remain the most sourced form of media in the UK, with some 14 million newspapers sold daily. It considers Julie Burchill's claim that the *Daily Mail* has created thousands more anorexics than *Vogue*, (*Guardian*, 8 July 2000) by analysing newspapers in order to assess the nature and extent of engagement in gendered discourses, direct or indirect. It looks both at coverage of 'thinness', particularly in relation to stars and models (Lena Zavarone/Kate Moss), and broader representations of women. It then focuses on the glossy magazines that have been blamed for the anorexic epidemic. Jess Carter-Morley, a fashion editor for the *Guardian*, epitomized the populist view of the role of women's magazines in causing eating disorders when she wrote 'surely it is time for the glossy magazines and designers who demand and promote an extremely thin body shape to take a more responsible attitude' (*Guardian*, 31 May 2000). The chapter explores the ways in which femininity is narrated for the reader in popular magazines for teenage girls and young women and asks what the implied value judgements are and whether women are being manipulated. Drawing on semiotics, narrative theory and critical discourse, the analysis interrogates the 'sites' so vehemently attacked by newspaper journalists, medics and MPs during 2000 for causing young women to emulate 'waifs' and 'heroin-chic' and assesses the evidence that magazines sell slenderness as part of sexual attractiveness and social success.

Chapter 5, Starring Roles: Screening Images, extends the analysis of the mass media from print to electronic forms by looking at television and the World Wide Web. It explores the ways in which stars move both across performance arena and between media forms and how their iconic status might make them influential on young women, particularly when few other women ever feature in the mass media in any positive way. It considers the contexts of representation, particularly looking at contemporary women's serials, and assesses the rapidly growing Web as both a source of information about femininity but also of interaction between women and girls.

Part Two of the book, entitled From Media Representations to Audience Impact inverts the focus of Part One on the media and texts by arguing that any account of media meanings is necessarily partial without concern for the audience. Research on the representation of body image in the mass media spans more than 30 years. Within the context of communication effects, studies of body image portrayals in print and broadcast media have raised a number of theoretical explanations of media influences on, and methodological approaches to, this particular domain of human experience. The section shifts from concern with analyses of body image representations *per se* and the interpreted possible reasons for, and consequences of, these to audience research that seeks to elicit evidence of effects or correlations from media users themselves.

Chapter 6, From Representation to Effects, focuses closely on the psychological processes that suggest that political, medical and public opinion that the media affects attitudes and behaviours is well founded. It explores why women seem more concerned with shape and size than men and why slenderness has positive connotations for the female self. The chapter looks at theories relating to role models, covetousness, aspiration and pre-existing mental schemas and assesses their validity and value as a means of explaining the role of the media in the phenomenon of self-starvation.

Chapter 7, Media Exposure and Body Image Ideals, moves from theoretical approaches linking the media to body image and self-identity, to considering the methods that have been used to test effects theory. It looks at what has been learnt by surveying audiences in order to test for correlations between role models and self-perception. It contextualizes self-image and represented image in cultural norms and contexts.

Chapter 8, Media Causation and Body Image Perceptions, turns to experimental methods of seeking causal relations between media models of femininity and young women's attitudes to and behaviours around their bodies. This chapter reviews studies designed to test cause–effect relationships between both magazine and television accounts of female shape and size and audiences' reported self-esteem and body perception.

Chapter 9, The Media and Clinical Problems with Body Image, moves to research on 'clinical' populations of women specifically diagnosed with eating disorders. It looks at the differences between 'disordered' and 'normal' eaters in terms of their attitudes to and behaviours around food and the media.

Chapter 10, Conclusion: Body Messages and Body Meanings, compares and contrasts the approaches to media images and self-perception explored in this book. Both approaches have their own particular strengths and weaknesses. We consider to what extent these might inform better theoretical models and methodologies relating media representations of the human body and public conceptions of body shape. We review what has been elicited from the research undertaken for this book and, in the context of calls for closer self-monitoring of body representations by the mass media and their producers, discuss whether there are any policy-related recommendations or other kinds of action or information that might usefully intervene in the process whereby 'looks could kill'.

PART ONE   Media Representations

2   Dying to be Thin

Eating disorders can include anorexic or bulimic behaviour; the first involves the rejection of food and the second purging after eating. In both the ultimate goal is to be thin. Moreover, although there are occurrences of anorexic males, the gender bias of the disorder is definitely female. Approximately 90–95 per cent of those diagnosed as anorexic are female and it is particularly prevalent among women in certain careers such as ballet, sport and modelling (Malson, 1998). There is no doubt about the contemporary problem, nor any doubt that interventions and research are both necessary and timely. Although obesity remains a far greater threat to British health than starvation,[1] during the past few years the problem of young girls systematically starving themselves to death has become a growing area of medical, psychological and finally political concern. In 1994, research in Australia amongst schoolgirls found that '16 per cent of the pre-pubertal girls and 40 per cent of the girls who had passed their menarche perceived themselves as too fat' (Abraham and Llewellen-Jones, 1997: 8). In the United States some estimates report that 20 per cent of young college females self-starve (Pyle et al., 1990).

Although primarily still a disease of the Western, and more affluent, white world, cultural imperialism is spreading the ideals of frail, pale femininity globally via the media, making the investigation of and explanation for eating disorders an urgent matter. The media have been repeatedly targeted as causal of the escalation of eating disorders:

> We now have damning evidence from Fiji of the impact of Western ideals of beauty where, in a three-year period after the introduction of TV (mainly US programmes), 15 per cent of the teenage girls developed bulimia. The penetration of Western images coupled with an economic

onslaught, had destabilised Fijian girls' sense of beauty, infecting them with a virus more lethal than the measles Britain exported to the colonies 100 years ago. (S. Orbach, 'Give us back our bodies', *Observer*, 24 June 2002)

Increasingly, the media are seen as somehow responsible for the apparent growth of eating disorders in a range of discourses including health, politics and, ironically, the media itself. Certainly the mass media are a relatively modern phenomenon and their rise does seem to parallel the escalation of a kind of thin fascism but whether they are causal of any phenomenon or merely reflecting socio-cultural issues has been contentious in many other areas of work on the media, most notably around the effects of sexual or violent material on audiences.

This chapter considers the historical context of eating disorders and the epistemology appropriate to them in order to assess why earlier work has not found ways of preventing self-starving illnesses and how the media have come to be a focus for concern. It explores history to clarify the similarities and differences between self-starving in different epochs. This enables a critical account of the contemporary context by eliciting the circumstances peculiar to the onset of the third millennium. It also looks at the evolution of theoretical and interventionist approaches to the illness, again critically, in order to explain the arguments for not just further work but work of a different kind to be done on why young girls are dying to be thin.

Dying to be thin: transcending the body

Eating disorders are not a millennial phenomenon. Orbach (1978) documented the history of problems in the UK and Bordo (1985, 1993) traced a long history of anorexia in the United States. This history merits attention because it informs a legacy of theory and associated practices of intervention that do not appear to be equipped to resolve the contemporary problem. Moreover, it is a history that clearly demonstrates the full extent to which the female body, whether desirable, displeasing or damaged, has been subject to and described according to the male gaze in a range of discourses. The history of the disordered female body is also necessarily the history of orderly femininity. It is also a history of gender relations because women's bodies were the object of male authoritative experience and knowledge until and arguably beyond the later twentieth century.

The body has always been a site of struggle, in that the mind can conceive of it, exists within its confines but can only partially control it. This duality of body/mind has generated much philosophical enquiry and remains a pivotal underwriting of contemporary debates not least within theories of anorexia. Deriving from Plato,[2] body and mind are seen as bifurcate: disjoined components irrevocably interdependent until death. The mind is the seat of the essential self bound to the material form of the organic body. The body thus becomes a problem, it is the 'other' the 'not self'; alternatively, it may be seen as a confinement or cage that traps the spirit or will. For Descartes,[3] control of the body was the intellectual pursuit.

More extremely, St Augustine saw the body as an enemy inhibiting spiritual truth and so requiring but resisting control. The goal was transcendence of corporal desires, hungers and functions in order to find the true self, the inner spirituality that in Christian terms is the route to God.

Bell (1985) cites 261 cases of female starvation for religious reasons between 1206 and 1934. Of these 261 fasting women, 181 (more than two-thirds) lived between 1200 and 1600 A.D. with many being elevated to sainthood. In addition to fasting (often to death) these 'holy' anorexics castigated their bodies, refused offers of marriage and sought refuge in religious orders. Many were sanctified for their alleged ability to communicate with Christ. (http://www.geocities.com/gina_rlp/history. html, accessed 20 February 2003)

Corporal greed, whether for food or sex, was viewed as evidence of the grossness of the flesh; it follows that control of such greed is evidence of the strength of self-will and the route to transcendence. In the fourteenth century chastity and fasting, occasionally until death, were symptomatic of sanctity:

Contemporary records construe Catherine of Siena's fast as an admirable and holy expression of piety. Her death was not presented as a regrettable or tragic culmination of disease or disorder. (Malson, 1998: 51)

Such religiosity is rare now in the Western Judaeo-Christian world but the philosophical legacy remains deeply embedded in our culture. Bordo even claimed that 'although dualism is as old as Plato, in many ways contemporary culture appears *more* obsessed than previous eras with the control of the unruly body' (1993: 149) and cites the diet and exercise industries as evidence of this. A spiritual explanation for the self-flagellation of starvation, extreme exercise and even self-mutilation does not sit comfortably in our largely secular and materialist culture in the twenty-first century but it may be that a memory of such routes to eternal approval sits deep in the Western psyche.

Ascetism is not a term that appears regularly in the literature on self-abuse and is almost totally absent in modern work on anorexia or bulimia yet both these are about purging the body, cleansing it and dimini-shing it, often in a highly disciplined regime. Excess of flesh or of fleshly pleasure or pleasure in flesh are linked to negative terms such as stupor, greed, passivity, placidness, poverty, un-attractiveness, lack of control, inactivity, idleness, idiocy and onanism. To be fat is to be the butt of jokes, to be viewed as a 'couch-potato', to be subject to the body. The real self is disappeared in folds of flesh and what cannot be seen cannot be known or valued or loved. For ascetics, controlling the appetite and paring away the flesh exposes and releases the spirit from the domination of the body. It is a route to self-knowledge and the start of the journey to God. Perhaps today it is even more difficult to gain a sense of self in a complex, polysemic world that denies unity, fixity and security. Moreover, in the agnostic, atheistic and multi-faith complexity of the early twenty-first century such goals lack the language of unchallenged Christian articulation. Instead, discourses of spirituality and self-reflection tend to be subsumed beneath the weight of meaning generated by two institutions that have largely superseded Christianity as the doctrine of personal growth and well-being, namely medicine and psychology.

Hysterical women

Self-starvation perhaps more than any other modern health phenomenon brings together the knowledge disciplines of the body and the mind. The rise of science and pursuit of scientific knowledge during the eighteenth century slowly brought self-starvation under the remit of medics. The growth of Protestantism during the period also saw the steady diminution of extreme Catholic practices of asceticism and by the nineteenth century fasting was being seen less as evidence of piety and more as a medical problem. Scientific scepticism and Protestant dislike of the extremities of Catholicism saw resistance to any idea that fasting was any evidence of godliness or a reason for admiration. Benson (1999) also suggests that the male priesthood resented the attention and adulation given to 'miraculous' girls and readily sought to expose them not as saintly but as sick or sinners.

Critics of those who associated fasting with religiosity argued that the early instances were less pious attempts at giving up food for Christ as evidence of devotion or purity and more evidence of a long history of the existence of anorexia nervosa. Some also suggested that many such famous cases were fraud or actually caused by disease. Malson refers to the work of Hammond (1897) who 'criticized the religiosity of many early descriptions of "fasting girls" as unscientific, claiming that they were probably cases of deception, fraud or organic disease' (1998: 52).

The early accounts of anorexia as a disease refer to it as a wasting illness, a form of consumption or distemper without the accompanying cough and fever. The early eighteenth century supported a buoyant and growing medicine, which theorized much illness as caused by the 'fluctuating equilibrium of internal fluids, spirits, appetites and "souls"' (Porter and Porter, 1988 in Malson, 1998: 54). These shifts in the humours of the body might be caused by nerves or imagination so illness was seen as a manifestation affecting the whole person. Although technically medicalized and a-theological, the similarities between explaining fasting as an act of will over the body to reach God and an act of imagination impacting on the proper function of the body are evident. Also evident in these diagnostic accounts was a recognition that remains in contemporary accounts of the role of the mind in disordered eating.

The relationship between body and mind was envisaged as enabled or disabled by the 'nerves'. Nervous sensitivity became almost a fashion in the early nineteenth century and was thought to indicate superior individuality. Nervous diseases and ailments were very much the symptom of the middle classes of Jane Austen's England. Hypochondria was seen as evidence of a suffering soul and treated with relative sympathy compared to our modern cynicism. Physical ailments of many kinds, but particularly gastric, were explained as resulting from nerves.

Commensurate with this development was the commercialization of the perceived problems that gave rise during the Victorian period to an interest in spas, health resorts and medical treatments. That link between body, anxiety and capital remains buoyant today and highly relevant to any enquiry into eating disorders or other body-changing processes. Also key to more contemporary debates was the gendering of nervous illness during the nineteenth century. The term 'hysteria' etymologically refers to a disorder of the womb that affects other parts of the body and is, by virtue of its association with women's reproductive system, quintessentially feminine. By association of nervousness with hysteria, nervous complaints readily became female ailments. Malson (1998) saw this connectivity as the origin of the discourses within which the contemporary phenomenon of anorexia nervosa would emerge.

> Hysteria was a condition assigned to women in the same way that eating problems today are considered endemic to women's existence. Although we are accustomed to thinking of hysteria as the disease of the bourgeois woman, it cut across class lines in both the United States and England. In the earlier part of the nineteenth century imprecise nosology meant that hysteria gathered into itself all manner of distress symptoms. Some of these by definition cancelled each other out, others meant that 'hysteria' became a convenient catch all for any kind of physical and mental stress experienced by women. (Orbach, 1993: 6)

Orbach points out that although hysteria crossed class lines it was middle-class women who frequented the medical profession and were perceived as frail and sensitive; working-class women were viewed with suspicion as deceitful and idle. Nervous dispositions became a marker of class sensibility associated with delicate and romantic femininity. The ideal woman was passive, pale, modest and maternal. She was seen as subject to her reproductive system, which rendered her emotional, faint and often confined to the home. It is possible to see such constructions retrospectively as conveniently oppressing and containing women within the burgeoning patriarchy of Victorian England.

In many ways hysteria was the nineteenth-century equivalent of eating disorders. Although men could and do suffer from both, they are usually seen as female complaints. They also tend to be associated not just with femininity but with female sexual attractiveness and reproduction. Even when hysteria was theorized as largely mental in origin the association of the condition with the uterus not only feminized the condition but constructed a model of femininity infused by sexuality, so long as that sexuality was related to maternity. The womb came to stand for the whole woman. Mort (1987) saw this representation as central to Victorian sexologists, theorizing that distinguished between the 'sexual bourgeois lady and the sexually depraved working-class prostitute' (Mort, 1987: 61). Respectable women were seen, according to the venerealogist Acton, *as not very much troubled by sexual feeling of any kind.* Acton was an active campaigner for the regulation of prostitution, which was viewed as a source not just of moral corruption but of disease. Women were effectively divided into good/asexual/middle-class and bad/sexual/working-class. In both instances they were seen as weak, morally, mentally or physically, and therefore in need of either care or control. The authority of patriarchy was well served by such constructions.

The closeting and controlling of Victorian women created narrow, limited lives, and towards the end of the nineteenth century psychologist Sigmund Freud (1856–1939) and women themselves began to theorize hysteria as relating to that suppression or repression. For Freud, hysteria might be the result of unexpressed and negatively evaluated sexual feelings, 'the "unspeakability" of such traumas was what led to their somatization' (Benson, 1999: 139). In writing about his patient Dora, for example, he states: 'gynaecophilic currents of feeling are to be regarded as typical of the unconscious erotic life of hysterical girls' (Freud 1905/1983: 98).

In contrast, for the emergent feminists of the suffrage movement hysteria was likely to be caused by the broader inhibitions enforced on women. Driven to law-breaking in their struggle for reform and the vote many went on hunger strike as a means of asserting control over their own bodies, rather than being subject to the control of men and the state.

> The government's response to this protest in the form of force-feeding is yet another example of the notion that control of the female body is not something that resides with its owner, the individual woman, but is an area to be contested. (Orbach, 1993: 7)

The suffragette hunger-strikes dramatically demonstrate the limited range of expression available to women at the turn of the century. Their actions were frequently labelled mad and 'hysterical' by the press (Young, 1988), enabling them to be ignored in Parliament and denigrated in popular opinion.

Hysteria came to be seen as a manifestation of Victorian culture; it was a means of expression for women otherwise repressed. In many ways it seems the polar opposite context to the contemporary quintessential female 'disease' – anorexia nervosa. Women today are sexually liberated and socially enfranchised. The problem seems to be not restriction of choice but explosion of choice. None the less, there are clear links between these two conditions: each is female, manifests during the reproductive years, tends to be viewed as middle-class, involves mental and physical symptoms and relates closely to identity and self-image.

Anorexia nervosa

Some of the major symptoms of hysteria are lack of appetite, vomiting, diarrhoea or digestive problems for no obvious physical reason. By the 1870s the phrase 'hysterical anorexia' was introduced into the medical vocabulary. Although the presenting disorders were gastric not uterine, the assumption that the cause was nerves informed the use of the term hysteric, suggesting once again that it was the womb which was somehow implicated and that this was a female disease. The absence of menstruation in sufferers further re-enforced the link to female sexual organs. The problematic relationship of the anorexic to food was seen as impacting on the whole family, wherein food and the family table were central to bourgeois life. So by 1880 links were being made between self-starvation, mental health, sexuality and family, links that remain the underpinning of the treatment of eating disorders today. Those links also underwrote the medicalization of family and sexual life:

> sex appeared as an extremely unstable pathological field: a surface of repercussion for other ailments, but also the focus of a specific nosography, that of instincts, tendencies, images, pleasure, and conduct. This implied furthermore that sex would derive its meaning and its necessity from medical interventions: it would be required by the doctor, necessary for diagnosis, and effective by nature in the cure. (Foucault, 1978 in Easthope and McGowan, 1992: 92)

That medicalization defined who had the right to 'control the body, define the parameters of sickness and health and to pronounce on sex' (Mort, 1987: 171) and, of course, to distribute authoritative representations about those areas.

Two medical papers, published by Lasegue (1873) and Gull (1874), placed anorexia clearly on the medical agenda[4] and defined the tropes for the following accounts. These tropes were that the illness was feminine; that it was a disease mainly of young women; that patients were middle-class or even wealthy; it manifested as a food aversion, usually because the patient claimed to suffer pain or discomfort after eating; there was no evidence of organic disease; childish behaviours were identifiable; obsti-nacy was a personality trait; and patients presented as nervous or rest-less, sometimes theorized as being due to young women's too great exposure to education and social activity. Missing from these was any sense that anorexia was caused by a desire to be slim; rather, slenderness was seen as a result of the disease rather than part of the cause. Throughout, 'the figure of the morally and physically weak woman in need of patriarchal control and medical authority was never far away' (Malson, 1998: 74).

The increasing scientism of the early twentieth century saw a strong shift towards explaining anorexia in organic terms. Because the disorder seemed to be seated in the digestion, the endocrine system became the focus for bio-medical research. A malfunctioning pituitary gland was seen as the likely cause because of its association with amenorrhoea, hair loss and fainting from low blood pressure – all evident in anorexia. Yet although the search for an organic explanation continued through-out the twentieth century, and continues, no satisfactory aetiology has been unearthed. None the less, the medical profession remains deeply involved in the explicatory, diagnostic and treatment processes. It is part of a twin approach to self-starvation in uneasy partnership with psy-chological approaches. The focus on nerves and mental states in early studies of anorexia inevitably led to the involvement of psychology in its diagnosis and treatment. Freud's work linking physical symptoms to mental distress was deeply influential and by the 1940s 'psychosomatic' illnesses were subject to international research. Self-starvation has been linked to personality disorders, hindrance of sexual maturity and lone-liness, but each of these may result from self-starvation rather than cause it. Psycho-medical discourses remain deeply influential because the fatal possibility of the illness necessitates their intervention, but by the point at which malnourished girls are brought to their attention, they are clearly dealing with the effect of the condition on the body and mind *in extremis*. The volumes of their representations of the body, health and sex remain authoritative and inform popular representations in our mass media. Yet no single satisfactory explanation has been achieved either for the illness itself or the apparent current escalation of its incidences.

Fasting girls: modern psycho-medical approaches

Despite the recent onslaught on the media as the source of all social ills, including anorexia, the area of self-harm remains mostly researched and theorized within a medicalized context, unsurprisingly given that most sufferers only come to the attention of the academic community when they are in desperate need of either medical or psychiatric intervention, or both. These approaches focus on either body or mind and remain dominant in informing treatment paradigms.

As with other conditions of illness, medicine and psychology act on the mind or body after affliction when it is the symptoms of illness that characterize the individual. For medicine the data that are presented are physical and the resulting theories of causes also tend to look for physical causes. The evidence of a starved body is explained as biological. In parallel, psychological theories for the construction of subjectivity necessarily inform theories for the destruction of self that is an eating disorder.

Contemporary medicine still seeks organic causes for eating disorders but is deeply compromised by the organic and bio-chemical malfunction that is actually caused by malnutrition. Recent work is inconclusive at best and contradictory at worst, which is worrying given that the US National Institute of Mental Health supports research showing *the mortality rate for anorexics is 12 times higher than the annual death rate due to all causes of death among females aged 15–24 in the general population* (Sullivan, 1995).

Medical interventions focus primarily on restoring weight loss and maintaining weight gain but remain active in seeking organic causes in the hope that they may find evidence that supports pharmaceutical treatments. Although the boundaries between psychological and biological pre-disposers to disordered eating are blurred there are some areas where organic cause can be identified as possible and worthy of research. One such area is genetic predisposition. The US website ANRED (Anorexia Nervosa and Related Eating Disorders) states:

> In fact, people with a mother or sister who has had anorexia nervosa are 12 times more likely than others with no family history of that disorder to develop it themselves. They are four times more likely to develop bulimia. (Eating Disorders Review at http://www/anred.com/causes.html, accessed 24 February 2003)

The Priory Hospital, Roehampton, London concurs. Its website states: 'There is an increased risk in families in which there are other anorexics and this probably indicates a genetic predisposition' (http:www.priory-hospital.

co.uk/htm/anorex.htm, accessed 24 February 2003). It may just be, of course, that anorexic learning environments stimulate eating problems.

Linked to this approach is some work on infant feeding patterns which suggests that mothers of anorexics tended to schedule their feeds more rigidly and wean those babies earlier than did mothers of normal adolescents (Steiner et al., 1991). However, whether such actions are due to mother/child genetics or taught/learnt syndrome seems impossible to ascertain.

Rare but more clearly organic is the phenomenon of Klinefelter's syndrome, which has been linked to anorexia caused by the gender identity anxiety accompanying the syndrome that is present in males and results in them developing female sexual characteristics (El Badri, and Lewis, 1991). Treatment with testosterone has been found to help such chromosome-disordered males.

In females the sex hormone oestrogen has also been researched as relevant to the fluctuating menstrual cycle and childlike characteristics of anorexics. It is certainly diminished in the body by starvation with possible consequences for fertility and bone density, and some studies recommend treatment with oestrogen to counteract such damage. At the specialist Priory Hospital Eating Disorders Clinic 'Patients may be offered supplements such as zinc, oestrogen, calcium or vitamins' (http://www. prioryhealthcare. co.uk/patinfo/eatprog.htm, accessed 27 February 2003). Confusingly though, another study claims that the *female sex hormone, estrogen, contributes to the symptoms seen in anorexia and underlies the sex difference in incidence* (Young, 1991: 327–331). This study argues for the prescription of progesterone to block the effect of oestrogen in anorexics.

Other work revisits the history of anorexia by focusing on causes that have a direct affect on appetite and digestion. Gastric motility studies have suggested that eating disorders relate to delays in intestinal transit of food (Kamal et al., 1991). Such delays may lead to pain, constipation and bloating. The former symptoms might lead to anxiety about food and its relation to discomfort. The latter might cause anxiety about weight gain. Yet again a further study refutes this claim by finding no difference between the electrical gastral activity in eating-disordered and normal children. (Ravelli et al., 1993). Other research found evidence of different electro-motile activity but concluded this was caused by, rather than causal of, the anorexic condition (Buchman et al., 1994).

Another approach, focusing on digestion, sought evidence of irregularity in the production of peptides associated with feelings of satiety. Korner and Liebel (2003) reported that peptides associated with feelings of satiety were more efficient in the anorexic subjects than in the control group. This may help explain why it is so difficult to reverse anorexic eating patterns. But the difference in speed of satiety may result from starvation and body adaptation to deprivation rather than cause it. Only a, probably impossible, trial that established accelerated levels of satiety peptides in normal weight individuals immediately prior to appetite loss and the onset of anorexia could indicate cause.

Glandular activity has also been investigated in the search for explaining anorexia. An over-active thyroid can result in weight loss but patients respond to treatment with drugs such as carbimazole or even to surgery to reduce the size of the gland and hence its production of thyroxine. Evidence of an over-active thyroid in anorexics may, however, simply be due to the anxiety associated with the condition (http://www.dotpharmacy. co.uk/upthy2.html accessed 28 February 2003) and the body's natural response to stress.

Irregularity in brain function and even tumour have also been related to anorexic outcomes. Brain tumour germ-cells were found in the hypothalamus of a sample of emaciated patients. As this part of the brain is associated with food regulation it has been hypothesized that such lesions might predispose towards anorexia (Chipkevitch 1994). Other work on the brain has theorized that serotonin levels could cause mood change including a tendency to obsessive and morbid behaviours that might result in self-starvation. Kaye et al. (1991) related such disturbances in serotonin in acute anorexia but point out that these might be due to a reduction in essential amino acids, precursors to serotonin production, because of abnormal diet.

As well as investigating biological reasons for eating disorders medics have studied the impact of substance abuse on body size and function. The abuse of drugs and alcohol was found to co-exist with eating disorders in a study presented at the International Conference on Eating Disorders 2002 by staff from the Harvard Eating Disorders Center. The study found that substance abuse alongside eating disorder was more likely to result in morbid depression and ultimate death (Dorer et al., 2002). However, it did not establish whether substance abuse contributed to the onset of eating disorder or whether the addictive processes of anorexia and bulimia indicate a personality disorder, making the patient more likely to be both a self-starver and a substance abuser.

Psychological interventions focus on the treatment of mental health disturbances which may either be causal of, or the effect of, malnutrition. These include personality disorder, addictive–compulsive behaviours, low self-esteem, anxiety or depression. The difference between such approaches and the medical model is that the latter concentrates on what physical event or component causes self-starvation whilst the former asks why an anorexic selects self-starvation and resists weight gain as treatment. The two approaches encapsulate the separate sides of the mind/body dualism that seems to lie at the heart of understanding the condition. For Crisp (1992: 78):

The diagnostic term anorexia nervosa is unsatisfactory. If it is to survive then it needs to be buttressed by a recognition that rather than nervous loss of appetite, there is a massive embargo on eating or retaining ingested food because of its implications for weight gain. The initial determination to diet and the progressively intense 'pursuit of thinness' (Hilde Bruch's term) crystallizes out as an overwhelming terror and panic of normal adolescent/adult body weight.[5]

The historical data on anorexia reveal how broadly the same condition can realize itself and be theorized differently in different cultural conditions. It is possible to argue that '[t]he discontinuity of history and the mutability of the individual are mirrored in the changes – of content as well as form – which self-starvation underwent throughout history' (Vandereycken and Van Deth, 1994: 9). The historiography of anorexia tells the story not just of the disease but of gender, culture and authoritative institutions. Of those institutions, psychology more than any has adapted and changed its conceptualization of the ailment. Today we hear little of saintly visions or humours or hysteria and rather more of personality/ identity problems and anxiety in accounts of eating disorders. One constant remains, that it is overwhelmingly an affliction of young women.

Psychiatric explanations for anorexia seek evidence of personality disorders of various kinds which might theoretically manifest in self-starvation. For diagnosis, personality disorder must include several symptoms from a range that features:

> Unstable relationships; impulsive behaviour, that is harmful to the person (including spending, sex, substance use, shop-lifting, reckless driving and binge eating); variable moods; undue anger or lack of control of anger; recurrent suicide threats or behaviour; uncertainty about personal identity; persistent feelings of boredom; and frantic efforts to avoid real or imagined abandonment. (Abraham and Llewellen-Jones, 1997: 40)

One of the obvious problems with this diagnosis is that many of these feature are socio-cultural rather than psychological; another is that some of these features may easily result from, rather than cause, eating disorders, for example due to the physical effects of malnutrition on sexual behaviour. Other aspects of personality theory include the idea that obesity is a compensation for loneliness and feelings of isolation: filling her stomach becomes a substitute for a full life.

In contrast, women with identity problems related to sexuality may refuse food in order to refuse growing up as starvation inhibits both menstruation and the physical shape of womanhood. This latter deeply Freudian model assumes a problematic relationship between father and daughter whereby either the daughter seeks to retain the affection a father who has become less demonstrative as his daughter becomes womanly or the anorexic senses the sexual interest of the father in her blossoming body and, fearing that, resorts to the safety of childhood by starving (Dare and Crowther, 1995: 131). Such theories may well inform understanding of eating problems but they are problematic in that not all or even many patients diagnosed with personality disorder demonstrate a consecutive eating disorder. Also they point to situations outside of mental health in the family and culture as contributive.

More pragmatically, cognitive approaches to eating disorders mostly start from a point where the teenage girl, often slightly subject to 'puppy fat', chooses to diet in order to achieve the slim figure that is very much the desirable norm in modern Western cultures. Initial success in rejecting food results in pleasure at the feeling of emptiness, in pride and self-satisfaction at dealing with the problem of food, then praise and admiration for the new shape and perhaps an end to being teased as fat, which in turn reinforce and validate the effort at dieting. The problem with such a simple model is that the kind of reinforcement it identifies disappears when the anorexic becomes clearly malnourished.

Other cognitive models suggest that the goal becomes not the slim shape but the sensation of starvation or the feeling of control. Anorexia is thus similar to an addiction and dependency disease like alcoholism: 'eating is seen as withdrawal, which leads to negative consequences, such as feelings of tension. The anorexic is afraid of, and avoids, this situation' (De Silva, 1995a: 143). So simple behavioural approaches work better at explaining anorexics' continuation of diet until ill health than they do at explaining the initial move to food avoidance.

Social psychological approaches begin to shift the focus from intra-individual issues to a concern with personal relationships, family, peer group and broader socio-cultural pressures on identity and behaviour. Anorexics are very often described as struggling with self-identity:

> People with eating disorders often lack a sense of identity. They try to define themselves by manufacturing a socially approved and admired exterior. They have answered the existential question, 'Who am I?' by symbolically saying 'I am, or I am trying to be, thin. Therefore, I matter.' (http:www.anred.com/causes.html, accessed 9 March 2003)

Part of that lack is addressed by perfectionism, by setting very high goals in all aspects of life. Typically, an anorexic will be an academic high-flyer, possibly a good athlete and very often slim and attractive, yet still feel valueless. The family has been theorized as in some way contributing to that sense of dissatisfaction with the self. In fact, the defining paper by Gull (1874) suggested that anorexics should be removed from the family for treatment.

Many aspects of family relations and behaviours have been cited as relevant to the low self-esteem linked to disordered eating: over-protectiveness, too much criticism, sexual abuse, marital discord, repressed emotionality, maternal food disorder, absent father and issues with siblings all occur in the literature (Bruch, 1973; Gull, 1874; Motz, 2001; Roberto, 1988; Stern et al., 1981). Such variety of family contexts suggests no single cause of or treatment for the illness that can be simply family-based. In fact, the complexity of the family as a system can confuse and mask rather than enlighten, or worse:

> Theories of family causation have also had the effect of blaming families, which only increases the paralysing guilt experienced by many families and hinders therapeutic endeavours to find solutions. (Colahan and Senior, 1995: 244)

So, although family context features frequently as in some way relating to disordered eating because eating disorders place a huge strain on family relationships, it is difficult to unravel cause and effect. At best it may be possible to say that in some families, some children (anorexia may affect just one of a group of siblings) find it particularly hard to move from childhood to adulthood and prevent that by body-inhibition. The normal need for a child to grow away from childhood may be curtailed by blurred and dysfunctional family boundaries that inhibit the develop-ment of self-identity – the resulting anger and sense of grief becomes inter-nalized leading literally to self-punishment (Motz, 2001).

An extreme family dysfunction, sometimes cited in the literature, is sexual abuse (Abraham and Llewellen-Jones, 1997; Motz, 2001; Palmer et al., 1990). The act of self-starving is viewed as a way of the victim of incest gaining back some control over her body, a way of punishing the abuser and a way of reversing the sexual development that the anorexic may blame for the abuse. At first glance, the reported rates of sexual abuse amongst eating-disordered patients seems significant; 'most cluster around 30 per cent' (De Silva, 1995b: 158), perhaps twice the rate for a mentally and physically healthy community. However, the disparate methodologies used to collect the data make any general conclusion impossibly hypothetical. Moreover, this rate of reported abuse 'is no higher than that found among patients suffering from other psychiatric disorders' (Abraham and Llewellen-Jones, 1997: 54), confounding any correlation between sexual abuse and the specific condition of self-starvation.

Refusing food simultaneously rejects a fundamental aspect of familial relationships whilst developing a parallel dependency around the illness; 'eating disorders generally weave a web from which it is difficult for family members to extricate themselves' (Colahan and Senior, 1995: 256).

But the particular turn to anorexia remains largely unexplained by mainstream family theory and therapy. As with other psycho-medical models, too many possible causal factors appear to exist to establish any kind of aetiology, and also as with other approaches, the presumed cause may even be an effect of the anorexic dynamic. A simple example might be that an anxious mother of a self-starving girl may become over-protective, or food faddishness may alienate and draw criticism from siblings. Although these approaches recognize the disease as peculiarly female, none really uses that major clue to inform theory beyond thinking about the biological essence of the female sex. But the distinguishing component of eating disorders is femininity (Malson, 1998) and by the late 1970s feminists were beginning to think about femininity in much broader terms than sex-type. They were looking politically at gender norms and roles and then most recently at the cultural construction of gender.

Thin is a feminist issue

Outside of the treatment discourses of medicine and psychiatry, which each deal with the effect of the disease and cure rather than prevention, much of the effort made to deal with anorexia focuses on trying to make sense of it. This has led to a critique of the psycho-medical model, and a further broadening out of discourses of explanation. The gendered nature of the sickness[6] has drawn feminist attention and theorized the body as a site of political struggle.

In 1970 Susie Orbach went to a group meeting in New York to discuss with women their body image and relationship to food. She describes the shock of discovery that, in the heady days of second-wave feminism with its illusion of liberation, so many women were obsessed with looking *right*, and so were both compulsive eaters and compulsive dieters. In *Fat is a Feminist Issue* (1978) Orbach focused on why women over-eat to the extent that they then need to lose weight. She argued that for many women fat was a kind of self-defence, a protection from the pressure on women to conform, to be sexual and to be attractive. For Orbach, the 1960s and 1970s were confusing and risky times for women. Expectations of them changed dramatically, particularly around sexuality, with women under pressure to both conform to their mothers' generation's model and be virginal brides and home-loving mothers but they were also being enticed by contraception and an increasingly sexualized culture to explore and enjoy their sexuality. Orbach argued that the explosion of sex into the public sphere alienated many women from their bodies and their desires – sex was for sale. For some, the anxiety about how to *be* sexually was resolved by not appearing sexual because they ate too much or too little to conform to an attractive image.

In the distortion of body size that follows the manipulation of hunger feelings, the anorectic and the compulsive eater powerfully indict sexist culture. The young woman takes herself out of the only available sexual arena and worries that should she express her sexual feelings her whole world will crack. (Orbach, 1978: 173)

Controlling the size of her body, Orbach argued, was an assertion of self and a protection of self in a world where the private and personal area of sexual identity was being commodified and publicized according to masculine needs and desires. Fat, and thin, became feminist political issues rather than issues of female biology or psychology.

In the decade from 1973 to 1983 many books on the politics of women's size were published (Boskind-White and White, 1983; Bruch, 1973, 1978; Chernin, 1981, 1983; Millman, 1981) and the feminist influence began to affect work on eating disorders. Although different in emphasis, these texts were common in their recognition that the social, economic and sexual situation for Western women in the late twentieth century was in some way related to the prevalence of eating disorders. Counihan (1999) defined that situation, affecting women's relationship to food and thereby size and shape, explicitly as:

The contradictory expectations of families for girls; the objectification of women and the degradation of their sexuality; the institutionalised cultural, political and economic powerlessness of women and the cultural slighting of female experience and female values. (Counihan, 1999: 77)

All authors saw obesity and anorexia as two sides of the same coin, as did Orbach (1978); each saw patriarchy as implicated in women's alienation but each still tended to focus closely on family and sexuality as the places informing identity. Each also argued that to overcome eating problems women need support to develop a strong sense of identity. Group therapy and support groups were seen as important.

In the 1970s and 1980s the message seemed to be that women had internalized a male view of themselves, on a micro level through the family and on a macro level through cultural forms that conflicted with a newly self-aware femininity, sexual liberation and growing social equality. Women were therefore caught between old and new discourses with the body the field of battle and food the weapon. The resolution presented in much of this work was to stop fighting: 'We need to revalue ourselves, supporting each other in our refusal to be blamed, framed or shamed any longer' (Fursland, 1986: 15). Nearly twenty years later eating disorders continue to increase, suggesting that either second-wave feminism achieved very little and women remain in the same turmoil about themselves, or that feminist models of eating disorders were wrong and the proposed resolution was inappropriate, or perhaps that the disordered body remains culturally central but not for the same reasons.

Although much of the early feminist writing commented briefly on the feast of femininity and food on offer in the media, shop windows and advertising hoardings as contributing to distorted concepts of the self and associated self-harm, there was still amongst this work an adherence to a psycho-medical approach to eating problems, not surprisingly as many of the authors were counsellors or medical practitioners who had been approached by affected women. That trend continued into the 1990s (Dolan and Gitzinger, 1991). What is left unexplained by such individu-ated feminist work is how women might be pressured to 'look' a certain way, why for only some that pressure leads to obvious self-harm, why some men appear vulnerable too and why eating disorders are so much a product, and an increasing one, of the contemporary Western world.

By 1986, Orbach was overtly blaming the promotion of a thin aesthetic for anorexia by suggesting that if the media began to promote fatness they would have the power to define a new aesthetic. In her introduction to the revised version of *Hunger Strike* (1993), she claimed journalists were part of an unconscious conspiracy to 'send women back' to domestic servility by claiming either that feminism failed, or succeeded so women don't need to struggle any longer:

> At the same time advertisements and media copy portray today's (Super) woman (for none of us are merely women any more) in the same hack-neyed and limited aesthetic. Slim, white and youthful. (Orbach, 1993: xxii)

Frequently, when other theories seem wanting, the mass media have been blamed as if they have enormous propagandizing power over people, and that has certainly happened around anorexia since the turn of the century, but that attribution rarely explains how the media might impact on the (de)construction of the body or why. That lack, or rather taken-for-granted model of both media content and media effect, is of course what underwrites this book. So much of what has been claimed about the role of the media in the construction of body image parallels the claims made about the media promoting violence (Barker and Petley, 1997; Gunter et al., 2003; challenge this) or the media causing sexual perversion or abuse (Dworkin, 1981, 1991 adheres to this). The first half of this book theorizes how media texts bear meaning and then analyses those texts – factual and fictional – to assess Orbach's (1993) claim. The second part explores how audiences might gain meaning from the media, and with what implications, in order to interrogate the effects debates in relation to body image.

Diet and discourse

Language as the vehicle of culture and identity has been the focus of a cultural turn in work on social relations, norms and roles since the later 1970s and 1980s. Increasingly, feminist work drew attention to, and continues to emphasize, the construction of meaning in a range of discourses – criminological (Heidensohn, 1985; Young, 1988, 1990, 1996); psychological (Holway, 1989); political (Weedon, 1987). Each of these has seen work on language as a route to understanding gendered norms and behaviours. Others concerned with different social issues such as racism (Fowler et al., 1979; Van Dijk, 1987), sexuality (Foucault, 1981) and political or class conflict (Glasgow University Media Group, 1976, 1980, 1982, 1985; Hall, 1973) also began to consider language as both a powerful technology and material data.

The turn to language inevitably meant a turn to the media, already a site of academic research and concern since the Frankfurt School.[7] The origin of effects theory lies in the model of the media developed in the 1930s as a response largely to Hitler's use of radio, film and photography. The Marxists of the Frankfurt School viewed the media as a hypodermic syringe literally pumping ideology into a supine audience on behalf of powerful groups. Media messages were seen as irresistible and the means by which in Marxist terms *the ideas of the ruling class became the ruling ideas.* The mass media for this model is a tool of the powerful and acts to gain consensus to the operation of power by affecting the consciousness of audiences. 'The signifying systems which constitute the sphere of ideology are themselves viewed as the vehicles through which the consciousness of social agents is produced' (Bennett, 1982: 51). So dominant groups maintain dominance not by brute force enabled by economic authority but by winning over to their view of the world the *hearts and minds* of the broader population.

The idea of ideology rather than economy as the means of social stratification and reproduction alongside the bourgeoning in breadth and frequency of the mass media after the development of television informed major theoretical shifts in social epistemology. These shifts were compounded by the significant socio-cultural upheavals of the 1960s and 1970s, including the struggles for equality by black people, women and gays. A simple determining model of class ideology shaping subjective consciousness via the mass media seemed to fall apart in the face of the industrial unrest of the late 1970s and 1980s. Also, civil rights and antiracist movements, second-wave feminism and gay pride drew attention to domination as working not just in economic terms but in a range of identity discourses. These struggles made clear that people were not simply propagandized into compliance by media messages but were active agents who could interrogate the stories they were being told and accept, reject or negotiate with them according to their other experience

(Hall, 1973). The idea that language as a sign system somehow just directly transmitted irrefutable meanings to audiences via the mass media could not explain the changes sought and wrought by oppositional groups. Nor could a model of society that preferred economics as the determining power explain the systematic oppression felt by women, black people and gays. Structuralism in the Marxist sense, whether economic or linguistic, was not working as an explanation for social relations in the late twentieth century.

For feminists, the major failings of Marxism were its lack of address to patriarchy and its fundamental pessimism and fixity, which suggested little hope for a more egalitarian society in any terms. Two redresses were necessary. First to look for evidence of patriarchal ideology in cultural texts, and particularly in the mass media, that might be reproducing masculine values and interests, and secondly to find a way of explaining and encouraging the difference and potential for change that inform feminist politics.

> To say that patriarchal relations are *structural* is to suggest that they exist in the institutions and social practices of our society and cannot be explained by the intentions, good or bad, of individual men or women. The social institutions which we enter as individuals – for example the family, schools and colleges, teenage fashion and pop culture, the church and the worlds of work and leisure – pre-exist us. We learn their modes of operation, and the values they seek to maintain, as true, natural and good. As children we learn what girls and boys should be, and later, men and women. These subject positions – ways of being an individual – and the values inherent in them may not all be compatible and we will learn that we can choose between them. Whatever else we do we should be attractive and desirable to men. (Weedon, 1987: 3)

For Weedon, recognizing the way patriarchal power operates on women's subjectivity is the essential first stage in the process of changing both social institutions and women's self-identity. That requires beginning by identifying meanings in socio-cultural forms that address gendered themes and assessing their potential to reproduce patriarchal power – the textual work of this book. Then the actual impact on women's lives and sense of self form the level of analysis for the second part of the book.

Eliciting meanings from text and evaluating them in terms of gender and power requires both a feminist approach that is politically conscious of and actively seeking patriarchy and a post-structural theory of discourse. Post-structural theory focuses on language as the mechanism through which social life is made sense of, communicated and contested. However, whereas structural models assume a shared, unitary and fixed set of meanings, post-structuralism recognizes differing, multiple and changing meanings, So, for example, British miners could be called the 'backbone' of the country during the years of World War Two but became the 'enemy within' during the strike of 1984–5 (Waddington et al., 1991). Similarly, anorexia was a means of meeting God in the middle ages but a slimming disease in the late twentieth century. Meanings are therefore not intrinsic to simple language forms. They depend on their structural place in syntagms of terms (clause, sentence and narrative) and on comparison within paradigms (girl equals human but not adult and not male), but more than anything on culture, history and subjective experience. Meanings therefore are a site of struggle wherein different groups try to express their experience and validate their identity. The ability of groups to attach their interest and values to language and disseminate them depends on the extent of their authority at any given historical moment. Once authority is challenged so the rectitude of the meanings generated will be questioned. They will be deconstructed.

Deconstruction is key to a post-structural reading of text. Post-structuralism recognizes that any text can yield a range of meanings but will tend to yield first and foremost the meanings conducive to groups with most power in everyday life. By deconstructing texts, by questioning meaning and looking for other possible meanings, it becomes possible to expose whose meanings are preferred in the reading. To do that requires a critical reading position that looks for evidence of dominant interests rather than accepting the ideas presented as fact. Clark (1992) does just this in analysis of news about sex crimes that exposes a discourse of blame in the courts and newspapers which labels women as provoking men to rape by their dress or drinking rather than criticizing men's inability to control their sexual behaviour.

A feminist, post-structural approach to writing about, and images of, women's bodies should similarly try to identify who benefits from that material and how and why is that happening now in the twenty-first century. Foucault (1981) argued that the *hystericization* of women by medical science, literally reducing them to an essential biological section of their body, the womb, was 'central to the reconstitution of social norms of femininity, the patriarchal subjection of women and their exclusion from most aspects of social life' (Weedon, 1987: 109) throughout the nineteenth century. For Foucault the body, as the site of sexual and social reproduction, is inscribed with meanings according to the needs of power. Analysing the inscriptions on the contemporary female body, therefore, may not only help with understanding the phenomenon of self-starvation but also reveal something about broader gender and social relations.

Blaming the media for self-starvation makes theoretical links between text, the construction of meaning and the construction of the self. Not only must this book identify possibly damaging media messages but it must also show how they might affect young women. Theorizing the potential impact of any such meanings on subjectivity involves understanding how language might construct subjectivity and, in the case of eating disorders construct it in ways that promote self-destruction. A post-structural theory of discourse necessarily leads to a post-structural model of consciousness and thereby identity. Because consciousness depends on language (Lacan, 1976), if meanings are not fixed in language then meanings are not fixed in consciousness either, rather the subject is always in a process of construction – always subject to discourse and open to change. This makes the subject the active agent making choices between discourses, learning, playing and contributing.

> In the battle for subjectivity and the supremacy of particular versions of meanings of which it is part, the individual is not merely a passive site of discursive struggle. The individual who has a memory and an already discursively constituted sense of identity may resist particular interpellations or produce new versions of meaning from the conflicts and contradictions between existing discourses. (Weedon, 1987: 106)

However, the individual who has little memory or a troubling set of memories or little sense of identity, however complex and polysemic, may find the struggle and confusion disabling and resist the inscriptions. Such an individual may even in anorexic terms try to evade the inscribing by ceasing to exist. A body that is a site of struggle for a confused and disabled self may simply become a problem to be removed.

The overt link to spiritual questing, the rejection of the material and the corporal sufferings that characterized the fasting of the late Middle Ages were redolent with meanings of transcendence and empathy with Christ's mortification.

> In contrast, what is striking about modern anorexia is its apparent *lack* of cultural meaning. Modern bodies can no longer be pressed into service as links to the divine; modern bodies appear to speak only to themselves. Thinness is an end in itself. (Benson, 1999: 138)

Or maybe the diminution of or annihilation of the body transgresses the problem of becoming feminine. ' "Fading away" may signify a resistance to a number of socially available subject (im)positions' (Malson, 1998: 186) either consciously (perhaps politically as a rejection of the roles available to women or possibly even spiritually in the search for transcendence from impossibly binding body roles that characterized ascetic fasting) or unconsciously as a means of easing the pain of identity crisis. If simple suicide were the goal there are less painful and quicker ways to achieve death; analysing discursive contexts and available meanings may help explain why so many young women are specifically dying to be thin.

Summary

Although self-starvation has historical precedents, when it was associated with religious ascetism and associated fasting (Bordo, 1993) or theorized as a nervous response to the oppressive patriarchy of Victorianism, it is arguably now both different from earlier examples and more pervasive than ever before in contemporary Western culture (Counihan, 1999). Yet it is also in many aspects the same. The act begins with self-starvation, either by fasting or purging; it is overwhelmingly performed by women; it is mainly associated with youth and pubescence; it effectively de-sexes the body; it is very difficult to treat, recurs and is often fatal. It is different now in that it seems to have become an epidemic rather than a rarity and the goals are perceived as slenderness not piety or respectable femininity.

The history of anorexia reveals both continuity and change. Change in theory led to change in treatment and yet increase in occurrence. That increase coincided with both the burgeoning of the mass media in the later twentieth century and the political thrust of second-wave feminism. These two have impacted on theories of eating disorders as feminists worked critically within the psycho-medical institutions to implicate patriarchy in women's struggles with themselves. Such approaches saw a problematic construction of gendered identity as implicated in anorexics and feminists first turned to the family and then to culture for evidence of the patriarchal ideology they felt was confusing and harming women's sense of themselves and their worth. Within that paradigm work on the construction of or, in the case of self-harming behaviours, destruction of the self increasingly turned to language and to the media as its most pervasive form of dissemination, rather than to essence and nature, either psychological or biological, to explain women's actions, relations and identities.

The further contemporary change is that eating disorders are understood as primarily, if only initially, related to the thin aesthetic that characterizes idealized contemporary woman. Whereas in earlier epochs thinness was a side effect of religious fasting or nervousness it is now seen as the goal of the anorexic, in fact of very many women. That change in perspective has occurred in a context since the 1960s of an expanding fashion and beauty market; increased female spending power; the growth of youth culture, feminism and mass media coverage of women's lives and issues.

In the next chapter the current construction of femininity is reviewed and anorexia is re-contextualized outside of psycho-medical discourses and within other discourses that shape the feminine in the contemporary West. The chapter considers who benefits from body-shaping, who defines what the shape is to be and why the media have become such a site of concern for those worried about young girls systematically committing suicide by self-starvation.

Notes

1   Over 30,000 deaths a year are caused by obesity in England alone. Adult obesity rates have tripled since 1982. Now 19 per cent of Britons are obese and 39 per cent overweight. http://www.bbc.co.uk/science/hottopics/obesity/fat.shtml (24.02.03). See 'Tackling Obesity in England' Report by the Comptroller and Auditor General HC 220 Session 2000–2001: 15 February 2001 HMSO.

2   Plato's fourth-century 'Allegory of the Cave' in Plato's *'Republic VII'* offers an example of the concept of dualism, with humans viewed as chained and shackled so that all they can see or know is via the shadows of themselves thrown on the wall they face. The goal is to be free from the shackles and go to the light which throws the shadow so that they can see reality.

3   Rene Descartes (1641) *Mediatones de Prima Philosophia* saw the knowledge of the self as the only certainty resulting in the familiar 'I think therefore I am' and the philosophical dualism that separates self/mind and body/matter. How these two interact and connect remains a central philosophical debate.

4   For a full discussion of these two papers see H. Malson (1998) *The Thin Woman*, London, Routledge, pp. 61–69.

5   Hilde Bruch has written extensively on eating disorders, including H. Bruch (1973) *Eating Disorders*, New York, Basic Books; H. Bruch (1978) *The Golden Cage*, Cambridge, Harvard University Press.

6   'Only an estimated 5 to 15 per cent of people with anorexia or bulimia … are male' (A.E. Andersen, 'Eating disorders in males', in K.D. Brownell and C.G. Fairburn (eds) (1995) *Eating Disorders and Obesity: A Comprehensive Handbook*, New York, Guilford Press, pp. 177–187.

7   Started by Marxists in the the 1920s in Germany, the group included Adorno, Marcuse and Horkheimer. They left Frankfurt for the United States in the 1930s, deeply concerned about the propagandizing potential of the mass media, especially radio and film. 'The Frankfurt School in general was profoundly pessimistic about the mass media. As Janet Woollacott puts it, their work "gives to the mass media and the culture industry a role of ideological dominance which destroys both bourgeois individualism and the revolutionary potential of the working class" (Woollacott, 1982: 105)', quoted by Daniel Chandler at http://www.aber.ac.uk/media/Documents/marxism/marxism08.html.

3 Body Matters

This chapter contextualizes eating disorders within other body-morphing activities to consider how our culture produces looks that threaten to kill those who aspire to them. Any proper understanding of behaviours and concepts, which, for many young women, are suicidal at worst, frequently socially disabling and even at the level of least harm, inhibiting and damaging to self-esteem, must look beyond the tip of the iceberg that presents itself as anorexia. Placing self-starvation in the context of other body design, dysfunction and displacement activities such as self-mutilation, drug abuse, over-exercise, fashion and cosmetic surgery makes it possible to view it as a symptom of a broader process of subjective (de)(re)construction. That contextualizing process clarifies what are presented as desirable, normal, acceptable looks in our culture. It also highlights what sustains an environment where many women see themselves as 'deviant' bodies.

The likelihood is that diagnosed eating disorders may only be the visible element of a contemporary obsession with body shape that engenders addictive and/or destructive behaviours as a means of weight and shape control. Smoking, drug use, over-exercise, cosmetic surgery, diet (Wolf, 1992) and the potential for self-harm may well be part of the profound subjective dissatisfaction with their body image that is evident and prevalent amongst young women in particular but not unknown amongst young men.

This chapter begins by reviewing the history of images of femininity to consider what, if anything, is so different about the current context that it might lead to blaming the media for self-starvation. The beauty ideal of Western cultures changed over time in the era prior to mass media and mass consumer culture. Between 1400 and 1700, a fat body shape was considered sexually appealing and fashionable. The ideal woman was portrayed as plump, big-breasted and maternal (Attie and Brooks-Gunn, 1987; Fallon, 1990). This ideal was prominently represented in art of the time (Clark, 1980). This standard of feminine aesthetics was associated with the socio-economic conditions. 'In economies oriented to subsistence rather than abundance, a plump figure was a sign of wealth, health and youth' (Polivy et al., 1986: 89). By the nineteenth century, the plump shape was replaced by a voluptuous hourglass figure, accentuating a generous bust and hips tapering to a narrow waist (Fallon, 1990). The voluptuous shape for women persisted through the early part of the twentieth century, eventually being replaced by the slender flapper of the 1920s (Mazur, 1986). With this new ideal, women began wearing binding garments and following strict diets, leading to the earliest concerns amongst the medical profession in the twentieth century about eating disorders (Fallon, 1990). A return to a fuller figure occurred in the 1930s, with an emphasis on leginess and business. This body shape ideal was exemplified by such film icons as Betty Grable and Mae West. The curvaceous ideal continued through the 1940s and 1950s, typified by Marilyn Monroe and Jane Russell, and other cultural phenomena such as the *Playboy* centrefold (Mazur, 1986). By the mid-1960s, however, fashions shifted once again towards the idealization of slender body shapes over curvaceousness. The same period witnessed significant change in gender roles, technological advances and the beginnings of global capitalism. Skinny fashion models, such as Twiggy, replaced shapely film stars as the dominant cultural icons. A preference for a body shape that mimicked this cultural ideal was increasingly reflected in the body image preferred by women, surveyed for their opinions about attractiveness (Cash, 1997; Serdulla et al., 1993; Streigel-Moore et al., 1996). Since then the only slight shift from extreme slenderness as the feminine ideal was the muscularization of the still very slender body during the 1980s. Coincidentally, and from some perspectives, causally, the mass media has increased in volume, spread and representative role.

Although the focus of this book is the problem of self-starving to slenderness and its hypothesized relation to media image, this chapter suggests food use/abuse is just one of a range of technologies working on women's bodies in order to alter shape, weight and attributes and can only properly be understood in relation to other theories and methods of body-morphing. It considers how meanings become associated with body image in ways that value-judge size, shape and type to provide us with models of the acceptable modern Ms and how that might impact on young women's consciousness and life choices. It asks who or what benefits from and therefore might contribute to discourses of malleable femininity. It places the media both in the cultural context of construction of ideas but also in the production context in terms of its relation to power and particularly to capital. It assesses the current anxiety about media meanings and self-image, to argue that the media work on the body in much more subtle and broad ways than simply the promotion of a thin aesthetics, and offers a methodology for exploring those by discourse analysis and considers that the pursuit and promotion of slenderness is in many ways a metaphor and sometimes a disguise for a whole range of represented gender norms.

Ways of seeing women

Writing some thirty years ago, the art historian John Berger explored the impact of images of femininity on audiences, from renaissance painting to modern advertising. He identified an astounding gender difference in ways of seeing women: 'Men look at women. Women watch themselves being looked at. This determines not only most relations between men and women but also the relation of women to themselves' (1972: 47). He explained the cause and effect of this:

> To be born a woman has been to be born, within an allotted and confined space, into the keeping of men. The social presence of women has developed as a result of their ingenuity in living under such tutelage within such a limited space. But this has been at the cost of a woman's self being split into two. A woman must continually watch herself. She is almost continually accompanied by her own image of herself. Whilst she is walking across the room or whilst she is weeping at the death of her father, she can scarcely avoid envisaging herself walking or weeping. From earliest childhood she has been taught and persuaded to survey herself continually. (Berger, 1972: 46)

In relation to the concept of dualism, discussed in Chapter 2, a key point is that a woman's sense of her body has not been hers to negotiate or control in order to find her essential self or God but has first and foremost been man's view of her body. Women see themselves through men's eyes. Berger (1972) notes that this is not an equal and opposite phenomenon but entirely related to male power to act on their own behalf, create images that flatter them and then elevate and promote those images in their own interest.

Figurative art re-presents someone who is no longer present so it transcends time and space. It also transcends reality in that it is not the original person but an artist's account of that person according to the gaze, craft and imagination of the painter. The art of the past is a record not of some truth of the past but of what might have been thought deserving of being painted, how and by whom. For Berger (1972), one particular kind of oil painting has much to tell about the gendered nature of the past and also resonates with the gendered contemporary, the European nude. He argued that a recurring theme in early nudes was the dominance of the female body and the allusion to the fall of Eve whereby the eating of the fruit of the tree of knowledge earns God's punishment for all women – subservience to men and the bearing of children. Early images showed the naked woman as aware she is the object of male desire and also aware of her own nakedness in his eyes. Frequently, the woman is displayed either directly to the spectator/painter/male or indirectly, via a mirror, viewing herself as the painter views her. The images are fecund, full-bellied and broad-hipped, yet passive and hairless.[1] These are male models of the female form which deny and disguise woman's active, adult passion by removing her active, adult sexuality and the hirsuteness which symbolizes it. Occasionally a man features in the female nude but the woman looks not at him but at the painter. She is often coquettish as she looks at her real love, the artist. For Berger these images record the inequality of gender relations and a sexualization of the female image that remains culturally central today. They reassure men of their sexual power and at the same moment deny any sexuality of women other than the male construction. They are evidence of gendered difference (although there is no need for this to be the case – men too could be painted thus) because any effort to replace the woman in these images with a man *violates* 'the assumptions of the likely viewer' (Berger, 1972: 64). That is, it does not fit with expectations but transgresses them and so seems wrong.

This act of looking is vital to understanding how images work to create meaning. It is not just that the content of the image offers meaning to the viewer but also that the viewer must find the content meaningful to them. To be meaningful, a painting must be looked at from a subject position that is enabled by the discourses offered by the image. It must have cultural consonance. So a viewer of either gender can arrive at a narrative explaining the seductive gaze of a naked, hairless, woman – it fits the gendered norms of an episteme, whereas a similar image of a man would not make sense. Foucault (1970) suggested that in this way the representation produces the subject and confirms knowledge about the world. Hall, in his analysis of Foucault's approach to representation, argued:

> For the painting to work, the spectator, whoever he or she may be, must first 'subject' himself/herself to the painting's discourse and, in this way, become the painting's ideal viewer, the producer of its meaning – its 'subject'. This is what is meant by saying that the discourse constructs the spectator as a subject – by which we mean that it constructs a place for the subject spectator who is looking at and making sense of it. (Hall, 1997: 60)

What is important here is the active role of the subject but it is also an activity already predestined by other cultural experience that is brought to the text. Meaning is therefore always intra-textual – a single new image cannot resonate unless it fits the history of the subject/viewers meaning experiences. In gendered terms, the historiography of these meaning experiences is embedded within a history of male power to define and to objectify, and a history of female subjugation and objectification. Woman has been represented as 'other' than man but also represented by man for man and represented for herself through his eyes. In a kind of cultural genetics 'this unequal relationship is so embedded in our culture that it still structures the consciousness of many women' (Berger, 1972: 63) and, of course, men – not because it is unequivocal truth but because it is utterly familiar and to engage with it critically requires an alternative viewing platform and conscious effort, difficult to embrace conceptually and achieve.

Although the nude coquette became less favoured during the eighteenth century, the representation of women remained within a particular paradigm of 'object of male gaze'. For Berger the eighteenth century focus remained on the woman, gazing out at the audience, as in Gainsborough's *Mary, Countess of Howe* (1764), but now she is modestly dressed and likely to be surrounded by her children, also gazing either at the audience or at their mother, as in Reynolds' *Lady Cockburn and her Three Eldest Sons* (1773). Alternatively the images are of the married couple or entire family, but still she tends to look out at the viewer. They are opulent images denoting wealth by dress, often showing land or property, as in *Mr and Mrs Andrews* by Gainsborough (1748), and, of course, the lineage of children who would inherit the newly emerging bourgeois money. The ultimate of these is perhaps Reynolds' *George Clive and his family with an Indian Maid* (1765) illustrating the wealth from trade and slavery. The woman and child look forward, the mother tilting the child's face to the artist, the maid kneels and looks downwards and Clive surveys all three. The women in these paintings are property, on display and valued as fertile, decorous and subjugated. These are less about the sexual attractiveness evident in the earlier 'nude' portraits and more about propriety: appropriate 'looks' and behaviour relating to monogamy, maternity and on the arm of masculinity.

These two traditions of representations of women, the desiring, sensual nude and the symbol of male material success, carried forward chronologically in recognizable though variable formats. By the nineteenth century the nude, or semi-nude, was usually either represented as myth or whore. In myth, whether in sculpture or painting, the early voluptuous images of figures such as Venus or Godiva gave way to images that Warner (1985: 31) described as 'comical maidens who clutch at drapes'.

> These late-nineteenth century versions have overlaid the medieval story with Victorian attitudes to female nudity, focusing pruriently on the disrobed woman, who is showing reluctance. (Warner, 1985: 310)

The moral climate of Victorianism and its oppression and containment of women, as discussed in Chapter 2, arguably rendered nakedness taboo. Berger (1972) went further still and argued that during the nineteenth-century the female nude was recast as prostitute. He cites Manet's *Olympia* as breaking the mould of traditional art by depicting the nude woman not as coy or classically sensual but realistically, contemporarily and as overtly sexual. The nude became the prostitute in the work of artists like Picasso and Toulouse-Lautrec – woman's body was for sale in image as in life. Buy the image, buy the woman.

By 1900 the 'first posters selling goods began to appear, and their visual style was determined by the conventions of official art, including the affixing of meaning – any meaning – to a pretty girl – any pretty girl' (Warner, 1985: 86). The message though was always the same: buy the product, get the girl; or buy the product to get to be like the girl so you get your man. The images from art were (and are) often reproduced in advertising either by direct reference to a traditional image or by allusion to it. Warner (1985) described an advert for bicycles in 1890 that depicts a chained and naked woman in classical style and pose, entitled *La Verité*. The sexual promise of the manacled woman is offered to the man who buys the bicycle. Such images pre-empted the now 'classic' use of naked models to sell cars. The art nude now features across a huge range of advertisements. Berger traces a line from the seventeenth century *Pan Pursuing Sphinx* by van Balen to a 1970s advert for fur coats depicting a woman in a bikini and fur coat about to be ravaged by a modern Pan. Buy the coat, get the man; or buy the girl the coat, get the girl. 'Buy' the image, 'get' the woman.

The link of images of women to products at the turn of the century added a second dimension to the possible impact of representation. Not only were women still consistently represented in high art forms according to the interest of patriarchy but by the twentieth century they were being publicly represented in popular art – publicity according to the interest of capital. The origins of these representations can be found not only in the art of the nineteenth century but in the plethora of magazines that served the newly literate late Victorians and the rapid commodification of print. Advertising was heavily taxed until 1853; print technology was expensive and journalism was serious and very much focused on the public sphere. Changes in technology and taxation impelled not only the commercialization of the press but also the search for new markets and new journalism to address these changes. By the 1880s magazines for women were popular and sometimes wholly dependent on advertising for profitability.

Magazines not only addressed women as consumers but also as readers, as in search of entertainment or in need of instruction in various social roles. From the start magazines which defined their readership as 'women' also took on, more or less overtly, the task of defining what it meant to be a woman, or what it meant to be a particular kind of woman. (Beetham and Boardman, 2001: 1)

This is nowhere more evident than in the juxtaposing of advertising amidst or alongside advice columns. This was specially common in the cheaper magazines and kept down the cost of journalism by replacing it with advertising text and images. Each discourse form added authority and legitimacy to the other. Women were at one stroke informed how to be acceptable women and sold the product to deliver them themselves. One example offered shows a woman 'classically' looking at herself in the mirror whilst she waves her hair with 'Hindes Hair Curlers'. Adjacent advice is given to a reader on how to colour grey hair with 'permanganate of potash' (*Woman*, 5 February 1891 in Beetham and Boardman, 2001: 164–172). Women in the Victorian period were addressed very much as wives and mothers. The role offered to them was closely allied to the home and to pleasing their husband or getting a husband. This role was sold to them both overtly and covertly and it was a narrow role. Yet the sale of goods to women as consumers may well have underwritten a major change because women began to shop, first from catalogues but soon from the newly emerging department stores, and shopping took them outside of the home into public spaces.

Prior to department stores like Macy's opening in 1860 in the United States and Selfridges in 1909 in London, women had only really circulated out of the home to find a partner or 'venturing out of the home was also allowed in the course of that century for the dispensing of philanthropy to the poor or sick' (MacDonald, 1995: 74). With extraordinary speed, by the time of World War One in 1914 women had become the major shoppers in the UK and the United States. This was recognized by trade, advertisers and the media. In the UK, Northcliffe added women's pages to the *Daily Mail* knowing a female audience would attract advertisers; in the United States trade journals 'regularly attributed between 80 and 85 per cent of all consumption to women' (MacDonald, 1995: 74) and women's magazines frequently devoted half their space to advertising. Women had the right to buy and also the right to vote. From 1918 this had been given to women over 30 and extended to women over 21 from the end of the 1920s. Advertisers were quick to entwine the two, for example the tobacco industry soon insisted on women's right to smoke in its slogans.

Film became what the historian A.J.P. Taylor called the social habit of the age. It was an entertainment arena which women could frequent without risk of moral condemnation. With film came the growth of the star culture, nurtured by magazines and the press. Images of famous actresses were used to promote fashion and make-up and names were allied with products leading to the sponsorship of radio programmes, initially by Procter and Gamble, hence 'soap opera'. Representations of women offered to women audiences in the inter-war years veered between housekeeper, mother and screen siren. Soap sells in all three dimensions: 'Persil' does the laundry; 'Lifebuoy' protects the family from germs and 'Knight's Castile' transforms the cleaner/mother with a 'complete beauty treatment' (MacDonald, 1995: 84) into an alluring young woman.

The first half of the twentieth century certainly saw a re-inscribing of women's bodies. Through advertising they were told clearly that they were women, what women should be, and what that particular product could do to help. Women were both given an identity and told they were not good enough *naturally* at one stroke. However, help was at hand *culturally* as just the right *commodity* to transform them was available for their *consumption*. Women were asked to buy themselves. As Berger wrote: 'The publicity image steals her love of herself as she is, and offers it back to her for the price of the product' (1972: 134). But the self offered back is always partial and each part she buys may soon be contradicted by another representation. Just as she buys the product that promises *domestic perfection* she is told she must instead be a *femme fatale*.

The onslaught on femininity within popular discourses continued and developed in sophistication during the early days of UK and US television in the 1950s and 1960s. The models of femininity on offer remained similar to those pre-war as the masculinizing effect of war, work and rations gave way to

> rounded shoulders, a close-fitting bodice emphasising the breasts, a tiny, nipped-in waist and long full skirts (often achieved through petticoats and crinoline-like constructions) a total contrast to the 'mannish angularity' of the war-time clothing. (Hollows, 2000: 148)

This was Dior's 'New Look' and it required high maintenance with diet, make-up, corsets and accessories, including the stiletto heel. The 'New Look' was decorative and sexy but the utility and practical clothes of working women during the war remained, albeit transformed into functional clothes for the busy housewife and mother. The male shirt became the shirt-waister dress and women were encouraged to move from functional to feminine by changing their looks. Women in the post-war years were sent back home to make room for the demobbed soldiers in the workplace and were encouraged to revert to traditional feminine roles by fashion and lifestyle representation. Moreover, the volume and frequency of representations increased dramatically with the introduction of commercial television and broadcast advertising.

> Research conducted between the 1950s and 1970s repeatedly found that television advertisements portrayed women as decorative, domestic, dependent on men and primarily concerned with personal beauty (Caballero, Lumpkin and Malden, 1989; Ferrante, Haynes and Kingsley, 1988; Knill, Persch, Pursey, Gilpin and Perloff 1981; Lovdal, 1989). (Gunter, 2002: 196)

The 1960s were a period of significant socio-political turmoil. In the United States the Civil Rights movement struggled to improve the situation for black Americans; pacifists took to the streets in the United States, UK and France to protest against the American war on Vietnam; universities and colleges were occupied by students and a second wave of feminism emerged that sought to 'intervene in and transform the unequal power relations between men and women' (Hollows, 2000: 3). That feminism was inspired largely by Betty Frieden's *The Feminine Mystique* (1963) and soon came to charge 'consumerism with constructing identities for women that were deeply conservative' (MacDonald, 1995: 86). Graffiti was regularly used by feminists to subvert the overt sexism of many billboards and hoardings. For example, an advert for the Fiat 127 Palio circa 1980 had its slogan 'If this car was a woman it would get its bottom pinched' embellished with 'If this woman was a car it would run you over'. New magazines like *Cosmopolitan* addressed liberated and career-oriented women and pressure on government for reform led to the introduction of the Sex Discrimination Act in 1975.

The range of identities available to women expanded in media representations beyond the bedroom and into the boardroom and in response fashion focused on the trouser suit. Women moved into male worlds and into men's clothing but men did not move into women's worlds and dresses. So although traditional ideas of femininity were challenged by women transgressing their gender, in effect this generally reinforced traditional masculinity as women adopted and endorsed its norms and practices. Arguably in the mass media feminism was paid lip-service in so far as it could be manipulated to deliver bigger and wealthier buying audiences. Women were spoken to as individuals and urged to consume all the products that had previously been markers of masculinity – cars; alcohol and financial services, though such advertising often still promised women either romance or domestic security as the reward for their purchase. 'Money management advertisements used more traditional appeals either to women's concern about their families' well-being or to their romantic desires' (MacDonald, 1995: 89). Moreover, women still remained the object of advertising for traditional feminine products such as fashion, cosmetics and perfume. Ironically, representations for these products now not only featured them as routes to romance but also as a route to success in a man's world of independence, travel and work. Women were being sold themselves re-constructed in a range of roles, 'transforming feminism's challenging collective programme into atomized acts of individual consumption' (MacDonald, 1995: 91).

During the late 1970s and 1980s feminists in academia were becoming increasingly analytical and critical of the way women were being represented in the media. The 1981 revised edition of Cohen and Young's edited volume *The Manufacture of News: Deviance, Social Problems and the Mass Media* included two such early critical pieces. Gaye Tuchman focused on 'The Symbolic Annihilation of Women in the Mass Media' and argued that media representations matter because they are not a truthful reflection of real lives but a symbolic account of what is *valued and approved* of that which appears to be fact. Her complaint was that women were both under-represented in media texts or, when depicted, either trivialized or condemned. The under-representation 'tells viewers that women don't matter much in American society' (Tuchman, 1981: 171) and that matters when 'by the time an American child is fifteen years old, she has watched more hours of television than she has spent in the classroom' (p. 170). Moreover, when women are shown they are seen as 'housewife, mother, home-owner, and sex object' (p. 175), in other words they are symbolically *divorced* from the economy and public life. Tuchman found similar patterns not only in television fiction and advertising but also in newspapers, where 'women are mainly seen as the consorts of famous men, not as subjects of political and social concern in their own right' (p. 182) and magazines, although these were more markedly variable in terms of the class of audience sought, including articles about work and career alongside 'stereotyped sex-roles in other sections' (p. 180).

Butcher et al., in the same volume, compared images of women in the media with those of men. The chapter focuses on the way in which parts of women – lips, breasts, legs, hair – signify sexuality whilst simultaneously denying women a holistic identity and role. Such representations refer in fact not to women's place in the world but to men's view of women's place in relation to their place in the world. An analysis of humour in the media 'tells us that male action, thoughts and words are the reality, the norm, and that women are deviant from that norm' (Butcher et al., 1981: 322) and found wanting. In the 1970s, women were only normal as sex objects, wives and mothers when they moved onto male territory as workers, drivers or voters they were poked fun at and negated. In each instance she exists 'through her relationships to men' (p. 325) and is offered as a means for men to consolidate their power in the world and in the bedroom.

Such representation and political critique supported significant resistance to some of the most degrading and sexist images of femininity and to the reduced status and potential for women in the socio-economic world. Legislative change and cultural sensibility certainly opened up apparent choices for women but without significantly matching these with changes in masculine roles and power. In representation, women were depicted as achieving success and happiness in love and work, aided and abetted, of course, by the purchase of the appropriate life-enhancing product.

In practice, the illusion did not match the reality. Women took on paid work but also retained the majority of childcare and housework duties. Moreover, women's work was and remains less well paid, more likely to be part-time and of lower status than men's. In practice, 'women could not share equally with men at work until men shared equally with them at home' (Segal, 1990: 304). In 1981 women in Britain earned 69 per cent of male pay and only 59 per cent of male pay in the United States (Norris, 1987). Early men's movements in support of feminism largely dissipated during the early 1980s. And during that decade the rampant individualism of Thatcherite politics supported an ideology of personal responsibility and meritocracy. The world was seen as changed – of course women could have it all was the message – if they deserved it and worked hard enough. 'Women could do whatever they pleased, provided they had sufficient will and enthusiasm' (MacDonald, 1995: 90). If they didn't have it all they only had themselves to blame and if they did have it all and couldn't cope they also only had their feminist selves to blame. These twin discourses assumed feminism had achieved real change, and so either women were personally lacking if they felt unequal, or feminism itself had failed women.

Before long women were also being bombarded with what Faludi (1992) called contrasting *backlash* messages. They were lured back into the home, barefoot and pregnant in the kitchen:

> Glossy magazines and commercials are currently filled with images of domestic, reproductive bliss, of home as a cosy, plant-filled haven of babies, warmth and light, skilfully managed and lovingly tended by women. (Bordo, 1993: 42)

Alternatively, pop videos showed images promoting strong, heterosexual, overtly seductive femininity. The male model of the sex siren was re-instated. Douglas described Madonna, for example, on the video for 'Open your Heart':

> It opens with Madonna as a dancer in a peep show who wears a black bustier and dances suggestively with a chair while pig-faced slavering men ogle her from individual cubicles. (Douglas, 1994: 287)

As the 1990s continued, another trend appeared, again revoking much of the shift towards adult, independent femininity promoted by second-wave feminism. Images of Madonna, Naomi Campbell and Courtney Love dressed up as sexualized little girls demonstrated the prevalence of cultural figures of infantalized femininity.

> Those media images emphasise one of the many profound contradictions in the category of 'woman'. For 'womanhood' is an ostensibly adult status, and yet the heterosexually attractive woman is frequently portrayed as child-like, dependent and passive. Cultural representations of this perversely infantilised femininity, of this diminutive child-woman

thus add to the discursive productions of 'woman' as inferior: For in phallocentric society it is size that counts ... (Malson, 1998: 109)

Such a range and pervasiveness of contemporary images of women (across not only the conventional media but the ever expanding World Wide Web, 24 hours a day), and the way they promote not only illusory but also disjunctive femininities, begs the question why and with what implications.

Beetham and Boardman's comment on the Victorian woman's magazines as treating women both as consumers and in search of identity holds broadly true today, not only for magazines but for a huge range of media outputs – from soap opera to the Web. There is more going on here than mere marketing, in fact the marketing could not work unless it fitted with already culturally resonant and acceptable models of femininity. It is ironic but true that although men dominate the prison population (over 90 per cent of UK inmates are male), it is women who are instructed how to be good, in terms of both behaviour and looks. In fact, 'women are involved in so little recorded crime and deviance that we need to look at their conformity' (Heidensohn, 1985: 108) in order to understand femininities. And to ask how that conformity in all aspects is normalized and who benefits from women's compliance.

For Berger in 1972 the attitudes that informed the painted female nude were now evident in the modern media: *advertising, journalism, television.* Certainly, in his book, he argued eruditely that in the 1970s publicity images offered women a means of buying the self that men desire just as art had once shown them a male view of themselves: 'the publicity image steals her love of herself as he is, and offers it back as a product' (1972: 134). The difference is that 'post' second-wave feminism, the model of femininity is polysemous and 'post' mass media the range of images is vast and constant. Art is now commerce and it is not just patriarchy that constructs woman's view of herself but capital.

Selling the body: the making of the modern Ms

Second-wave feminist theory did theorize a politics beyond the interpersonal, particularly in the UK where socialist feminism was influential in arguing that capital was central to both women's and men's exploitation and oppression, but it did not always embed the personal in a broader political analysis. Such an analysis should contextualize the personal and private in a politics that is based on capital, markets and commodification, whereby the economy and those with economic power are served by cultural forms and the human behaviours they promote. In work on eating and the body, although Bruch (1978) saw self-denial at a time of food a-plenty as a powerful rejection of the commodification of food she did not explore that commodification critically. Similarly, Boskind-White and White (1983) commented on the cheapness of America's junk food, making binging and purging viable, but did not ask who benefited from that process. Only Counihan (1999: 87) suggested that 'the economy depends on manipulating consumers to buy as much as possible, and one way is to project simultaneously the urge to eat and the need to diet'. That manipulation depends on the mass media not just to purvey advertising, and of course the mass media for the most part depend on advertising – it is a symbiotic relationship – but to support a climate wherein women's bodies are an apparently legitimate site of reconstruction and thereby an apparently legitimate market in re-constructive products is reproduced.

Women learn to reconstruct themselves. It is second nature to disguise themselves, dress themselves and decorate themselves with a huge range of materials. Over the past 30 years they have gone further than ever before in this process. They can re-arrange some of the organic material that is their body – sometimes without any harm to health, sometimes with devastating consequences. Thin fetishism is just one aspect of body morphing. Nearly 30 years after Orbach (1978) identified the unreal feminine picture purveyed in the mass media there are even more ways of achieving what remains an unreal ideal. As well as fashion and diet there is exercise, rejuvenation, surgical re-modelling and chemical maintenance and it permeates all of our popular culture and much of our purchasing. Some goods and processes are merely temporary body adornment, others are more permanent body modification. Just one magazine, the May 2003 issue of *Marie-Claire*, supplied all the examples that follow.

Artefacts to adorn include cosmetics, perfumes, fashion, jewellery and prosthetics.[2] Cosmetic advertising straddles twin discourses of science and beauty whereby the beauty is the goal and the science the means of achieving it. With treatment cosmetics, the authority of science lends credence not just to the efficacy of the product but the legitimacy of the beauty that is the product's goal. This is most clearly evident in the huge range of anti-ageing creams and treatments now being sold as the newly liberated consumers of the 1970s become the forty-somethings of the new millennium. Women are being sold youth but alongside that beauty constituent is the opposite sales pitch that ageing is unacceptable femininity. So two different meanings are enabled by the beauty is youth myth – the represented one and the connoted difference – 'age is ugly'. Shiseido offers 'renewing serum' that minimizes 'signs of early ageing such as visible pores and fine lines' immediately whilst L'Oreal's 'Visible Results' moisturiser has 'technological breakthrough' 'activa cells', uses computer graphics to indicate the improvements to the model's (a well-known actress) face in eight days, is acclaimed by scientists and suggests it should be used from age 30 'Because You're Worth It'. That last phrase both suggests that the product is expensive and that women have an obligation to care for themselves. Ironically information about dermatological tests demonstrating little effect from such potions is also sometimes discussed in feature articles adjacent to the advertisements. What is rarely aired is why ageing is such a denigrated stage of femininity that women will spend large amounts of money to disguise or deny it.

Disguising or embellishing cosmetics typically add colour or hide blemishes. The preferred discursive themes here are less science and age and more 'nature'. So a Maybelline advertisement for lipstick with added metallic glitter asks 'Maybe she's born with it'. Avon's 'Lash Designer Mascara' offers 'lashes you didn't know you had' – so not fake just hidden – and No. 7 'Intelligent Colour Foundation' gives a 'sheer veil of natural looking colour'. Timotei shampoo invites readers to 'wash your hair in sunshine' for 'natural looking highlights' while Silvikrin offers 'fuller looking hair' alongside an image of a woman in a bra pushing her breasts together to create a 'full' cleavage. Perfumes also tend to be linked to 'nature' and to sensuality, usually indicating both aspects with copious amounts of flesh and little text. So Alexander McQueen's scent 'Kingdom' features eight naked very young, very slender women inter-twined. Chanel instructs the reader to 'take it' referring to the perfume 'Chance' and depicts a near naked, very young model. Deodorants focus on 'feminine' smells, offering 'Always' sanitary pads with smell 'neutralizing properties'. The reality of women bleeding is not part of any sales pitch only the disguise and containment of it. Other adverts are for lifestyle 'accessories' such as mobile phones, bags, watches, deodorant, coffee, alcohol and food. Again the overt meanings also connote different meanings in their interpretation – youth versus age; nature versus artifice; slim versus fat; sensuality versus frigidity; girlfriend versus single woman; purity versus soil.

Fashion and beauty features dominate the non-advertising text – though the frequent allusions to brand names actually make these read very like the adjacent overt promotions. Fashion and beauty in the May edition of *Marie-Claire* focused on the coming summer. Readers are told 'a bright mouth in summer is gorgeous' and 'weight gain is a symptom of dehydration' and fashion is skimpy frocks and tiny bikinis – 'small is beautiful'.

Many of these adornments appear harmless to women, even fun and aesthetically pleasurable, but they are not free (a silk-chiffon Jill Sander dress is £2,307) and they are not constant but must always be updated (last year's colour is so 'out') and they are not universally applicable to all women. Rather certain kinds of women are marked out as appropriate to such products – in advertising, television drama and shop windows, embellishing products are normally displayed on the young, the slender, the sexually alluring, the white and the wealthy. Such constituents are allied to beauty adornments and overwhelmingly such products are accoutrements still to femininity rather than masculinity. Those who do not comply with such beauty constituents are placed outside of the discourse of feminine identity represented in much of our culture. For them there is exclusion to the dark zone of non-conformity or an expensive or even painful search for ways of fitting the femininity on offer.

Some ways of fitting involve changing the body and appearance in relatively minimal ways that are none the less at best deceptive and at worst uncomfortable. Between adornment and modification lie activities such as hairdressing, hair removal, corseting, skin treatments and piercing. Hair colour frequently addresses age. Clairol asks: 'Why fade to Grey'? Self-tans are everywhere in the May issue of *Marie-Claire* and the advertisements return to scientific authority to convince the reader: L'Oreal fake tan cream offers 'dermo-expertise from research to beauty' and Clarins cream has 'vitamins and minerals'. Teeth can be whitened by 'Orbit' chewing gum and every body displayed is hairless.

Finally, there are the products and processes that actually act to change the body by modifying shape, size and/or attributes, from diet to hormone replacement therapy to cosmetic surgery. These texts were clustered towards the end of May's magazine, after women had been clearly shown their failings. Cosmetic dentistry is offered, on a full colour half-page, to 'create your perfect smile', with Dr Joe Oliver. The actress Pamela Anderson confesses to her 'boob' job and adds 'I've bought boobs for friends and believe me their lives have changed completely'. The classifieds are full of clinics offering fat removal, breast reshaping, nose-reshaping, lines and wrinkles removal, lipo-sculpture and laser treatment. 'Unwanted hair' is addressed by waxing and electrolysis; poor eyesight corrected and skin lightened – 'scars ... patches or whole body'. At the very end are lonely hearts adverts, astrology and, rather oddly, adverts from abortion clinics. Whatever situation women find themselves in and however they look they are always found wanting and needy.

Any space remaining outside of advertising of one form or another is filled by articles on men, relationships, diet, size, food, holidays and health. These fill the 108 of the 347 pages that have nothing for sale on them. Women are being, as in Berger's (1972) description, sold themselves in order to achieve a self whom the men in the features might choose. These features include one on eligible bachelors, three on male sex symbols, one on men's identity crisis, one on women's looks that men fancy and one on men who have been betrayed by women alongside the 'man of the month' and the 'hero of the month'. All these ads and features are in one month's edition of one magazine.

There has always been a feminine aesthetics but now it is not about natural beauty but unnatural beauty or rather cultured beauty. Also, there is no longer a unitary and relatively stable model of beauty but one where the body itself is less an object of beauty than a structure to be adorned beautifully. That adornment may vary too – both chronologically from year to year and situationally from place to place or activity to activity. The opening up of women's lives has equally opened up a range of femininities each of which has its own aesthetic and a market to support that. The ideal woman was once knowable and relatively stable now she is ever-changing and elusive.

It may be too that the gradual expansion from linear masculinity which necessarily accompanies an empowerment of femininity – gay culture, male fashion, active fathering, domesticization and reflexivity – will see an increasing tendency towards male body objectification and resulting obsessions with shape, size and looks and dysfunctions in identity, although there is as yet little evidence of such a trauma of masculinity. The opening up of gender identity following second-wave feminism, and enabled by the mass mediation of images, has also opened up a huge marketplace just as the opening of borders by travel and communication has generated a global trade in national identity and attributes.

> Commodification is the mode through which contemporary Western societies seek to ensure a minimal continuity in how people present themselves. That is, the means for managing the self have become increasingly tied up with consumer goods, and the achievement of social and economic success hinges crucially on the presentation of an acceptable self-image. (Shilling, 2003: 81)

Wolf (1992) discovered that the skin-care industry alone grossed 20 billion dollars worldwide, despite the opinion of Body Shop owner Anita Roddick that there is 'no topical application that will get rid of grief or stress or heavy lines … there is nothing, but nothing that is going to make you look younger' (Wolf, 1992: 110). Alongside the face, women are sold their bodies. 'Gym scenes are increasingly portrayed and glamourized in an ever widening range of adverts' (Sassatelli, 2000: 228) and, of course, all the garments and accessories that go with the work-out must be bought and kept up to date.

Changing ourselves is big business and much of it is fun: 'adornment is an enormous and often pleasing part of female culture' (Wolf, 1991: 75). We modify ourselves because that is what women do; it is part of femininity, part of the construction of identity, and it is an extraordinary revenue strand for commerce. Moreover post-feminism has taken issue with the strongly feminist critique that sees the cultural construction of femininity as in the sole interest of patriarchy and capital. Hollows (2000) documented the theories of those who see women's buying of beautifying goods and processes not as exploitation but as about the celebratory, pleasurable and empowering potential of fashion, make-up and the consumption of all manner of body-altering products. Radner (1989) viewed choice and subversion as making women agents of their own identity with *beauty practices predominantly aimed at the self* because the impact of any products is 'imperceptible to anyone but the practitioner herself' (Radner, 1989: 311).

However, choosing between one diet drink and another; one skimpy, belly-revealing top and a cleavage-exposing blouse or the gym rather than cosmetic surgery arguably only offers choice amongst similar models of attractive femininity. The problem seems to be that so many of the images offered to women in the media are the same – slender, fair, fit, young, sexual – and the goods sold to women are sold to 'help' them achieve that image whilst, at the same time, women are expected increasingly to occupy a large variety of roles – sex symbol, career woman, mother, wife, housewife, athlete. For girls entering adulthood the discontinuity between their 'real' selves, the representation of women and the range of roles they are shown occupying must present as at best challenging, certainly confusing and possibly confounding. All women modify, some morph and some mutilate in the effort to define themselves – all of us are subject to the same pressures and so to some extent all women suffer as subjects of social construction.

> She attempts to make herself in the image of womanhood presented by billboards, newspapers, magazines and television ... She is brought up to marry by catching man with her good looks. To do this she must look appealing, earthy, sensual, virginal, innocent, reliable, caring, mysterious coquettish and thin ... In the background a ten billion dollar industry waits to remodel bodies to the latest fashion. (Orbach, 1978: 20–21)

Knowing what is an 'acceptable' self-image and which 'consumer goods' might help an individual 'present' themselves is inextricably connected to the representation of those images and goods. Yet despite the plethora of publications and consistent reference to the role of cultural representation in the construction of the female sense of self, research has barely addressed the issues addressed by Orbach over twenty years ago. Meanwhile, multiple billions of dollars are being made in the re-construction of body and image:

> The dieting industry has never been so sophisticated, so aggressive or so popular. Nor has it ever been so rich. More than 800 new diet books weighed down bookshop shelves this Christmas, membership of health clubs rose by an average of 59 per cent in the new year, and supermarket sales of low fat products grew by more than £300 million in the past five years. Overall the 'well-being' sector – which includes organic products

and vitamin and mineral supplements as well as beauty products and health and fitness – has soared by over 60 per cent in the past five years, faster than any other retail sector. (*Observer*, 6 January 2002)

Thin is beautiful according to the cosmetic, health and diet industries and also according to fashion. Liz Jones resigned as editor of *Marie-Claire* in 2001 after campaigning to use larger models in fashion shoots. She was resisted by the fashion industry, modelling agencies and other magazines all of whom believed that thin was the most beautiful way to display clothes. Jones revealed not only how dramatically underweight the models were but also the amount of retouching and fakery used to achieved the final images for magazines; even legs are stretched by image manipulation software. Jones commented:

> I had simply had enough of working in an industry that pretends to support women while it bombards them with impossible images of perfection day after day, undermining their self confidence, their health and their hard earned cash. (*Mail on Sunday*, 15 May 2001)

This book not only begins to address and analyse such images, but also tries to assess in Part Two how young women actually react to them.

Mediated meaning and method

Concern with the way women are represented is not new and informs theories of representation, identity and behaviour. Since the 1970s, sexualized or trivializing representations of women were and remain seen as not only degrading but likely to incite male oppression and even sexual violence. This concern led to a wide range of anti-pornographic feminist work during the 1980s, focusing on the impact of debasing and titivating sexual imagery on male attitudes to women and often calling for censorship (Dworkin, 1981, 1991; Zillman and Bryant, 1991, 1994). Alternatively, research developed that looked more closely at the relationships between such images and women's sense of themselves, their self-esteem and life choices. Much of this work was psycho-analytic and had a significant impact on the way that the media was theorized as acting on audiences. It necessarily also impacts on how any relation between media image and self-image might be understood and helps address the issues raised in the past few years about the media causing self-harm. In an article on 'heroin-chic', Arnold asks:

> Given the role fashion plays in defining and redefining our bodies … should the image makers be censured? Are they creating role models for the vulnerable that speak of desolation and self-abuse? (1999: 280–281)

Orbach saw a clear causality between media images and self-identity. She identified two areas – the role of the media and the construction of identity – and linked them to claim that the media affected the self, and in the case of the female body did so negatively for many women. Such a hypothesis depends on a theoretical model linking the media to identity and empirical evidence of the typology of 'body image'. The theory remains contentious whilst methods of investigating media representations of the body and their possible affect on audiences have tended to accept at face value the 'shock-horror-probe' reports in the media themselves of 'starving celebrities' and 'cat-walk waifs'.

Media theory originated with the work of the Frankfurt School on propaganda during the 1930s and the years following World War Two. Members of the group left Germany for the United States to promulgate work on the role of the mass media as a tool of power and included influential Marxists such as Adorno and Marcuse. They proposed a pessimistic effects model whereby the media operated as an ideological state apparatus manipulating defenceless mass audiences towards consensus with dominating views either fascistic as in Nazi Germany or capitalistic as in the 1950s United States. Research was designed to 'measure the potency of media messages in relation to shaping political and consumer behaviours' (Gunter, 2000: 11) and underwrote a strong effects model of the media's role in society.

That model still informs much public, press and political opinion on both sides of the Atlantic, as is evidenced by the regular furore and panic over explicitly violent or sexual media material in the case of copy-cat criminal responses or moral breakdown. However, though remaining deeply influential, the early theory was doubly criticized, first because of its assumption of an effect with little reliable work on actual audiences (Katz and Lazerfeld, 1955) – this lack and the shifts in research intended to improve effects theory are addressed in relation to representations of body image in the second half of this book. Secondly, the Mass Society or propaganda model was criticized for an over-simplistic model of communication processes within which meaning was assumed to be a straight transfer from author via text to recipient. That second shift led to more subtle and less pessimistic work on text and theoretical developments that are ongoing and inform the analytical approach used in the next two chapters to investigate representation of body image.

During the 1940s methods of content analysis were developed which dominated work of mediated communication until the 1980s. Because the assumption was that messages were manifest and transparent in meaning, research developed to systematically count and label textual events according to predetermined criteria. The effort was to 'code' events and features as if their meaning was unequivocal in order to quantify content and then infer effects. It works best on minimally unambiguous tasks. For example, the commission for racial equality carried out a content analysis of British television in the early 1980s to map the representation of ethnic minorities and found 96 per cent of actors could be labelled as white.[3]

In simple number terms, that analysis indicated an under-representation of the racial diversity of the UK though even at that level the labelling of whiteness might arguably be a less than straightforward assignment. However, what such quantification meant and what impact it might have would require going beneath the surface of skin colour-counting to explore the resonance with reality, roles played, stories told, values implied, interpretations assigned to programmes by audiences and effect on behaviour or attitude. So systematic a quantification of denotative features might indicate an area meriting further research but critics of the method pointed out the dangers of over-simplifying media representation and its relation to the real.

A simple example might be the phrase 'red rose' or the corresponding image. It is perfectly possible to count all occurrences of the phrase or image in a collection of material but what those mean may vary according to whether the context is about gardening, rugby, the Labour party, rivalry between the counties of Lancashire and Yorkshire or a romantic drama – all of which can be signified by a red rose. Meaning might also change according to whether the representation is actual flowers, photographs, drawings, oil paintings, fabric, speech, writing, graphics or abstract, and according to historical period, genre, narrative, interaction and actors. Finally, audiences themselves bring to the medium a whole lifetime of interpretative schema that may or may not correspond fully with either the meaning frameworks of the programme maker, researcher or other audience members according to other variables such as age, race, class, gender, biography and so forth. In other words, the textual context of any representation and the cultural context of any interpretation can vary its meaningfulness so both are relevant to any analysis of the media.

So, two key components to analysing the media or in fact any 'language' event or product, are textual consonance and reality resonance … ideas, values, stories can only make sense if they 'fit' both within and between texts, that is with what audiences bring to a piece of text from context and from other 'texts' – represented or lived. So any piece of textual representation can be counted as material form but any interpretation of meaning depends on that form's relation to others in the same representation and also its relation to culture beyond the immediate text. The recognition of the subtlety and complexity of meaning marked the end of a structural paradigm in linguistics and the recognition that meanings are not fixed to lexes and syntax in use but culturally conventionalized.

Barthes' (1957, 1977) work was seminal in calling into question the transparency and fixity of the sign's (visual or verbal) relation to reality and effectively began the shift away from a structural model of communication in academic work on the media. Roland Barthes argued that signs only become signifiers in accordance with the intent of the interpreter and the 'nature of society's conventional modes and channels' (Hawkes, 1977: 131), which are the vehicles of that interpretation. Hence a 'bunch of red roses' is merely a horticultural sign without the cultural conventions of 'romance' for roses and 'danger' for red. Commonly in the West, red roses signify 'passion'.

Barthes argued that over time and with repeated use, signs become emptied of their original denoted meaning, retaining a mythic meaning. In this process denotative or literal meanings may be underwritten or even superseded by connotation providing a second order of signification which may even substitute for the literal. For example, the term 'blonde' refers literally to a shade of hair but connotatively to a woman, probably sexually attractive, perhaps sexually available, probably young, possibly 'dumb'. It is hard to interpret the term literally because of the pervasiveness of the connotations which tell quite a complex story about gender.

Barthes theorized relations between sign, sentence, narrative, social world and psyche, clarifying a connection between text and subjectivity previously merely assumed by effects theory. For Barthes (1977), meanings are derived from consciousness which in turn is patterned by language forms, and he suggested:

> Without wanting to strain the phylogenetic hypothesis, it may be significant that it is at the same moment (around the age of three) that the little human 'invents' at once sentence, narrative and the Oedipus. (Barthes, 1977: 12)

His concept of narrative structure was that text-types/genres include the systematic selection and reproduction of components of composition which make texts familiar due to their conformity to templates. Familiarity with such patterns in cultural forms may play a part in the process of meaning generation and interpretation central to understanding the relations between language and the social world. Media texts are realized as complete texts, stories or narratives, and Barthes argued:

> A set of sentences is organized and that through this organisation it can be seen as the message of another language, one operating at a higher level than the language of the linguists. Discourse has its units, its rules, its 'grammar': beyond the sentence and though consisting solely of sentences, it must naturally form the object of a second linguistics. (1977: 83)

Although complex and expanded, compared to single words or phrases, there are recognizable characteristics to narrative as identified by Vladimir Propp (1968), who described narrative as a system that might include all, some or several sets of 'villain, hero, lack, search, struggle, resolve, happiness'. Repeated through the history of story-telling this common organization imposes a logical structural law on the synchronic or content level which Levi-Strauss (1958) argued renders it accessible to an audience in a way which over time makes it 'naturally' predictive. Narrative offers more in that it is a means of connecting texts, both over history through repetition and cumulatively across texts with particular genres or types sharing structural templates. In Levi-Strauss' terms, a reader may have differing sets of expectations of genre-topics like romances, biographies or news and also different pre-emptive expectations of the format-type in which they appear, such as novels, documentary film or the popular press. Such texts, over time, become institutionalized. Certain literary forms constitute the classic texts of cultural heritage; the 'BBC News' constitutes our 'unbiased, objective' source of information about our contemporary world; women's magazines tell us what is fashionable and beautiful, whilst the Web appears anonymous and interactive.

Hall (1973) illuminated and politicized these interjections in the seminal article on television messages, 'Encoding–decoding'. Hall added power and value to Barthes' model of meaning interpretation. Recognizing that meanings are conventionally linked to language forms, textually and culturally, and are potentially therefore variable and changeable, Hall pointed out the likelihood that dominant social groups are likely to have more power over that process and therefore may well imbue forms with meanings conducive to their own interests. Focusing less on the text and more on the audience, he none the less brought issues of power, dominance and hegemony into work on the media, returning to the Marxism of the Frankfurt School but softened by the strong influence of cultural theorists such as Richard Hoggart (1958, 1972) and Raymond Williams (1958, 1961, 1981), with their empowering political model of human agency. Hall argued class and race resonated in media texts in accord with the class and race of those producing (encoding) messages, who would prefer their own interests and values. This dominant cultural order makes the potential for connotation in Barthes' terms unequal. Rather, in discourse our social life is 'hierarchically organized into dominant or preferred readings' (Hall, 1973: 46) and then disseminated via institutions such as the media but also education, law, medicine and so forth. Repetition and familiarity render these versions of the world normal and other versions are excluded, or even denigrated should they present as a problem for dominance. The process is necessarily never complete and always a struggle for power as those whose identity does not comfortably fit with dominant norms and values may become critically aware that their subjectivity and social experience is negated or made invisible and fight for a positive sense of self. Particularly concerned with class and race, Hall embraced meaning as socially constructed according to power and always in process. Such an approach was deeply political in that it deconstructed representation always according to what else might have been 'meant', as always value-laden, and as responsive to social pressure from human agency but normally acting in the interests of those with power over discourse.

Also deeply political, for Foucault language was a *technology of power* which reduces the need for real physical control of the populace by orchestrating a symbolic order.

> Each discipline marks out an area of body and mind for control. First the mad and the sick, then the children and the criminals, domestic life and its great untameable, sex. Each is brought under the terrible domination of language – the discourse of power. (Inglis, 1990: 107)

Through language, power infiltrates every aspect of our social lives and subjective selves but not in any straightforward unitary way because each of us occupies differing identities (class, race, sexuality, age, religion and so forth) whilst different social situations may require different operations of power (family, court, street, work, classroom and so forth) and each of these may have differing meaning associations at different historical periods or *epistemes*. Foucault's post-structuralism accounted for the normalization of dominant identities as appropriate for all through the power of dominant groups over discourse. He related discourse to the construction of subjective identities but saw these as not fixed, nor determined, nor finite and unitary but subtle, variable, acting on and responsive to the will to power. Methods of social analysis must take account of the fact that 'Relations of power–knowledge are not static forms of distribution, they are matrices of transformations' (Foucault, 1981: 92–102). Importantly, the analysis of discourse according to its values, themes and historical context becomes a means of revealing the operation of power, the state of social relations, areas of conflict and challenge.

Discourses construct our sense of self and the media are frequent, pervasive and invasive sources. The body may be material but it is the mind that interprets that corporeality and makes meaningful its contours, appearances and sensations and it does so through the language of the cultural community within which the body is situated. Old models of the self tended toward determinism, with the essence of subjective identity fundamentally fixed or innate, either according to God, or class or biology. During the 1960s, 1970s and 1980s, identity politics, deeply rooted in anti-racism, Marxism and feminism, challenged the fixity of views that fail to allow for human agency and change and legitimate social stratification and inequalities as natural. Central to such challenges was the epistemological turn to language and the concept of the subject and social world as 'constructed' rather than 'essential' (Gilroy, 1999). That concept is vital to a model of media messages affecting subjective identity and consequent behaviours.

Lacan's (1977) work on the unconscious articulated the role of language in identity formation and profoundly relates to Barthes' semiotics as well as psychoanalytic theory. For Lacan, language, both verbal and visual, is an integral component of self. The infant is seen as coming into consciousness of itself as separate and different from the mother as it enters the symbolic world. This process splits the young self into an unarticulated unconscious and the represented 'I' that the child learns exists as it becomes aware of separateness from the mother. Lacan calls this phase the 'mirror stage' because the child sees itself reflected in social intercourse as a subject. It becomes conscious of its difference from the mother through language and thereafter a split exists between the unconscious and conscious self. Following Freud, Lacan theorized this stage as central to sexuality and the development of gendered identity, with boys and girls entering the symbolic order differently. This difference is socially reinforced because the masculine is socially dominant and so masculinity in the symbolic order is positively valued whilst femininity is valued as lesser or lacking. Girls enter the symbolic order as 'not-men rather than as women' (Woodward, 1999: 46). Lacan's explanation for gendered subjectivity as culturally constructed underwrote work on language in identity theory and informs media effects theory, but it remained a determinist approach in that he viewed gendered identity as formed and fixed at infancy through language and merely reinforced thereafter.

Feminist interjections took issue with the accepted privileging of the male order as fixing the subject that characterized Lacan because that theory necessarily also fixes gendered identity as inequitable, denying the possibility of change in the socio-sexual order. Such work resisted structured unitary models of subjective identity as determined by the symbolic order, citing change as evidence of agency. Feminist psychologists like Holway (1989) took a post-structuralist position on identity, opening the potential for the change in subjectivity that Lacan denied. Holway saw the life-course as a constant process of self-identity establishment rather than the self being shaped at the moment that language enters the child during infancy. She suggested subjectivity is a constant process of negotiation of power relations according to the various discourses encountered during human life, not just the privileged masculinity of gendered discourse, in order to arrive at a sense of self at any moment that is appropriate to the context.

Weedon's (1987) position was similar but deeply concerned with who has the power to define and to disseminate discourses, rather than how individuals might negotiate their way through these to a sense of self. Weedon feminized both Hall's work on the media and Foucault's on subjective identity whilst retaining their focus on language and adding a feminist and socialist critique to psychoanalytic work on subjectivity:

> Language is the place where actual and possible forms of social organi-
> sation and their likely political and social consequences are defined and
> contested. Yet it is also the place where our sense of ourselves, our sub-
> jectivity is *constructed*. The assumption that subjectivity is constructed
> implies that it is not innate, not genetically determined but socially
> produced. (Weedon, 1987: 171)

She was also politically committed to a feminist critique of that power and the more equal reconstruction of gender relations. She recognized the diversity of feminine identities on offer in discourse:

> A glance at women's magazines, for example, reveals a range of often
> competing subject positions offered to women readers, from career
> woman to romantic heroine, from successful wife and mother to irre-
> sistible sexual object. (Weedon, 1987: 174)

And like Holway (1989), Weedon believed that subjectivity is 'precarious, contradictory and in process, constantly being reconstituted in discourse each time we think or speak' (1987: 175). Weedon, however, focused on the social subject and adapted Foucault's account of discourses as histor-ically situated and hierarchically organized to both explain, and seek means of changing, women's continuing subordination. Weedon (1987) recognized that gendered discourse 'post' second-wave feminism was, and arguably remains, fraught with contradiction, bearing both the con-servative legacy of traditional patriarchal models of femininity yet also incorporating the political shifts that had opened up new modes of femi-ninity to women. These latter were/are not only responses to women's demands for liberation and equality but also a recognition and reorgani-zation of markets, audiences and consumers. Cynically women's buying power ensured that their requirements for change were to some extent at least met. Yet of all the shifts in women's roles called for since the 1970s, the one arena that remains unaddressed in any 'liberating' way is child-care. Here the patriarchal nuclear family remains the norm, extolled in advertising, policy and moral discourses. For Weedon, the different demands imposed on contemporary women from capital and patriarchy make her the 'subject of a range of conflicting discourses, she is *subjected* to their contradictions at great emotional cost' (1987: 176), perhaps partic-ularly subject at times of vulnerability, dependence and uncertain identity – for example during adolescence, when choices about self and future are of paramount importance.

Summary

Foucault's theory of discourse theorized behaviours and values as made normal through language as it *penetrates each subject in cultural intercourse*. Language use arguably exercises ideological power over the subject's psyche making unnecessary the exercise of real force over the physical body. The individual 'body' – self, identity, sexuality – is central to this thesis. The body is both the object of knowledge, the site of social/sexual control and the material evidence of the self. Language is both a vital part of how we interact with others and the world but also the means by which we know ourselves and our world through the mental concepts enabled by language. It is a truism to then argue that the mass media, with their constant, repetitive and familiar 'languages', are acting on identity, both directly in our reading, viewing and listening and also indirectly, as media content is so much part of our conversation, gossip and educational interaction with others. If language is part of who we are and how we see the world, then mediated language must also contribute to the self.

For young women, media images are implicated increasingly in the phenomenon of the starved self. The argument is that looks could kill but looks are just one aspect of the gendered discourse – for looks to shape ourselves they must comply with other aspects of the feminine and with our willingness to continually monitor and reconstruct that. The extent of the willingness may be all that separates those who are dying to be thin from those who are dieting to (be) fit in order to be buying to be beautiful and subscribing to what Wolf called the 'beauty myth'.

The beauty myth arguably works, in Foucauldian terms, just as other normative discourses, both as a technology of power and trope of subjectivity.

> The beauty myth tells a story: The quality called 'beauty' objectively and universally exists. Women must want to embody it and men must want to possess women who embody it. This embodiment is an imperative for women but not for men, which situation is necessary and natural because it is biological, sexual and evolutionary. Strong men battle for beautiful women, and beautiful women are more reproductively successful. Women's beauty must correlate to their fertility, and since this system is based on natural selection, it is inevitable and changeless.
>
> None of this is true. 'Beauty' is a currency system like the gold standard. Like any economy it is determined by politics, and in the modern age in the West it is the last, best belief system that keeps male dominance intact. In assigning value to women in a vertical hierarchy according to a culturally imposed physical standard, it is an expression of power relations in which women must unnaturally compete for resources that men have appropriated for themselves. (Wolf, 1992: 12)

The outcry against the media has assumed that the media portray images which suit the interest of both capital (particularly the fashion and diet industries) and patriarchy (in the portrayal of women as frail, young and sexual), but rarely has it researched these assumptions on the theorised effect.

Language is the means through which we understand what it means to be 'good' and 'bad' but such value associations themselves are malleable and meanings sometimes contradictory, as Weedon (1987) described. So constructed within and pre-dated by discourse, subjects too shift and slip and struggle for a sense of self, particularly perhaps socially subordinate subjects, like young girls, whose identities may neither be privileged nor positively valued nor perhaps even visible – and particularly if those already frail identities are subject to a bombardment of largely illusory modes of self that are not only contradictory in their variety but ever-changing. Moreover, should such girls fail to *have it all*, the implication is that they only have themselves to blame because 'post-feminism' gender inequality has given way to meritocracy. In truth, the old requirements of women remain in place but now these are joined by new and conflicting ones. At a time when young women have little access to a feminist critique (because it is seen to have achieved its goals and perhaps even overstepped them – Faludi, 1992), it is perhaps unsurprising that some either shrink, literally, from growing into the maelstrom of contemporary womanhood and/or see their inability to identify with the discontinuity of femininities as personal failure.

Impossibly women are being asked to be sexual, independent and careerist yet still also childlike, docile and maternal and always young, white, beautiful and thin.

> The female form metamorphoses from one sign into another, and this flux of signs, each succeeding generation's variations on the ancient topic, is accepted as a sequence of statements of the truth. The body is still the map on which we mark our meanings; it is chief among metaphors used to see and present ourselves, and in the contemporary profusion of imagery, from news photography to advertising to fanzines to pornography, the female body recurs more frequently than any other: men often appear as themselves, as individuals, but women attest the identity and value of someone or something else, and the beholder's reaction is necessary to complete their meaning, to find the pin-up sexy, to desire the product the housewife poses to vaunt. Meanings of all kinds flow through the figures of women and they often do not include who she is herself. (Warner, 1985: 331)

And

> Publicity is the life of this culture – in so far as without publicity capitalism could not survive – and at the same time publicity is its dream.

Capitalism survives by forcing the majority, whom it exploits, to define their own interests as narrowly as possible. This was once achieved by extensive deprivation. Today in developed countries it is being achieved by imposing a false standard of what is and what is not desirable. (Berger, 1972: 154)

Such assertions from Warner and Berger are arguably even more apposite in the early twenty-first century, with its declining markets for traditional industries and expanding leisure, culture and media industries. The themes and discourses central to such assertions and the specific question informing this book – can media representation be causal of self-starvation? – are tested out in relation to the nature of representation in the following two chapters: first through an analysis of print media and then by focusing on television and the World Wide Web. The second half of the book addresses the second component of the question by studying the ways in which audiences make sense of and construct meanings from such representations.

Beauty is and always has been cultural currency because it has always been a particularly desirable attribute of femininity for men, as this chapter has shown. Women's sense of themselves is the sense men have made of them through their domination of gendered discourses. During the twentieth century, beauty first became big business and now is simultaneously a site for the working out of sexual politics within which second-wave feminism has challenged the patriarchy of earlier epochs. As with other powerful discourses, the beauty discourse, is regulatory, representative of particular interests and restless. Beauty can never be achieved; it must always be sought and now that we have newspapers, magazines, 24-hour television on many channels and the World Wide Web, the media more than any other discourse source tells us what to seek to make us beautiful, where to buy it and how wonderful life will be when we have.

The analyses that follow in Chapters 4 and 5 focus on the gendered discourses in samples from a wide range of popular media selected since the panic about images in women's magazines emerged at the turn of the millennium. The aim was to try to establish whether there is a 'culture of thinness ... adopted purposely or accidentally through the media and advertising' (BMA, 2000: 25), how that is represented as desirable and what might make it acceptable. It is a qualitative analysis that seeks evidence of the perpetration of 'beauty myths' by exploring the femininities offered in representations in terms of absence and presence, values, narratives and themes in order to map the discursive context within which so many young women *find themselves dying to be thin.*

Notes

1   Berger cites the work of Tintoretto, Rubens and Memling from the fifteenth
    and sixteenth centuries.
2   All the advertisements mentioned in this chapter were in the magazine *Marie-Claire*, May 2003.
3   See *Television in a Multi-Racial Society* (1982) Commission for Racial Equality,
    discussed in O'Sullivan et al. (1994).

4 Print: Selling Sex and Slenderness

At the close of the twentieth century a new 'moral panic' seemed to be emerging in the news media which broadly claimed there was a crisis in femininity and blamed the fashion industry. In the United States the *New York Times* (22 May 1997) published President Clinton's rebuke of fashion designers and fashion magazines for depicting models in photo-shoots 'glamourizing the strung-out look' associated with heroin use. 'Heroin-chic' imagery featured emaciated, sunken-eyed, young models in extraordinarily expensive clothes and marked the end of the fit/muscled/though lean/healthy body fetishism that had characterized much of the 1980s; a look that was perhaps a response to panic about AIDS. Instead, during the 1990s, the

> façade of healthy strength [was] replaced by images of bodies that appear to have given in to illness, thin corpses that appear to have given in to the mortality of flesh instead of fighting its inevitable decay. (Arnold, 1999: 285)

In place of health and strength, the 1990s showed frail femininity – models seemed very young, sometimes closer to children (Hartley, 1998) than women (as in the advertisement for Calvin Klein underwear that also drew Clinton's attention in 1995). These images spawned an anxiety about child pornography that continues to fill our news media – though now in relation to the Internet (Ndangam, 2003). Later in the decade, if not actually children and vulnerable, models were nevertheless as small as pre-pubescent girls but apparently so by choice.

The clothes that characterized 'heroin-chic' were 'designer' but the setting was depravity, dirt and emaciation. These were not images of real squalor but of lifestyle; images of girls apparently self-abusing with drugs rendering them skeletal and semi-conscious. Young women appeared to be risking death for the sake of looks. Nor was it mere appearance, as several high-profile models 'came-out' as addicts and stories of the use of drugs to control weight filtered into the news. The class of models emerging from heroin-chic left behind the bruised, semi-conscious, grubby image but did not put on weight. Thin was in, and soon so it seemed was any means of achieving it, including anorexia or bulimia nervosa. By the end of the century claims were appearing that eating disorders were becoming 'more prevalent in Western industrialised countries' (BMA, 2000: 23). Though a lack of longitudinal studies makes this difficult to establish, it is certainly true that

> [t]he aggregate annual mortality rate associated with anorexia nervosa is more than 12 times higher than the annual death rate due to all causes of death for females 15–24 years old in the general population and more than 200 times greater than the suicide rate in the general population.[1]

Obesity is actually a much greater problem: 'In the UK, 17% of men and 20% of women are currently obese and over half the adult population is overweight' (BMA, 2000: 14) but obesity has very negative associations with greed, sloth, poverty and lack of self-control, particularly in the West and particularly amongst the upper socio-economic groups to which many people aspire. On the other hand, slenderness is linked to sexual attraction, fitness, success and self-control, all highly prized in Western culture and suggesting a certain cultural anxiety linking body shape with identity and self-esteem. This alongside the changing role of women and a long history of patriarchal representations, now vastly expanded by advertising and the mass media, constitute the socio-cultural historical specificity of eating disorders recognized in the British Medical Association (BMA) report in 2000 as follows:

- A changing female role, in which women find themselves struggling to strike a balance between new ideals of achievement and traditional female role expectations;
- A pre-occupation with appearance and body image that is associated with rise of mass fashion and consumerism, and:
- A culturally pervasive pre-occupation with weight control and obesity. (BMA, 2000: 22–23)

For each instance the media is perceived as playing a significant part in disseminating ideas that suggest acceptable feminine identity and the BMA call was for the analysis of such media representation and investigation of effect.

In order to contribute to that, this chapter analyses a range of women's magazines – fashion, beauty, health, lifestyle – in order to determine exactly how women are depicted and in what contexts, but argues that to some extent glossy magazines, although not innocent of promoting a thin aesthetics, are none the less not solely responsible for constructing gender norms and values and that the slender-is-sexy norm would only be 'saleable' if it fitted into wider concepts of gender and identity. So, this chapter begins the analysis of gendered imagery in the print media with the British national press, because that remains the most accessed form of print media in the UK with some 14 million newspapers sold daily. It then considers the most popular women's fashion glossies and those designed for teenage girl readers to explore the ways in which femininity is narrated for the reader in the print media. What are the implied value-judgements? Why might they be there? Are women being manipulated and if so for what purpose or to whose benefit? Drawing on semiotics, narrative theory and discourse analysis, it interrogates the 'sites' so vehemently attacked by newspaper journalists, medics and MPs in Britain and the United States, during the early twenty-first century, for causing young women to emulate 'waifs'.

Those 'sites' are communication, both verbal and visual, between media producer and media audience. They are a significant source of the language of our cultural community. As infants we both enter and are entered by language. It is the means by which we make sense of our world, of others and of ourselves. Language is also a *social barometer* (Fairclough, 1992), in that it indicates something of the climate of a culture according to pressure applied to it. That measure becomes part of knowledge about the world and informs actions and beliefs. The way language is used, who uses it, what meanings are associated with it and the ways it changes (or stays the same) can offer insights into what a culture values at any time and whose interests are represented. Language is both affected by or reflective of socio-cultural issues, and active on them, in that language constitutes our subjective sense of self and therefore our attitudes and actions:

> Language is a socially and historically situated mode of action, in a dialectical relationship to other facets of the social. … it is socially shaped, but it is also socially shaping – or socially *constitutive*. (Fairclough, 1995: 54–55)

Language is both material form and social practice: as the former it is neutral shapes or syntagms; as the latter it is constitutive of the discourses which are the mode through which social groups assert their values and express their experiences. As such, the values and stories elicited from language can offer a means of mapping social relations in terms of whose stories are told at all, whose interests are positively evaluated and therefore who has power to imbue that discourse with meaning. Such an approach is critical discourse analysis in that it does not merely describe the form of a language event (the textual constituents) but considers also the practice of the event (who created it and who interpreted it) and its relation to the broader historical and socio-cultural moment within which it occurred. On the one hand, this is an impossible analytic task requiring the placing of all language data in a production/reception context and appropriate social history but on the other hand it can enable the close investigation of a specific topic or social event (in this case young women and eating disorders) according to a particular discourse production genre (the mass media) at a particular time (the early twenty-first century). The approach is an extended semiotics (Barthes, 1957, 1977) that is not merely descriptive but politically critical (Hall, 1973; Weedon, 1987) and specifically socio-historical and subject-centred (Foucault, 1970, 1978).

'Skinny models send unhealthy message'

'Skinny models send unhealthy message' (*Guardian*, 31 May 2000) is a new anxiety but the shifting fashions in body-shape ideal have been researched previously, in relation to the body measurements of beauty parade contestants and models depicted in fashion magazines and soft pornographic publications. This work has indicated a thin-ward trend in Western body-shape ideals but that trend had not, previous to the 1980s, been significantly problematized as detrimental to health. Archival data of the reported height and weight measurements of Miss America pageant winners from 1960 to 1978 indicated that weights had decreased over time. A similar trend towards slimmer build was also noted in an analysis of *Playboy* centrefolds. While female models had been getting slimmer, average women of similar age in the United States, where this research was conducted, had become heavier (Garner et al., 1980). This trend was also illustrated by an analysis of the average bust-to-waist ratio (representing curvaceousness by dividing bust size by waist measurement) of models appearing in *Vogue* and *Ladies Home Journal*. This ratio was observed to decline significantly between the mid-1960s and mid-1980s. A similar decline in bust-to-waist rations was also noted among popular movie actresses (Silverstein, Perdue et al., 1986). The same year, Gagnard (1986) reported a significant increase in thin models in popular magazine advertisements from 1950 to 1984.

An update of the Garner et al. (1980) study by Wiseman et al. (1990) reported that the slimming trend continued from 1979 to 1988. Sixty-nine per cent of the *Playboy* centrefolds and 60 per cent of the pageant contestants studied weighed at least 15 per cent less than expected (as suggested by actuarial tables). This is noteworthy because being at least 15 per cent below one's expected body weight is considered symptomatic of anorexia nervosa (American Psychiatric Association, 1994). At the same time, the number of dieting and exercise articles in popular women's magazines increased year by year during the same period, while the normal weight range of American women and the reported prevalence of eating disorders in the United States both continued to rise.

Singh (1993) observed that while there was evidence that media role models had exhibited a trend towards weighing less and a slimmer build, there was another important aspect of female body shape that apparently had not shifted to any significant degree. The waist-to-hip ratio (WHR) is a key factor in judgements of feminine physical attractiveness. The significance of the WHR is that it represents a key determinant of a woman's attractiveness to a man by acting as a signal of her fertility. Singh observed that healthy fertile women normally have a WHR of 0.6 to 0.8. This means that their waists are typically 60 to 80 per cent the size of their hips. Singh noted that earlier studies of female body shape trends in the media had ignored the WHR measure. Mazur (1986), for example, reported that from 1940 to 1985, the average hip size of Miss America beauty pageant winners changed from 35 inches to 34.5 inches; waists from 24.5 inches to 23.5 inches; and breast size from 34 inches to 35 inches. Thus, the average body measurement of 1940 contestants was 35–24.5–34 (WHR = 0.70) and in 1985 was 34.5–23.5–35 (WHR = 0.68). The WHR hardly changed at all (Singh, 1993).[2] Waist sizes were never found to approach either hip or breast measurements in either group, as would be required to suggest a shift towards a more tubular body shape (Garner et al., 1980).

Despite the claims of other authors that there was a clear trend towards a more tubular shape (e.g., Morris et al., 1989), the WHRs of the models examined in such research have generally shown little change over time. Furthermore, research has also shown that females with tubular body shapes are not rated to be as attractive as females with hourglass figures (Furnham et al., 1990). Curiously, however slender women become, the fecundity factor that makes them sexually appealing to men, the WHR, remains intact, whether maintained by diet, exercise or, of course, surgery. Whereas the firm muscle of buttocks and thighs may resist starvation, the fat of waist disappears quite readily, improving the WHR. Breasts also shrink very quickly through diet but rank high enough on the attractiveness quotient for many very slender women to turn to padding or surgical implants to boost their sex appeal even, ironically, when they may be too thin to menstruate or conceive.

By June of 2000, the Blair Labour government's Women's Unit in London, England, was concerned enough about the apparent rise of health-damaging efforts at slenderness to convene a meeting to discuss a possible link between apparent increases in eating disorders, mostly amongst young women, and magazine images of 'super-waif' fashion models. Psychotherapist Susie Orbach (1978, 1993) was consulted alongside academics, magazine journalists and medical practitioners. The so-called Body Summit was presided over by Tessa Jowell, Minister for Women.

The impetus for the summit on the media and the body was, rather ironically, a growing media-led articulation of concerns, largely emanating from medical and psychological discourses, that 'magazines' feature significantly and detrimentally in the construction of body image amongst young women. The effect was theorized as negative due to magazines' consistent preference to depict fashion and beauty as inexorably linked to extreme slenderness with the effect of creating self-destructive attitudes to food amongst young female readers in particular. The *Guardian* (31 May 2000) reported that some '7 million women and 1 million men in the UK suffer from eating disorders' (unsourced). The article said that the British Medical Association 'claimed that the promotion of rake thin models, such as Kate Moss and Jodie Kidd, was creating a distorted body image which young women tried to imitate'. It also printed the response from a leading model agency, which argued that 'women who bought magazines featuring thin models were as much to blame as their editors and the advertisers'. In other words, consumers not producers were normalizing waif-like women.

This argument parallels the claims by many in the tabloid press after the death of Princess Diana in 1998 that they only hounded her because the public demanded to see her image in the news. This view of the role and content of the media raises complex issues about media ethics and professional practices, and it invests audiences with both blame for and authority over media messages. This acts as a counterpoise to theorizing the media as empowered to affect cultural norms and values by bringing the audience into meaning construction as already primed to expect, accept and perhaps even demand or desire only particular versions of the world. Despite this account, popular, and often in consequence policy/political,[3] accounts of many social ills – violence, delinquency, sexual 'perversion' and now self-starvation – have frequently been explained by effects models of the media. A curious result of this has been a fragmenting of the media from within about its own practices, as various sections have sought, at different times and in different circumstances, to extricate themselves from blame. This diversionary castigation was evident after Princess Diana's death when the 'quality' newspapers and broadcast news launched a critical assault on the tabloids and their obsession with Diana; an obsession that made profitable the activities of the freelance 'paparazzi' photographers, who followed Diana everywhere.

A similar assault on the media as causing 'bad' effects happens in other arenas, especially crime and sexual *deviance*. Violent crime is often blamed on the fictional media by the factual media. The murder of toddler James Bulger in 1993 was enthusiastically linked to a video called *Child's Play 3* (Wykes, 2001). Stanley Kubrick's film *A Clockwork Orange* was banned in the 1970s after being blamed in the papers for a series of so-called copycat rapes. Questin Tarantino's film *Reservoir Dogs* was cited in a case where three youths tried 'to cut off a 15 year old boy's ear before stabbing him to death with a broken bottle' (Michael Winner, *Guardian*, 9 July 2000). As Winner goes on to point out, the evidence for such causality is tenuous at best. Rather:

> People do not go into cinemas angels and come out to slash their mothers-in-law. There are other causes of evil and the fascination with blaming film simply detracts from the research that should go into the genuine causes of violence. (ibid.)

Sexual morality, or rather perceived immorality, has frequently been blamed on the media too. From the banning of *Lady Chatterley's Lover* in the first half of the twentieth century, to 'legislation proposed by the British Conservative Member of Parliament (MP) Peter Luff, February 1996, which would require publishers to place age suitability warnings on the covers of young women's magazines because of their use of "sexually explicit" material' (Tincknell et al., 2003: 47).

Here, as elsewhere, it is women who are *instructed how to behave* (Heidensohn, 1985). Tincknell et al. note that there was no 'comparable panic over the proliferation of sex in men's magazines' (2003: 48).

In the case of the crisis of anorexia, it is magazines featuring advertisements and articles promoting fashion and beauty that the mainstream news media have singled out to target, and again it is young women who are perceived as particularly at risk. Jess Carter-Morley, a fashion editor for the *Guardian*, exemplified the holier-than-thou view of newspaper journalists when she wrote 'surely it is time for the glossy magazines and designers who demand and promote an extremely thin body shape to take a more responsible attitude' (*Guardian*, 31 May 2000). One powerful response came from another journalist who pointed the finger not at magazines but at newspapers:

> The *Daily Mail* has created thousands more anorexics than *Vogue*, because *Vogue* simply shows thin women while the *Daily Mail* keeps up a non-stop commentary on the weight gain of famous women and links it to their sexual orientation and career success. (Julie Burchill, *Guardian*, 8 July 2000)

Less obvious than 'fashion photos', news too relies on and reproduces cultural norms and values, as Julie Burchill's quote above so neatly demonstrates. It is more complex, more frequent, more subtle and more popular than magazines. News is narrative;[4] it tells a whole story embedding events in words and pictures and juxtaposing them with other complementary news. It offers explanations, often by 'experts', to support the journalistic 'angle'. It also connects stories to extra-news knowledge and events, often other stories or myths and not always ones that are either suitable or even relevant to the event being reported.[5] News in the papers also has to make sense quickly and efficiently to an audience that is only likely to read it once and may well be eating or standing on a train simultaneously. News has to fit prior cultural knowledge to make sense.

For all these reasons news is, as Julie Burchill claimed, far more likely to resonate meaningfully with an audience than a few dislocated images of thin women. As Cartner-Morley commented, 'a well adjusted woman does not starve herself to death just because she sees a picture of a skinny model' (*Guardian*, 31 May 2000). However what if that image is just the clearest rendition of a whole accumulation of messages, pervading our culture and frequently reproduced in communication, which suggest to women that to be lovable, successful and sexually attractive, they need to conform to a very narrow set of body measurement criteria? Orbach's 1978 comment on women has continuing relevance:

> She attempts to make herself in the image of womanhood presented by billboards, newspapers, magazines and television. ... She is brought up to marry by catching man with her good looks. To do this she must look appealing, earthy, sensual, virginal, innocent, reliable, caring, mysterious, coquettish and thin. (Orbach, 1978: 20–21)

That self-starvation is a problem is demonstrated by the evident rise in the problem of and anxiety about the incidence of eating disorders, both professional and popular. Yet that professional concern has resulted mainly in a medicalization and psychologization of the conditions associated with food obsession. Furious medicalization (without any evidence of a cure for anorexia and bulimia) and psycho-analyticization (with no obvious reduction in incidence or curtailment of the tendency for 15–20 per cent of anorexics eventually to die as a result of the effects of their eating disorder).[6] Each approach has also failed to provide any kind of generic cause or preventive strategies except for that favourite scapegoat of social ills, the media. Failing to account for the condition within their own knowledge disciplines they turned outward to the broader culture; found a preponderance of 'thin is beautiful' fashion aesthetics in women's magazines and declared them guilty. It was against this background that the British Medical Association and UK government's summit on the body was held.

A sometimes crude cause and effect model (seeking in the socio-cultural world a similar pattern to that central to science-based disciplines) accused the fashion world and its magazines. Arnett claimed 'magazines are a medium where gender role identity formation is an especially common theme, particularly in magazines for adolescent girls' (1995: 522). *Serious* journalists have rapidly joined the medical scientists and psychologists in a tirade against fashion magazines. Such journalists have agreed that 'anorexia is powerfully fuelled by media images' because women 'measure themselves against the ideal images captured on camera' (*Guardian*, 19 June 2000) and distributed in the fashion and beauty magazines and find themselves wanting. These quotes came curiously from the journalists on the women's page of the *Guardian* who seemed oblivious to the fact that by using the term 'ideal' of images of very thin women they too were indicating a very narrow – literally and figuratively – concept of appropriate femininity. The use of the term ideal both suggests that there is such a thing as an ideal shape for/type of women and that shape is starvation-thin, tall, young and probably blonde.

If magazine fashion images are culpable, if they can distort women's self-image and impel self-destruction, it would seem relatively easy to cure eating disorders, but such a theory raises far more questions than it can answer. Why don't all women who regularly see thin images suffer from eating disorders? Do all women suffer from thin obsession but not all succumb to extreme self-mutilation? What impact do other thin images such as female shop window mannequins – usually too physically distorted to make menstruation a possibility or even to stand up should they be real – have on the passing multitudes? How can images alone be so powerful? We have to have learnt what they signify, what they connote, other than thinness, from somewhere. The profile of anorexic girls is very often middle-class high-achievers. Could such young women really be persuaded into ritual suicide by a few pictures of strangers alone?

It may be satisfying to be able to offer some resolving account of eating disorders but to accuse magazines with images advertising the products of the fashion industry is to target merely a symptom of broader social norms and values which are already gendered. Magazines form a mediating part of an already gendered discourse. That discourse is the broad cultural representation of sexual identity and activity. It generates the symbols that signify what is valuable and desirable in the feminine and pre-empts but informs and is reproduced by the content of magazines and the cut of clothes. That symbolic order is also the means of signifying self-worth, identity and subjectivity.

On the day after the UK government's Body Summit, the national daily press provided extensive coverage of the issues – sometimes seriously, sometimes scathingly. A sample of mediated images of femininity immediately followed that summit: the *Daily Telegraph* (923,815), *Daily Mail* (2,327,732) and *Sun* (3,447,108) represent the highest circulation publications for each of the quality, middle-brow and popular sectors of the UK newspaper spectrum respectively.[7] A further sample from the same papers was taken three years later to explore any long-term effort journalists might have made to address the British Medical Association's calls for urgent action to be 'taken to reduce the pressure on young women to be thin, and to reduce the number of young people who develop anorexia and bulimia nervosa' (BMA, 2000: 2). For each date the analysis also looked at the *Guardian*, whose female journalists were so outspoken and accusing of magazine journalism, just to explore the kind of femininities on offer in an apparently at least liberal if not politically feminist newspaper.

Another print sample was taken from the 2003 July editions of the best-selling teen and fashion glossy monthly magazines, spanning the audience age group most vulnerable to eating disorders, 13–25 years. These fell into two categories: teen titles aimed at older schoolgirls, of which the best-selling are *Sugar* (321,258), *Bliss* (255,653) and *J17* (143,308). Teen titles are in many ways primers for the 'real' adult glossies and their advertising spiel:

> Women's glossies are as seductive to teenage girls as a gaggle of loud-mouthed adolescent boys smoking outside school. Magazine publishers know this – the National Magazine Company's research shows that 94% of teenagers buy a magazine every month. They also know that teenagers have more disposable cash now than at any time in the past. And they know, crucially, that readership of magazines by adult women has been declining for nearly a decade.
>
> It's this situation that has given birth to the latest marketer's dream, the 'baby glossy' – a new generation of magazines for teenage girls which aims to harness the 'reading up' tendency of teenagers to the proliferation of new products targeted at them. (*Guardian*, 2 July 2001)

Further editions were also collected of the most popular glossies – the fashion/lifestyle magazines aimed at young, independent women in the 18–35 age group. Best-selling of these are *Glamour* (537,474), *Cosmopolitan* (463,058) and *Marie-Claire* (400,038).[8]

'My body and me':[9] women in the newspapers

In their onslaught against magazines and television as causal of all manner of social harm, newspaper journalists have always been curiously unreflective about what goes on within their own pages. This was, and remains, the case in news reports concerning eating disorders and body image. Yet newspapers are deeply gendered both in terms of production context, content and audiences and are produced more frequently and circulated to larger numbers than magazines or most television programmes. Burchill, in the *Guardian* article quoted earlier, argued that news can present women in ways that make body image of central importance to feminine identity. It also clarifies that although 'a well adjusted woman does not starve herself to death just because she sees a picture of a skinny model'

(*Guardian*, 31 May 2000), such images may actually be consonant with the cultural climate of what are very desirable attributes of femininity – attractiveness, wealth, career success, popularity – through association across a range of discourses, and should not be viewed as simply solely causal of self-harm but as evidence of broader constructions of feminine subjectivity.

Much research has highlighted the masculinity at the heart of newspaper journalism, both in terms of ownership and control of the industry and journalistic practices and profiles (Holland, 1998; Tuchman, 1981; Tunstall, 1996; Van Zoonen, 1994, 1998; Wykes, 2001). Women remain under-represented in the profession and those who do achieve are under no illusion that they have to be 'one of the boys' to get on (Christmas, 1997).

> While real, embodied – if invisible – women continue to have only minimal roles in the shaping of our popular media, the men who produce the pages will continue to build their power on the decorative excess of the women who are pictured on them – just like the eighteenth century academicians and their voluptuous models. (Holland, 1998: 32)

Moreover, masculinity comes to the media already trailing clouds of hegemonic glory through its long history of authority in other discourses and practices. Our everyday meanings are anyway deeply masculinized. Berger (1972) argued that in 'art' men act and women appear in ways that suit the male. Arguably his point could be made of all representation. Masculinity already empowered physically, culturally and economically, through the mass media, becomes discursively so, reproducing and legitimating its place in the world because '[m]oney and power are able to filter out the news fit to print, marginalise dissent and allow the government and other dominant interests to get their message across' (Herman and Chomsky, 1988: 2). In the process of news-making those mostly male journalists 'provide interpretations, symbols of identification, collective values and myths' (Chibnall, 1977: 226) on behalf of all of us. Women who do enter the profession

> often get very stereotypical assignments which relegate them to marginal areas of journalism. They also have to live up to a double requirement: they have to show in their daily performance that they are good journalists as well as 'real' women. (Van Zoonen, 1998: 37)

Such research suggests that Burchill was right to criticize the *Daily Mail* but needed to go further and look at journalism as a whole as likely to produce gendered discourse according to power – masculine power. That power is dominant twice over in the media industries – in the bedroom and the boardroom as both journalism and media ownership are male-dominated. The likelihood is that representations of femininity in the press will be conducive to male interests.

Yet there was clearly a news focus on the dangers of fashion for females at the turn of the millennium and a consequent government summit about the problem. The newspapers published on the day following the summit (22 June 2000) did cover the debate and consequent policy recommendations but none considered their own part in the construction of femininity as in any way relevant to the way young women feel about themselves and their bodies. The four newspapers – the *Sun*, *Daily Mail*, *Daily Telegraph* and *Guardian* – looked at closely at that time and again three years later have a combined circulation of about 6.6 million daily – a good proportion of the reading population of this country. It is impossible to collect a breakdown of audience in terms of gender and age but the goal of this section is to explore how femininity is represented, rather than how it might be received – which is the business of the second part of the book – in one of the potentially most influential discourse types, the media, in the modern world.

The *Sun* has long been targeted by feminists for its portrayal of women as semi-nude pin-ups on its notorious page three which it claims resolutely are just 'fun' (Holland, 1998). Its response to the anorexia summit was broadly similar on 22 June 2000. The editorial was headlined 'Thin Joke' and Minister for Women, Tessa Jowell, who chaired the summit, was accused of wanting to waste public money by counting the 'number of waifs on TV'. On page 24, a further very brief article referred to the decision of the summit to ask the Broadcasting Standards Commission to 'scan soaps, dramas and even game shows for images of women, however tricky it might be "to decide which women were fat or thin"'. The remaining references to women in this edition were few and either negative, sexual or about famous subjects (also often negative unless portrayed semi-naked and sexual). Of the 64 pages, only 12 had 'news' featuring women, including the front page and two inside pages, which were devoted to 'Nurse is probed over 18 child deaths'. Curiously the article never says she was a woman but labelled her 'an unmarried nurse in her forties' who had 'mood-swings'. The connotation is not 'normally' feminine, perhaps menopausal – maybe lesbian. A further brief article features a woman victim of crime whose murderer has never been caught. The only other news featuring women was about Royal Ascot, the major UK horse racing meeting, and depicted four female lottery winners wearing ridiculous hats covered with net and lottery balls. *Sun Woman* had a fashion spread of four young blonde women in brief bikinis entitled 'String's the Thing'. The remaining references were all to famous women, either pop stars, including Kylie and Madonna, members of the royal family or soap opera actresses and there are several semi-clad models used in adverts.

Twelve pages of sport featured an eighth of a page article on a young, blonde tennis player.

Three years later, the *Sun* (10 June 2003), now in support of the Labour government and edited by a woman, Rebekah Wade, is nothing if not consistent. It still had 64 pages of which 12 feature women in stories. Again there were 12 pages of sport – this time two featured women. One page contained a brief reference to the pride felt by the mother of young footballer Wayne Rooney and the second, yet again, concerned young blonde tennis player Anna Kournikova. The latter included a very large photograph, showing her with midriff exposed and captioned: 'Does my bum look big in this?' Other news featured celebrity women, either getting married (Kate Winslet), having babies with partners ('Big brother star looks happy and trim') or separating: 'It's all gone tong: DJ and wife split' and 'Amanda is still apart from Les'. Alternatively to being accounted for according to their relations with men, the famous females were either 'sexy' – yes, Kylie was there again: 'The pop princess famed for her perfect rear' is shown in bra and brief outfit – or criticized for not being sexy: 'Movie star Melanie Griffiths looks like a living doll after years of cosmetic surgery'. A double page about stars seeking publicity by posing with snakes was titled 'Celebrity Reptiles'. There was also a photo of bikini-clad Miss Great Britain and a fashion spread showing only women's legs and feet and titled 'Sole Stars'.

Women in the *Sun* are valued only if young, decorative, fertile, famous, heterosexual, white, slender, preferably blonde, or they have famous male partners. The *Sun* appears to feel quite at liberty to comment on women's size or shape. All the women featured positively are young. None is black. Any deviation from that narrow norm was either ignored as 'news' or somehow denigrated in the paper either directly or humorously (Butcher et al., 1974). Many of the women were associated with men, as if this was the prize for their beauty, or shown as if on offer to male readers – the male partners were rarely foregrounded whilst the women, either alone or accompanied, gaze at the reader or feature merely as 'parts'.

The *Daily Mail* (22 June 2000) had a massive headline taking two-thirds of the front cover: 'LUNACY OF THE TV WEIGHT WATCH POLICE'. As with the *Sun*, this focused on just one aspect of the Downing Street initiative, the monitoring of television images of women. Only on page 2 were the issues of magazines, models and the fashion industry addressed – though this did improve on the *Sun*, which only wrote about the televisual images. The *Mail* also quoted psychotherapist and eating disorder expert Susie Orbach saying: 'We no longer have images of models as they look themselves, they are often digitally enhanced'. None of this article criticized journalism at all; nor did the *Mail* reflect on its own contribution to a cultural construction of feminine identity, as described by Burchill. Indeed, next to the large front page titles was an image of a young blonde woman, cleavage exposed, gazing at the reader, parted lips glossed, entitled: 'My drug rape ordeal'. The full story on page 11 depicted her again in a different, strapless dress and high heels as a victim of date-rape who warns women of the danger of drinking alone in bars. A further front page image showed the Prince of Wales' partner and asks: 'Camilla: was that a dress too far?' An inside article by Ann Leslie revisits the body summit and is titled: 'Nanny Tessa, you're just being absurd'. Whilst criticizing teen magazines for their constant focus on the question: 'Does my bum look big in this'? (a textual cross-reference to the *Sun*'s Kournikova article), Leslie claimed that the Labour government is simply vote-catching and the summit is 'gesture politics' seeking 'moral brownie points'. The newspaper had 96 pages, including 14 in the 'Femail' section. Thirty pages feature women prominently but only one of these is amongst the 11 pages of sport and yet again it is Anna Kournikova. A half-page photo showed her in brief tennis dress and was titled: 'Anna stops the traffic but starts winning: poster girl Kournikova shows that her tennis is as eye-catching as her looks'. Other stories included Royal Ascot, this time with *Daily Mail* women journalists looking absurd in lampshades in place of hats. On page 5 was a story titled: 'Devastated PC shoots himself as policewoman brands him a sex-pest'. He was described as a 'biology graduate'; 'a well-respected and popular officer' who was a victim of the 'politically correct culture sweeping police forces' and was 'gentle, friendly and dedicated to his job'. She was 'an Asian PC' who went 'mad' at a 'minor incident'. Most other feminine references in the paper were to royalty, including Caroline of Monaco, Princess Diana, Camilla and Sarah Ferguson and focus on their looks, relationships and health. 'Femail' is mainly about fashion – young, blonde, white but less flesh-exposing than the *Sun* with a special on outfits for a summer wedding. There was a long article on the effect orthodox Judaism can have on marriage, 'Wives from another time', and another on marital infidelity. Shopping features as 'therapy'. Beauty advice is on dental cosmetic surgery.

In 2003, the *Daily Mail* had 80 pages. There were 10 on sport and yet again the only substantial piece on a woman showed Anna Kournikova. Two photos were sub-titled 'Mixed emotions: a downcast Kournikova leaves the Edgbaston practice courts in contrast to her delight at a recent fashion shoot'. As in the other coverage her tennis brilliance was given less attention than her looks. There were 14 other pages with woman stories, of which nine featured celebrity relationships – all white, all young – the other five featured health stories, three of which showed young, white women, one of whom was singer Britney Spears – midriff revealed.

The *Daily Mail* is a humourless and slightly prudish *Sun*. Most women were missing from its pages: none shown was black; one elderly woman and one plump woman were both ill. There were three crime stories that referred to women: one was a victim; one a possible witness and the third featured the Soham case, which involved the murder of two small girls in Cambridgeshire, England. The story likened Maxine Carr, in prison awaiting trial for the killings, to Rose West. West is currently serving life for the murder of young girls in 1995. The comparison implied Carr's guilt 5 months before the murder trial[10] was due to take place. Extreme castigation of women whether as victims or perpetrators of violence is common in the press, which tends to try women twice, both for their crimes and for their failure to be 'feminine'.[11] Otherwise women in the news were royal, stars, blondes, pregnant (or wanting to be), in love, heterosexual and 'looking after their bodies and their health'. Again the inference was that these were the women who get on in life (many are famous and wealthy) and certainly these were women who get their man.

The *Daily Telegraph* also featured women at Ascot – this paper placed them on the front page, looking foolish and unsophisticated clinging on to large hats in high winds. The conservative and traditional broadsheet had 48 pages on 22 June 2000, an inside article on the 'thin summit' was flagged on the front page with 'Goodbye Perfect Bodies'. Fifteen pages had a significant female presence – but only a very brief article amongst seven pages of sport covered women's tennis. Page 3 was virtually totally devoted to the body image summit and foregrounded a photo of Susie Orbach (therapist), Liz Jones (magazine editor), Tessa Jowell (government minister) and Rebecca Martin (teen-magazine editor) and was headlined 'Magazines ban anorexic models'. The article was factual and lucid. It focused closely on the portrayal of skeletal models in magazines and the need for a code of practice to depict a 'diverse' range of women. Unlike the tabloid *Sun* and *Mail,* the piece only mentioned television in passing and pointed out that the Broadcasting Standards Commission was merely considering research into broadcast images – a very different interpretation to that offered by the tabloids, which suggested that government was impelling controls. However, the serious, thoughtful though uncritical tone of this main piece was diminished by an article immediately below it by the *Telegraph's* fashion editor, Hilary Alexander, titled: 'It all went pear-shaped for the body politic'. Like the *Mail,* this claimed the government was trying to 'nanny' the population and was engaged in 'spin' and 'sound-bite'. Alexander even ended by arguing that clothes look best on thin models and women diet because they want to 'look their best'. The article on page 28 by the editor of *Vogue,* Alexandra Shulman, picked out the 'blame-storming' nature of the summit and the self-promoting activities of those in attendance. Shulman is herself brutally derogatory of Liz Jones, editor of *Marie-Claire,* whom she says has too many 'weird insecurities' to 'spearhead a movement designed to encourage young women to feel good about themselves' and ended by saying women will not give up the 'quest for a flat stomach'. The effect of this was to present the summit as little more than a cat-fight and seems to confirm stereotypical ideas about 'career' women as bitchy and competitive.

There were no bikinis in the *Telegraph* and young women featured only in advertising. Most articles about women were health-related or featured royalty and either their clothes or relationships. Two exceptions both featured women and sex – one was about an Oxford scientist who was cleared of sleeping her way into an academic post; the second was the same date-rape case featured in the *Mail* but in the *Telegraph* the photograph used was of Nina Richards' face only. She looked tearful, hands clenched to her mouth, eyes averted and in her middle years. There were two pieces – the first about her case and the second more generally about drug-assisted rape. As in the main story about the summit, both articles were factual, well-researched and non-judgemental and therein lies the problem with the *Telegraph's* account of femininity. The story of the status quo was told but the legitimacy of that status quo is not questioned – it is a truly conservative newspaper.

In 2003, three women featured on the front page but only as images – the Chancellor's wife and two famous women whose romances are detailed in the inside pages. The main paper was 32 pages long. Nine pages featured women but there were none on the sports pages. There was, however, a long obituary on Elsie Widdowson. As in the tabloids, the marriage of Kate Winslet took pride of place on page 5 – much of the text referred to the previous relationships of the couple – with a typically *Telegraph* factual headline, 'Surprise for family as Winslet weds Mendes'. A large photo of the return of three young WRENS (women serving in the British Royal Navy) from the Gulf is on page 6, though most of the commentary is about a male officer. An article about Broadway featured actresses, including one of Sarah Jessica Parker nearly wearing the top of her dress – this was the only slightly sexy image of women apart from advertising. Page 11 has a feature on Vita Sackville-West that discussed her lesbian affairs and page 13 had Hillary Clinton discussing her husband's affairs. In the features section actress Anna Chancellor revealed intimate details of her affair with 'an Algerian cab-driver' for most of a page. A style section featured shoes, 'Simple slippers, fit for a star', and lipsticks for the 'perfect pink pout'. Two further brief pieces focused on stars.

The *Daily Telegraph* at first glance did offer more space to women and more serious space but much of it is photographs – albeit tasteful ones. Also two substantial pieces were about dead women. When examined though it was the same type of women who feature here as in the tabloids: royals, stars and victims. As in the tabloids the accounting discourse was very often sexualized though here it is about relationships rather than looks. The curious thing about the *Telegraph* is how descriptive it is – there was no passion, no irony and no criticism, even of rape. It seemed to be saying to readers – these were the few women of interest, they are mainly interesting because of their relationship to men and that is simply how it is. Even the coverage of the body summit reduced the power of a straight piece by offering two rather dismissive and slightly humorous accounts. In fact in this paper women seemed only to be newsworthy at all if they could somehow be depicted in relation to men.

The *Guardian* is by reputation a liberal, quality newspaper and certainly its women journalists spoke out against the emaciated images being offered to young women. It reported the summit on 22 June 2000 with a front page piece that emulated the line taken by the tabloids, 'TV plan to monitor images of ultra-thin women', but included a discussion of the role of magazines, though not newspapers. Part of the editorial also covered the summit but oddly it added a sexual dimension to the debate by focusing on early pubescence, pregnancy and sexually transmitted disease and then confusingly talking about the 'flat-chested, slim-hipped androgynous model favoured on the catwalk' as a form of misogyny. The piece did little to clarify the debate about the relationship between media image and eating disorders. Moreover, the main paper, at 28 pages, featured barely any women at all, except two obituaries. There was some reference to women as victims: a long piece entitled 'Policeman gets 18 years for sex attacks'; the drug-rape case featured in the other papers, but without any photograph; about 200 words on Kate Winslet (again) as the victim of a stalker; and a brief item on a woman victim of racial insults. International royals were featured, including wives, on page 16, as was the actress Jane Fonda. There was also a long piece on the Queen Mother. The G2 supplement had 24 tabloid size pages. It included a joke piece on Jane Fonda; a long story on a headmaster who abused girl pupils and an interview with an Asian woman novelist who had been attacked by men in her community for caricaturing Asian culture. The arts section featured singer Juliette Greco but concentrated on her looks, her relationships with Camus, Sartre and Miles Davis and her 'free-living'.

In 2003 there were 34 pages in the main section and 24 in G2. Only three pages in the main paper have stories about women: Kate Winslet's marriage again, the singer Shirley Bassey, and the mother of a murdered Gypsy boy who is photographed and interviewed. Each of these was primarily an image. All the sport was male. No women featured in G2 except for a picture of singer Cilla Black linked to a quiz. For all its protestations, the *Guardian* perhaps serves women least of all the newspapers – in that it 'symbolically annihilates' them (Tuchman, 1981) rather than denigrate, laugh at, sexualize, victimize, or represent them in traditional roles and relationships as happens in the other papers.

The newspapers have little to boast about in terms of how they represent women. They feature rarely unless sexually attractive and/or linked to a famous man. Whether famous or not in their own right, it is their sexual role (mother, wife, mistress, rape victim) that tends to be newsworthy. Moreover the typology of those featured is very narrow: young, slender, white, blonde, famous and under-dressed, and the representation tends to be visual rather than verbal. Just as older men choose such women as 'arm-candy' so our national press presents women as 'news-candy' – to please the eye and sweeten the business of reportage. In our newspapers, implicitly and sometimes explicitly, women's size and shape do appear to correlate with sexual attractiveness, sexual role and/or fame (Burchill, *Guardian*, 8 July 2000). Discursively, many people access such connections and implicit value-judgements daily, constructing myths of femininity that may well cognitively prompt them to accept other instances of information that fit those patterns and also contributing to their communication, action and self-perception.

'You can get rid of cellulite' and 'make any man better in bed'[12]

The representations most singled out as harmful at the body summit were those in glossy fashion magazines and certainly this medium makes overt connections between 'looks' and 'sexual love' to a largely young, female audience. But such a connection must make sense to readers on the basis of other experience; it has to have cultural consonance in that it fits prior knowledge that may have historical origins (as in the long history of representations of femininity) or occur elsewhere in the contemporary shared culture (newspapers, television, the Web) or social practices (family units, religion, employment). Magazines are part of broader discursive practices and power relations; they fit ideas within those and those ideas come from that context.

From the 1960s, women's glossies have apparently reflected the sexual liberation and career ambitions that had been nurtured by second-wave feminism. Magazines addressed the aspirational desires of young women at a time of economic growth, reliable contraception and individual freedom with *pride of place given to sex* (MacDonald, 1995). Those aspirations though were still presented as revolving around men: how you dress for work; freeing yourself from an unreliable man; meeting Mr Right; asserting yourself during sex; how to make your body attractive and where to be seen, all related to getting sexual satisfaction and very often dependent on buying a product – if only the magazine itself. In many ways the old models of 'coupling' were barely challenged despite the 'feminist claims' of magazines like *Cosmopolitan*, which launched in 1972 in the UK. It was just that instead of settling for one man women gained the freedom to try several – it was as if all their new-found financial independence was worth was the ability to buy versions of themselves that more men would desire. This was the intense contradiction of the post-feminist magazines and remains evident, perhaps even less feminist, in the new millennium.

Magazines were not and are not charities, and the dependence on advertising ensured considerable contradictions were at play within their pages. Wolf even argued: 'What editors are obliged to appear to say that *men* want from women is actually what their advertisers want from women' (1991: 73), particularly in relation to thinness, which she points out is rarely cited by men as an attractive attribute in women. But in the magazines it is always there – thin is the body on which the clothes, make-up, relationships and lifestyle of successful (that is desirable) femininity are hung. It is the essential structure of the sexual subject on which gender is inscribed. If a woman's body is not the right size and shape nothing else will fit – certainly not any positive self-identity.

In women's magazines three discursive institutions appeared to be in competition for readers' attention: two were overt in their ideology, if uncomfortable bedfellows – patriarchy and feminism; the third was covert, and profitably exploited the disjunction between the other two – capitalism. It is advertising and its role that is the great unspoken in the equation, yet no women's magazines could survive without it and it is reasonable to assume that, even if unconsciously, choices of content will be made sensitive to advertiser's requirements of consumers.

Glamour is published by Condé Nast, *Cosmopolitan* by the National Magazine Company and *Marie-Claire* by European Magazines Ltd. I analysed the editions on sale in June 2003, to correspond with the second batch of newspapers and to see whether the calls for change from the Downing Street summit, carried in the press three years previously, had been realized. The June magazines are in fact dated July. Each was very focused on summer holidays but when compared with the editions of the previous three months for each magazine, the overall format remained static in terms of volume and genre of material, only the fashion and beauty advice varied, seasonally. Each of these best-selling women's fashion and beauty glossies has a reference to re-shaping the body along-side one on how to get, keep or please a man on the front cover of the July 2003 edition. All have more space devoted to advertising in some form or other than to other content.

Glamour has stormed into the magazine market. It won 'Consumer Magazine of the Year' in 2003. Its front cover featured the three young, thin, female stars of the film *Charlie's Angels* (Figure 4.1). At £1.80 in Britain, its cover price is cheaper than many; it is small enough to fit into a hand-bag and yet has 290 pages. For July 2003, the contents page indicated only 31 of these 290 pages were 'feature' pages. It also claimed some 50 pages of fashion and beauty, all of which list prices and stockists. Eighteen pages had collage arrangements of *Glamour* recommended fashion and beauty purchases. It had 125 pages with nothing on them but advertising. The advertising conformed to the kind in the edition of *Marie-Claire* (May 2003) already discussed in Chapter 3. Women were broadly told they

Figure 4.1   Glamour

should smell 'sexier' (perfumes and deodorants), colour hair, lips and
skin 'naturally' but 'scientifically', deal with menstruation 'discreetly' and
shape and smooth their bodies (cosmetic surgery and depilation).
Glamour had no adverts for diet products and only four for foodstuffs
(two for chocolate products). There were several promotions for mobile
phones.

Features divided between film and pop star-focused reports (20
pages) that integrated sales with gossip and comment and were
heavily image-based. The remainder were lifestyle-, relationship- and
beauty-based. The section *You, You, You* offered the advice 'play match-
maker and you might get your fingers burned'; 'how it feels when lust
turns to love' and 'what his sleep style says about him' foregrounding

relationships with men. The L'Oreal cosmetics company slogan 'Because You're Worth It' headed a discussion on salaries, followed by a brief piece on 'Find out if your type gets to the top' at work. Next came 'De-jelly your belly' and 'Identify your stress personality'. These brief pieces each offered a self-help book to achieve the particular goal, in fact they were arguably adverts for self-help books. A serious piece on women involved in working in the Iraq conflict was followed by a glamour promotion for 'combat chic' sponsored by Nivea Deodorant. An article on arguments in relationships preceded one titled 'Get more of everything you want in bed', and again suggestsed a self-help book purchase. Three pages offered film, music and book reviews and then pages 193 to 254 were devoted to fashion and beauty. These featured very slender, young, white girls either wearing very little and/or very expensive clothes, and beauty advice featuring the same body-types and many pages of products necessary to achieve 'pretty perfection'. The section completed with 'Why don't these women have cellulite?', with advice on how to 'kiss goodbye to your lumpy bits' with 'fish and exercise', 'veggies and green tea' and 'seed oil and supplements'. Again this foregrounded images of slender, young, white women, wearing only brief underwear. There was very little text. A fifth page offered 'cellulite busters' for sale, including 'Phyto-sculptural' for £57. *Living Glamour* ends the magazine with four pages on home and garden and five on holidays.

Marie-Claire for the same month (July 2003) had a beautiful, young, white, blonde, slender actress on the front cover: 'Angel Cameron: sexy, stylish and sussed'. It contained 354 pages and the editor admits: 'Oh dear, I've come over a bit star-struck this month'. There were several pages of 'Celeb Sightings' to introduce the edition and a long interview with the cover star. Next came an article on sexual compatibility, one on women drug mules and one on a celebrity with breast cancer. An article called 'Real Lives' gave tips on how to deal with 'odd' body-shapes and 'flatter your assets'. This piece, by implying that it is/was a problem to be 'too tall', or 'busty' or have 'wide hips', reinforced the slender boyish stereotype of perfect femininity. The women featured mention having 'unbalanced shapes' and one is told 'wearing loose cuts will make your bum look bigger'. It was followed by an article on 'Sex Lives of the Rich and Famous' about 'sexiest soap male' Shane Ritchie and his young, thin, blonde girlfriend who 'gets up at dawn and goes to the gym'. *Marie-Claire* offers readers a consistent diet of appropriate men and warnings about inappropriate men. For the magazine, David Beckham is the ideal and in April they placed him on the cover as the dream man. Editor Marie O'Riordan commented: 'He represents something for every woman: father, husband, footballer, icon. In a word he's the ultimate hero' (http://media.guardian.co.uk/circulationfigures/story/0,11554,689337,00.html).

In the July 2003 edition an article exposed the villains – men who cheat in love. Although this article seemed to warn women about male duplicity and lack of commitment, the next exhorted them to 'change' themselves (not their men) to save their love affairs. It suggested therapy as a way of changing yourself and so improving your sexual relationship. In this feature, one woman said she risked losing her boyfriend because she put him under pressure with 'unrealistic expectations' and another claimed 'therapy has made my relationship with Simon possible'. Soon after *Marie-Claire* offered the 'Man of the Month', with the chance to date an 'eligible man'. Then came 'flavour of the month' featuring 'Australia's newest sex God'. Next were film and music reviews then fashion and beauty. The fashion pages again featured young, slender, white models in swimwear. Many images were sexualized: wet T-shirts, pouting lips and topless shots. The beauty pages had similar images but included male models – two males and one female in overtly sexual and near naked poses – with sub-headings such as 'crazy, sexy, cool' and 'burning desire'. Essential products to achieve these looks (and presumably 'attract' the men featured with them) were depicted in a 'shopping' section. Little seemed to have changed since Berger (1972: 144) wrote 'To be able to buy is the same thing as being sexually desirable'. Towards the end of the magazine there were a few pages on health, the Agony Aunt page on 'Sex and relationships', eight pages on 'interiors' with product listings, some information on recipes and holidays because, of course, once you've got your man by 'looking right' this is the kind of support for your lifestyle you will need as a couple. The narrative was flawless; the whole magazine works as a story in Proppian terms; the lack was the man (or happy relationship); the heroine's journey was to seek a hero (avoiding or destroying or changing villains on route); her journey was arduous requiring much self-improvement, discomfort and hard cash as she transformed herself into 'Cinderella' but the resolution is 'love' and 'marriage' or at least the modern equivalent. The motif that moved her through each stage to success was beauty.

Cosmopolitan is A4-sized with 334 pages but is structured very similarly to *Glamour* and *Marie-Claire* so the narrative order of the product feels very familiar. Each of these three glossies had only one serious but still woman-centred article: 'Women in the Line of Fire' (*Glamour*, July 2003: 66–74); 'I thought we were friends then he raped me' (*Cosmopolitan*, 2003: 87–90) and 'From Bolivia to Olivia. On the cocaine trail' (*Marie-Claire*, July 2003: 91–96). The remainder of the content in each was beauty, fame and relationships, with *Cosmo* most overtly selling the myth that buying looks is a means of getting love. Each magazine seemed to feature 'stars' in the early pages, followed by a serious piece, then relationship features. The central bulk was beauty and fashion with lifestyle pages towards the end. *Cosmo* was typical. The effect was to set up a desirable

Figure 4.2   Cosmopolitan

scenario (romantic, heterosexual love) featuring attractive young people (often 'stars' discussing their love-lives). In *Cosmo*, it was a bikini-clad Geri Halliwell who tells readers 'I have fantasies of the ideal scenario – the happy ending and finding true love' but believes her own 'needy streak has attracted the wrong men' (pp. 58–64). Once again, women were urged to change themselves in order to find a man. The following pages provided an apparent means of achieving the lives of the stars or at least their fantasies, via the purchase of beauty and fashion products. A cynical reading of the inclusion of the 'serious' article in each magazine might be that it lends authority and therefore 'credibility' to the 'fairytale' remainder.

Cosmo was the most sex-centred of the three adult glossies, as was evident from the cover of the July version (Figure 4.2). Even *Cosmo*'s serious article was often sex-related and it had featured naked men in both June and July (but for some kind of 'fig-leaf' genital cover – 'cocktails' in the June edition).

Cosmo (July 2003) featured 'Confessions', which was a sexual exploits letters page (p. 15) An article on 'single and sexy' was actually about 'meeting a gorgeous man' and asked 'Where are all the single guys?' The next feature (pp. 16–19) was on dating a new man! Then Agony Aunt Irma Kurtz offered advice on 'love, sex and relationships' (p. 25) followed by pages of celebrity women and advice on what to buy in order to look like them: one of these told readers 'why being single gave her the chance to meet the perfect man' (p. 32). Next was a 'make-over' of a young blonde woman and then came 'the kind of man we all want to date' (pp. 39–40).

Each foray into relationships was followed by some kind of advice column indicating what a struggle romance is and how women can act appropriately to make it work for them. *Cosmo* offered lots of information about how men think, what men want, as in 'Man-ual: Everything you ever wanted to know about men' (p. 52) and how to 'Turn Mr Holiday Fling into Mr Forever' – an extended collection on finding your man on holiday (pp. 76–82). Agony Aunt Irma Kurtz returned on p. 96 to caution against 'free-love'. Then a light piece on mums and daughters (pp. 100–103) preceded the male pin-ups posing as 'sexy, naked bar-men' (pp. 104–110). After which readers were assured that 'just because you have fantasies about making love to a woman, that doesn't make you a lesbian' and 'lesbian fantasies' can turn on a boyfriend (pp. 115–116) leading to the dramatic 'Tragedy strengthened our marriage bond' (pp. 119–120). The section before fashion and beauty was called the 'passion package' (pp. 133–152), which describes sexual encounters in 'Anouska's sex diary' and my 'Changing room encounter' and 'cybersex'.

The fashion and beauty section began with a lingerie spread 'to get his pulse racing' and then dresses for a 'summer of love' (pp. 162–174). The next fashion spread suggested readers 'cast off their inhibitions' (p. 188–193). As in *Marie-Claire,* the next piece dealt with 'problem' figures and how to disguise and minimize, so reassuring those who do not conform to the bone-thin models that they too can 'buy'. Beauty features focused on tanning, hair removal and 'wow him locks' (pp. 202–238). There was a 'youniverse' on health, which included a thinly disguised piece on how to lose weight entitled 'What's your food personality?' (pp. 255–260) The magazine ended, as did *Marie-Claire* and *Glamour,* with a lifestyle section.

The similarity in content and narrative structure across these three different and most popular magazine products reinforces the messages in these magazines about what women should want (a man forever); how they might get it (beautiful looks); what difficulties they might encounter on this quest for looks in order to get a man (weight, lumpy bits, hairiness, age, expectations, mis-shaped features, odour); how to overcome these (buy products or services); and the resolution or prize that results in holidays, homes and happiness. In each magazine the 'classifieds' come at the end. For those really desperate or with serious shape and size problems the classifieds offer surgery, astrology, sex toys and love phone lines.

Aimed at adult women, these magazines cannot suddenly impose sets of ideas and aspirations that have no cultural consonance either previous or parallel. What they offer in terms of values, themes and stories must resonate with the expectations of women who buy and read them, or they simply would not make sense. The fact that a horizontal sample of different products at the same time showed so many similarities between textual structures and meanings suggests it must reproduce the 'preferred' gender conditions in the culture. To be popular requires acceptability. Certainly these narratives fit alongside the representations of femininity in newspapers but girls must come into womanhood already discursively and cognitively armed with the beauty myth for such adult texts to be meaningful. There are many sources of such mythic ammunition: our mothers, films, literature, families, school, television and, of course, teen-magazines such as *Sugar, Bliss* and *J17*, which form the next sample for analysis. Again the edition is July 2003. These are the most popular magazines of their type and the July edition's format is broadly similar in volume and organization to the previous three months.

'What boys love about you'; 'sexy hair and beauty tips'; 'bag a boy by the week-end'

These quotes are from the front covers of three magazines for teenage girls: *Sugar, Bliss* and *J17* (July 2003). Each magazine featured the face of a young girl, all are white, fair, long-haired and made up. Hachette Filipacchi publish *Sugar,* which claims it is 'what being a girl is all about'. www.emap.com stated: 'Inspiring and reassuring, *Bliss* is the voice of teenage girls today' and *J17* is for:

> Girls with attitude. Alongside sex, snogs and advice in J17 confidential, to cutting edge street style, sorted careers info, cool celebs and text message fun – it's the original teen mag and the best!

The age of teen-mag readers is hard to estimate, but *Sugar*'s website sex advice section includes 'Lots of people talk about sex but less than a third of under 16s are actually doing it' (www.sugarmagazine.co.uk), which suggests it is aimed at under 16s. In fact another teen-magazine, *Cosmopolitan*'s baby sister *Cosmo-girl*, is aimed at 12–17-year-olds and focuses on the usual teen magazine fare of boys, beauty, fashion, pop stars and real-life stories' (http://www.englishandmedia.co.uk/publications/categories/ks4%20Media%20Pack%20Notes/Cosmointerview%20.pdf). This is disconcertingly similar content to the adult glossies and is readily seen as grooming women for the more adult material. Teen magazines 'participate in the construction of particular meanings about what it is to

Figure 4.3   Sugar

be an adolescent girl' (Gonick, 1997: 71). Teenage girls know they will grow up – they may desire that and seek enlightenment or fear that and seek reassurance, but whichever, they know they will change their being, and the magazines offer them glimpses and possibilities of what that new self might be. As Berger (1972) said, 'we are as women sold ourselves'.

Sugar is A4 format and has 240 pages. The front page image is nearly always 'pin-up' style full gaze and sexually suggestive, both in text and image, as in Figure 4.3.

The editorial welcome stated: 'Ever wanted to ask a load of fiery fellas about sex?' Advertising differs from the adult magazines in that there are many ads for sports clothes rather than designer fashion, few for hair colour and few for perfumes. *Sugar* read to me as if aimed very much at the younger end of the teenage market; I would be surprised if many girls over 14 read it. None the less, deodorants, sanitary products and hair removal feature strongly as do acne cures and mobile phones. There were far fewer adverts than in the glossies but many fashion and beauty pages actually 'advertise products', embedded in advice.

Sugar seemed much less orderly in a narrative sense than the adult glossies, although most of the same constituents are there on the contents page: Your Lives: real life; Your Looks: we love beauty; Your style: we love fashion; Top celebs; Top totty: boy-watching and problem pages, star-signs and letters. The key missing theme in *Sugar* (July 2003) was a sexual relationship as the ultimate goal of all the flirting, beauty and fashion. The content of each theme was dispersed throughout the magazine in mini, rather incomplete vignettes – there is, of course, no 'climax' of finding Prince Charming as these girl readers are below the age of sexual consent. Without that ultimate goal of sexual love that supports and rationalizes the fairly coherent, linear fashion of the women's versions, each little pallet merely offers tasters of adult life to familiarize the reader with what is of value: stars, clothes, make-up, attracting the opposite sex, boys, shopping and slenderness. Instead of a single narrative the magazine works as a collation of mini-narratives: a series rather than a serial. Instead of giving a completed story, *Sugar* (July 2003) offers the necessary ingredients but without divulging the final product. So, for example, pages 10–13 feature cartoons and photos of 'celebs' in embarrassing or funny situations; pages 14–15 print readers' own embarrassing moments; pages 16–18 opens the theme of 'boys' with pop stars the 'Leading Ladies' followed by boy skateboarders offering their flirting tips; girls are then offered fashion and beauty tips and a serious account of family life (pp. 28–29), then a guide to boys moves to 'Swimfans: set temperatures soaring' with young, blonde, white, slender models in bikinis (pp. 32–37).

The magazine has several similar clusters offering much the same content not necessarily in the same order. Nearly all of it is about how to make the most of your looks or what boys think and like, so it is not dissimilar to the glossies but the final coming together of 'looks' and 'man' that characterizes the holy grail of women's magazines is deferred here. There is in fact quite a strong prohibitive moral and sexual health line that closes *Sugar* in many of the responses on the problem pages: 'You and your heart'; 'You and your body'; 'You and sex' and 'You and your life'. Girls are advised: 'Fingering … it's best to leave it until you are aged 16 or over'; 'My advice is wait until you feel 100% ready to have sex'; and 'He doesn't feel ready for a proper relationship just yet' (pp. 123–128). Finally, after these admonitions the horoscopes return to 'hot dates', 'boys', 'flirting', 'lurve' and 'crushes'. The magazine teases, excites, promises and does not fulfil several times over, then warns and finally defers to the future. Arguably, it is seducing young girls with extracts from the fuller narrative of adult femininity.

J17 seems a little older and wiser than *Sugar*. July 2003 featured a pull-out of the 100 hottest boys of summer. It is A4 size, 124 pages and, like *Sugar*, has relatively few adverts compared to its big sisters – 16 full pages of deodorants, sanitary protection, mobile phones, shampoo and acne cures – but a great deal of product endorsement. Where it, and *Bliss*, differ from *Sugar* is that each endorses more clearly the progressive, linear narrative style of the adult magazines. *J17* (July 2003) began with a 'Celebs' cluster that was less about their relationships than the adult versions and more about their looks and 'attitude' (pp. 11–24). The 'You' section is on a theme that intersects the others a little and deals with parental divorce, fashion in Leeds, put-downs for bullies and being mates. 'You' (the reader) is still treated as a child with childish experiences rather than adult (sexual) ones. *J17*, like *Sugar*, has embarrassing stories from its readers, and the next cluster in July 2003 was 'Real Life' on couples (though no sex is mentioned), pregnancy (the story of abortion ends with a warning: 'when it comes to contraception you can never be too safe), asylum and drugs (pp. 51–58), then 'Boyology' (pp. 66–75), Fashion and Beauty (pp. 30–36 and 77–96), and finally reviews, horoscopes, problem pages and two ending pages on boys. This tighter structure made the magazine feel much more like the women's publications. Although the goal of 'sexual love' is still deferred, as in *Sugar*, the logic of the myth that results in it is beginning to firm up as girls are romanced and groomed for womanhood. Again the magazine is overwhelmingly white, blonde (the girls anyway) and slender.

As in the mature magazines, men/boys feature a great deal. They are dubbed 'hotties' but remain clothed and *J17* tells its readers how to 'bag a boy by the weekend' but there is no inference that this will result in sex. Rather, by the Sunday 'you should have kissed your fella and are well on the way to making him your boyfriend'. Fashion borders the adult and beauty even more so. In a shoot called 'Six in the City' girls model dress and make-up like the cult 30-something actresses from the raunchy television show 'Sex in the City'. As with *Sugar*, there were several problem pages at the end of the magazine and the tone was similar: again girls are advised not to have sex until '100% ready' but several readers' letters refer to sexual worries or relationship problems indicating an older readership. This age difference was also reflected in a brief section at the back on using 'Feng shui' in your room. It tells readers: 'Scented candles are specially good at promoting romance' (p. 117). The horoscopes, more overtly than *Sugar*, have a 'love stuff' comment. *J17* is closer to the adult format. The themes are all present, albeit with very little sexual or relationship content, and in its place more child-centred issues of friends and family, but the narrative is becoming much more like the adult formula: look at famous people; famous people are desirable; how to look famous (and what to buy to achieve it); who to desire but not what happens when you achieve your desire. Again there is deferment but the process and goal are much clearer here.

Bliss is the same format as *Glamour* and has a very similar look although, like *J17*, it is produced by Emap. It even claims a 'glam' look in the editorial. Like *J17* it had a coherent narrative akin to the adult glossies under the section heads: trends; celebs; girl; boys; glam; coaches (problems); and regulars such as reviews. It seemed closer in tone and style to the grown-up narratives. In the July 2003 edition Bliss like the other teen-mags, was still fairly ad-free. It did offer perfumes (including Chanel). Its male pin-ups looked mannish rather than boyish. Again the focus was white, slender and usually blonde, and fashion emulates what famous, adult women wear. A makeover piece transformed three schoolgirls aged 15 and 16 into 'glammed up' young women in high heels and strapless dresses (pp. 158–162). The tropical beach shoot for fashion showed girls with attentive boys/men either touching them or gazing at them (pp. 124–133).

Embarrassing readers' stories featured as in the other teen-mags; there was also an unwanted pregnancy story and associated warnings: 'remember it is illegal for a boy to have sex with a girl under 16' (pp. 94–95) and a cautionary article on holiday sex: 'Summer loving – will it happen too fast?' (pp. 86–90). But Bliss also offered a clearer view of the prize at the end of the process of constructing femininity that it narrated. The star of TV's Buffy the Vampire Slayer says of her new husband: 'He's a true partner in every sense of the word' (p. 46). Readers were told that 'lads have ways of sussing whether you're a fling or the real thing' (p. 116) with advice on how to 'pass' the rating game and keep his interest. The coaching sections too were more adult with advice on careers (pp. 174–175), contraceptives (p. 172), help to find a boyfriend (p. 176), jealousy (p. 177) and penis phobia (p. 168). Letters mentioned 'A' levels (end-of-school examinations), suggesting some readers were at least 17 or 18 and on the threshold of independence. Horoscopes also assumed that readers actually have a 'man' rather than just daydream about one (pp. 183–190). In Bliss, with its proverbial link to 'wedded', the assumption that adult femininity was also heterosexual and couple oriented was overt, as was the means of achieving that state. Girls were even advised: 'How to fake it * Act your way sexy' (p. 76). 'Pick someone – a celeb or a mate – who has the effect on boys you want: "Analyse her" says life coach' (p. 79) and spice up your bedroom with sequins and silk to 'get ready for some sultry Arabian nights' (p. 62). Bliss still cautioned but also encouraged its reader's sexuality as it literally 'coaches' them for womanhood – and that womanhood was depicted as white, slender, mostly blonde and often either touched or looked at by men. There was nothing in Bliss that decried or derided 'other' models of adult womanhood – no diets, exercise or cosmetic surgery – but there was nothing that depicted them either.

In the rites of passage to femininity through teen-mags men become the prize of looks but only certain kinds of looks achieve men. If you do not conform you can buy many products – clothes, make-up, cosmetics, services – to change yourself by adornment so long as the underlying structure of your body is the 'acceptable and desirable' size and shape to fit these. If not, the covert message may well be – change your body.

Summary: Lose 4lb in 48 hours[13]

During the early 1980s, research emerged to show the preoccupation of women's magazines with nutrition and fitness and aiming for an 'ideal' body shape. Appearance-related themes centred on subjects such as dieting and exercise were found to have become increasingly prominent and prevalent, especially in long-established magazines aimed at women (Parham et al., 1982; Weston and Ruggiero, 1985/86). Indeed, this trend continued throughout the decade with advertising and feature copy placing emphasis on being slim to be beautiful (Hertzler and Grun, 1990). Further evidence was reported by another content analysis-based study of traditional women's magazines (*Ladies' Home Journal, Good Housekeeping*), fashion magazines (*Cosmopolitan, Glamour*), and modern women's magazines (*New Woman, Ms*) published during 1980–81. Although the number of exercise articles per six-month period was similar for men's and women's magazines, the women's magazines published 13 times as many weight-loss articles and six times as many articles on beauty or improving one's appearance (Nemeroff et al., 1994). Wiseman et al. (1990) examined the number of diet-for-weight-loss, exercise and diet and exercise articles from 1959 to 1989 in leading women's magazines (*Harpers Bazaar, Vogue, Ladies' Home Journal, Good Housekeeping, Woman's Day* and *McCalls*). An overall increase in the emphasis on weight loss was found to occur in these publications over the 30-year period examined. Klassen, Wauer and Cassel (1990), who studied food advertisements aimed at women, found an increasing trend for food advertisers to incorporate weight-loss claims in magazine adverts for their products from 1960 to 1987. In addition, Anderson and DiDomenico (1992) found that a sample of popular women's magazines contained at least 10 times as many dieting advertisements and articles as a similar sample of men's magazines. They suggested that this correlates[14] with the incidence of eating disorders in the dominant female target audience.

Further research with magazines aimed at young girls and young women also found explicit images of slimness as attractive. Content analyses have shown that 45 to 62 per cent of articles in teen fashion magazines focused on appearance and that only 30 per cent or less of the articles focused on identity or self-development (Evans et al., 1991; Pierce, 1990). A further analysis of a single issue of *Teen* magazine found that every one of a sample of 95 images of girls or women depicted thin models (Levine and Smolak, 1996). Guillan and Barr (1994) studied the nutrition and fitness messages presented between 1970 and 1990 in a magazine for adolescent women, to evaluate whether these messages changed over time, and to assess the body shape portrayed as desirable. Both nutrition-related and fitness-related coverage emphasized weight loss and physical appearance. Half the major nutrition-related articles presented a weight loss plan, and weight loss was frequently addressed in other nutrition articles. The primary reasons presented for following a nutrition or fitness plan were to lose weight and become more attractive. Statements that the product or service would promote weight loss were found in 47 per cent of nutrition-related advertisements.

These studies suggested that the cultural demands placed on women to be thinner, and the accompanying standards of attractiveness portrayed by the media, played a role in observed increases in eating disorders among young women (Garner et al., 1980; Morris et al., 1989; Silverstein, Striegel-Moore et al., 1988; Silverstein, Perdue et al., 1986). Although perhaps rather crudely assumptive about meanings and effects these studies do record a long and systematic printed discourse of idealized, slender femininity.

The modern print media are perhaps more covert operators on the body rather than explicitly overt as they were suggested to be in these earlier content analyses. At the outset of the twenty-first century, there are, of course, publications like *Shape* which are explicitly engaged in re-constructing women's bodies, but the print media analysed here are not, and are even critical of the diet and slimming industries. Despite this, the stories that they do tell about femininity are insidiously, repetitively and systematically engaged in a very particular construction of femininity that is deeply body-conscious and embedded within a particular gendered narrative. In a sense the 'morphed' female body is not the 'real me' but merely the symbol that connotes both 'normal' femininity and 'normal' gender roles and relations. As Butler argued: 'Identity is performatively constituted by the very expressions that are said to be its results' (1990: 25). Gender is done to us not by us; literally it is written on the body. It is not done to us by a few images of skeletal models but by a whole discursive context within which those images have cultural currency and in which the mass media have a very salient part to play, partly through their pervasiveness, partly due to the vastness of their audience, partly through their relation to advertising and partly through their expression of continuing masculine hegemony.

In these terms, what is shocking about the British press is how little it has changed since Tuchman and Butcher wrote about it some 25 years ago (published in 1981). Women, even when famous and successful in their own right, though most of these are 'glamorous stars', are still usually sexualized, served up as body 'parts' or in relation to men – as partners, ex-partners, mothers or victims of sex crime. Serious gender issues are still treated humorously and independent, successful women rarely feature unless there is something of interest about their sexuality or some detail about their sexual relationships that can be added to the story. Stars seem to feature more than Butcher and Tuchman noted, but only in the same context of sex and men. Alternatively, women barely feature at all, perhaps because, as seems to be the case with the *Guardian*, women are not newsworthy unless sexualized, so if it is not politically correct to publish sexualized stories then women simply are not news. The story being told through these papers to millions of men and women readers each week is that women can be successful but must also be 'sexy' and associate with, or appear to want to associate with, men, in a normal heterosexual manner. Such women are also normally young, blonde, slim and preferably scantily or provocatively dressed. Otherwise women are not depicted at all or belittled at best, ridiculed at worst or only featured if victims. This is the daily narrative of femininity in our newspapers where repetition and frequency and authoritative sources lend stories what Levi-Strauss (1958) called a mythic quality that lends them the appearance of truth. Newspapers systematically represent a view of the world to us and the view of the world of femininity offered is narrow, traditional, white and patriarchal – it is a view in men's interest. That is what myth does: it supports 'systems of belief that sustain the power of the powerful' (MacDonald, 1995: 3).

It does seem that the feminist thrust of the 1970s has merely embellished the old models of femininity with an extra dimension – women must still be monogamous, heterosexually available, maternal, slender and fair but also financially attractive, even famous too to get good press. Men no longer expect to pay for dinner. Women expect to earn their own money to spend making themselves attractive to men (incidentally but perhaps not coincidentally making the beauty and fashion industries very profitable). In Barthes' terms that process robs them of their diversity and complexity as they collude, even take pleasure, in reshaping themselves to fit a femininity fetishized by male interests.

And they start learning young, how and why to do this. Prior to the advent of an advertising-driven mass media, art certainly showed women as men wanted to see them. Now, and increasingly as electronic information and entertainment alongside more traditional forms all but overwhelm us with representation, girls develop into women bathed in discourses of stereotyped femininity played out in masculine narratives and marketed in the mass media, even, it seems, in the generalist British national press. 'In the absence of mainstream journalism that treats women's issues with anything like the seriousness they deserve, women's magazines take on a burden of significance – and responsibility' (Wolf, 1992: 73). Yet the UK government's body summit arose because many women, including those working in the magazine industry, feel that what should be a woman-centred media space is actually doing women a gross disservice.

The overwhelming experience of reading these magazines is, first: women are expected to be aspirational; to aspire to images that are relatively uniform – particularly in body-type; to aspire to heterosexual relationships and to spend a great deal of time and money in order to attain those things. Paid work is valued but depicted as a means to those ends, via the purchase of beautifying products and processes, not a goal in itself. Work generates money and then: 'Savings offered when you pay by direct debit could be up to £132 per year = Sunglasses £105 *Gucci* (leaving change for a few bottles of suntan lotion)' (*Glamour*, July 2003: 30).

Second: the magazines are little more than vehicles for advertising with many of the features actually promoting products, books or services. What is connoted throughout is that the goal of a heterosexual relationship can literally be bought by adorning the body, which must be shaped appropriately in order to bear the advertised goods.

Third: each magazine works, in narrative terms, as a story in the same way – although the narrative in the teen-mags is either fragmented or remains unresolved it has the same constituents. This convention in the women's glossies creates inter-textual referencing across time and space which reinforces the story told across magazines. That story is also shockingly similar to the one made available in the newspapers. It may well be that 'a well adjusted woman does not starve herself to death just because she sees a picture of a skinny model' (*Guardian*, 31 May 2000) but she sees little else that appears to promise success or happiness.

The print media are not literally selling diets and slimming but promoting a particular body aesthetic as relating to both sexual desirability and marital happiness and career success – the latter is promoted as giving women the independence to buy products and services to pamper and improve themselves so that they will attract the man, just as the famous women stars featured have done. This is subtle and implicit beauty mythologizing. The goal is not the 'thin' body but feminine identity which is still narrated as dependent on a woman's sexual role – the thin body is promoted as the means of achieving sexual fulfilment by attracting a man. The means is looks and is sold to us directly and indirectly, but the end is love.

The print media overwhelmingly represent women visually and within very particular narratives. The following chapter expands the role of the mediated image and considers two visual electronic media, television and the World Wide Web, and analyses their contribution to a culture that depends on supporting women's desire for independence and income because of their value as consumers, whilst simultaneously persuading them to dislike their bodies and faces so they spend copiously on conforming to the beauty myth in order to be sexually loved. Wolf (1992) referred to this as a culture with a split personality that requires women to comply in order to enjoy. Simply women are told that their real selves are not good enough but they need not worry because now that they are liberated workers they can purchase the represented self – a feminine facsimile – in order to make themselves sexually desirable, which is the route to heterosexual love. Cinderella may go to the ball and find her handsome prince but only if she can fit into a size 8 designer dress, but that's not a problem because she can also buy a diet and 'Lose 4lb in 48 hours'.

Notes

1 P.F. Sullivan (1995) Mortality in anorexia nervosa, *American Journal of Psychiatry*, 152: 1073–1074 quoted in BMA, 2000: 8.
2 Singh (1993) examined published data from various body measurements for *Playboy* centrefolds between 1955 and 1965 and 1976 and 1990; body measurements for centrefolds were not published between 1966 and 1975. Data for Miss America winners from 1923 to 1987 were obtained from Bivans (1991). Percentage of ideal body weight and WHR were calculated for each sample. There was a clear trend towards slenderness for both *Playboy* centrefolds and Miss America contest winners, as indicated by decreasing percentage of ideal weight. WHR for *Playboy* centrefolds increased slightly from 0.68 to 0.71 over the years examined, whereas Miss America winners had a WHR decrease from 0.72 to 0.69. Breast and hip measurements were practically identical for both *Playboy* centrefolds and Miss America winners for all the years examined.
3 The relationship between crime, news and political and cultural issues in relation to the media during the Conservative years from 1979 to 1997 is the subject of Wykes (2001).
4 News tells a story. It embeds pictures into words, into broader verbal contexts that make sense of events according to the cultural-at-large and our experience of it. Moreover it does so according to the ideologies and practices that sustain British journalism and derive from the profile of journalists, the commercial demands of media institutions and the political context. See Wykes (2000) for a full account of the way in which news as narrative necessarily prefers a patriarchal, consensual and conservative model of explanation for socio-cultural events such as familial violence and public disorder.
5 For example, in accounts of the case of the killing of Oxford student Rachel McLean by her boyfriend, John Tanner, in April 1990, news about the trial in the *Sun* had the headline 'Fatal Obsession' connoting inaccurately both '*crime passionel*' as an explanation for murder (there was no reason for Tanner to be jealous) and Rachel as murderously violent. It coincided with the very popular film *Fatal Attraction*, featuring obsessive female violence.
6 See note 1.
7 These figures were for May 2003: http://media.guardian.co.uk/presspublishing/tables/0,7680,973798,00.html, accessed 10 June 2003.
8 The magazine circulation figures are monthly examples from 2002 and were all obtained from http://media.guardian.co.uk/circulationfigures, accessed 10 June 2003.
9 *Guardian*, 19 June 2000.
10 The story was front page news on 10 June 2003 because Ian Huntley, accused of the murder of two Cambridgeshire schoolgirls in 2002, had attempted suicide. Maxine Carr, his girlfriend, was due to stand trial for 'conspiring to pervert the course of justice'.

11 See M. Wykes (1995) 'Passion, marriage and murder: analysing the press discourse', in R. Dobash, R. Dobash and L. Noaks (eds), *Gender and Crime*, Cardiff, University of Wales Press, pp. 49–77; M. Wykes (1998) 'A family affair: sex, the press and the Wests', in C. Carter et al. (eds), *News, Gender and Power*, London Routledge, pp. 233–247.

12 *Glamour*, July 2003.

13 *Shape*, front cover, July 2003.

14 This ratio matched that proposed by Stropp (1984) and Bemis (1987) as representative of the difference in the prevalence of eating disorders between females and males.

5 Starring Roles: Screening Images

The contemporary small mass media screens of the television set and personal computer are also relevant sources of representation about the body and each has been targeted as a dangerous influence for the young and/or vulnerable. This chapter explores some of those accusations as they specifically relate to 'looks' in order to provide a holistic account of the way contemporary media promote body image.

A number of content analysis studies have previously focused on the representation of body image on television. Such studies revealed a preoccupation with beauty, thinness and food (Garner et al., 1980; Silverstein, Perdue et al., 1986; Toro et al., 1988; Wiseman et al., 1990). While female characters displayed fluctuating curvaceousness, weights were estimated consistently to be below average. Fewer than one in ten women in television shows and advertisements[1] were judged to be overweight (Gonzalez-Lavin and Smolak, 1995; Silverstein, Perdue et al., 1986). Kaufman (1980) found an interesting twist to the ideal body image as represented in television commercials and programming. Analysing 600 minutes of videotape, Kaufman's study rated 48 per cent of the 537 characters viewed as thin or average. Fifteen per cent of the men were found to be overweight, as compared to 8 per cent of the women. Teenagers were never depicted as obese, and only 7 per cent were found to be overweight. Of the 537 characters rated, the vast majority of whom were slender, 509 (95%) were presented in situations involving food. Characters were shown with food, eating food, or talking about food.

Examining 4,294 network television commercials, Downs and Harrison (1985) made several findings involving the frequency of 'attractiveness-based messages'. On average, one out of every 3.8 commercials involved some form of an attractiveness-based message. Based on this frequency and average viewing habits, Downs and Harrison estimated that children and adult viewers were exposed to some 5,260 attractiveness messages per year (an average of 14 messages per day). Of these, 1,850 messages dealt directly with beauty.

From the media messages that were identified, emerged stereotypes of beauty, success and health (Downs and Harrison, 1985; Garner and Garfinkel, 1980) linked to the slender body. At the same time, negative stereotypes of poor health and a lack of control have become associated with obesity (Ritenbaugh, 1982). Together, these positive and negative stereotypes play a role in the cultural formation of the ideal body. This ideal body may be internalized by young women and become a goal in a programme to transform their body shape to match their internalized ideal body (Banner, 1986; Spitzack, 1990).

The focus of this first part of the book is how ideas about women's bodies are formulated in discourse and particularly how the contemporary mass media, with their systematic and pervasive discursive presences, operate as institutional sites in that formation. Historically through art, advertising, newspapers and magazines, knowledge about women's beauty, bodies and 'brains' (this latter largely only mentioned in its absence) has been constructed very much according to the operation of male power to inscribe, and the power of capital to generate consumption – each upholding the interest of the other. At the outset of the twenty-first century mass-mediated discourses now include 24-hour multi-channel global tele-visual and Web-based multi-media forms including text, chat, music, images, video, film, animation and graphics. Each also provides images that a more traditional mass medium, the newspaper, reproduces, embedded in the very particular narratives of femininity discussed in the previous chapter.

This intertextual cross-referencing is an interesting aspect of represen-tations of women as it strengthens the authority of each discourse by making it appear as part of a continuum of knowledge. Further, the more repeated a version of the world is the more it garners the appearance of truth or reality. This repetition and consolidation is the business of myth-making, which Levi-Strauss (1958) identified as *messages* about a culture. By analysing the cultural references prompted by the constituents of myth it is possible to reveal the practices and values that produce meaning. Those constituents are the signs that make up language and the systems or codes of representation that provide the arrangement that makes such signs meaningful – that may be a code of dress or of syntax or of news-making. In a mass-mediated culture where reality is interpreted, medi-ated and then endlessly re-interpreted and re-mediated in differing formats, times and contexts, the distinctions between the original truth of the cultural event, the mediated interpretation and the interpretation of the mediated interpretation become endlessly intra-informing. In the extreme, text may only be the inter-play between signs, which in sub-stance or relationship cannot be construed as telling anything about the world. Representation is arguably what Baudrillard (1983) called a *simu-lacrum*, bearing no truth relation to real events, so not a means of accessing knowledge about actuality. Postmodernist theory effectively refutes the link between sign and referent, preferring a model of signs as 'pastiche, self-referential and explicitly inter-textual' (Easthope and McGowan, 1992: 182). Analysis of text from this theoretical perspective becomes, as Derrida (1981) argued, merely more writing rather than any claim to revealing truth.

At least it does if that analysis operates only within the closed parameters of mutually re-interpretative and self-sustaining sign systems. But those systems and the myths they generate are not simple closed systems but both productive of and produced by social subjects. So those inscriptions and interpretations in the cycle of meaning are not just enclosed within a system but the means by which we act on the world and each other. Text is practice but in effect text is also our only actuality because everything is represented. As Barthes (1957) suggested, texts denote our world for us and connote its values.

Whereas the semiotics of literary criticism tends to analyse text in its own terms without 'drawing on any corpus of information, biographical social, psychological or historical *outside* the work' (Hawkes, 1977: 152), an analysis of text as discourse is not merely about the language but the power of it in practice at any historical moment – in that it appears as knowledge 'across a range of texts, and as forms of conduct, at a number of different institutional sites within society' (Hall, 1997: 44). For Foucault (1980), this production of knowledge or discourse cannot be explained as simply dialectical in Marxist terms because power does not just operate in economic ideological determination, nor is it explicable by semiological analysis that avoids discourse's 'violent, bloody and lethal character by reducing it to the calm Platonic form of language and dialogue' (Foucault, 1980 in Hall, 1997: 43). Rather, analysing discourse requires attention to both the language and practice of meaning construction. Just as social subjects are not always over time or place entirely equal in either status or power to inscribe meanings, so the meanings available via sign-systems will vary according to the power of language users which in turn relates to their social orientation (Hall, 1973). Mapping meaning therefore provides a method of identifying power relations.

Furthermore, meanings constitute the basis for practice that is knowledge about the world and also ourselves, as self-consciousness depends on language (Lacan, 1976). So seeking to identify the operation of meaning also potentially identifies the range of subjectivities through which it is possible to conceive of a self. When different contexts embody the same knowledge about the same event or subject then they are, in Foucauldian terms, a discursive formation that practically confers meaning on the real and material, which in fact cannot have existence free of discursive formation because we cannot conceive of reality without language. Hence, real and material bodies also become meaningful only in representation.

Moreover, discourse not only defines what should be the object of our knowledge and who we are as subjects, but also, by exclusion or denigration, what is not worthy of knowledge and not acceptable as self. The mass media are both institutions in their own right and also major sources of representation of other institutionalized representation. In a sense then they doubly represent, in that they self-refer – print to film; television to the World Wide Web; news to fiction – and cross-refer to other institutions – news about medicine; television drama about family; magazine features about work; and in each case the broad subjective categories of gender, race, class, age and sexuality are represented and reproduced creating meaningful spaces within which social subjects are invited to interpellate themselves. That interpellation, or the way in which young, female, social subjects as audiences experience media representations of the body, is the focus of Part Two of this book. This chapter continues the analysis of the textual data on the body that the mass media contributes to the discursive formative of femininity to try to identify and account for the meanings offered by the representation of looks.

There are many connections and borrowings between the print media and the now overwhelming moving visuals of television and the invasive interactive qualities of the Web. The first sample explores those relations by looking at articles on 'stars' in print whose stardom lies in other media such as pop, film and television. This enables both a consideration of the potential role of icons of femininity in the representation of the body and makes a connection between the print media and the much more contemporary forms of global television and the Web. The chapter then focuses on the modern television soap opera in relation to modern femininity, the popularity of food and health programmes, and the World Wide Web.

'The egg-timer dieters (or how long it took these celebrity women to lose their unwanted pounds)'[2]

'The *Daily Mail* keeps up a non-stop commentary on the weight gain of famous women and links it to their sexual orientation and career success' (*Guardian*, 8 July 2000). This raises a particular issue about the use of celebrities in body representation and the extent to which a focus on the famous might have a more significant impact on women audiences than images of unknown women.

Since the creation of cinema, 'stars' have been used to sell products and endorse ideologies and lifestyles. Moreover, the rapid popularization of cinema in the first part of the twentieth century was matched by the burgeoning of women's magazines, and the recognition by commerce of the consumption power of the female audience. The way stars leak between and blend mass media discourses makes them the perfect mythic symbol, binding together through their image each place of representation and instantly also confirming their fame and the legitimacy of their exposure and message. The transfer value of stardom is clearly evident in the pages of newspapers and magazines where stars from other media – and particularly the highly visual media of pop music, film and television – feature regularly as news.

Female stars of the stage, cinema and small screen dominate the representations of femininity in newspapers and magazines. It is not surprising, therefore, that during the focus on anorexic femininity since the turn of the millennium, the shape, diet, desirability and sometimes deaths of famous women have been newsworthy. Slimming and slim stars have dominated both the press coverage of beauty and desirability, and self-starving and harming activities linked to shape and weight manipulation. The association of stars, rather than ordinary women, with such issues is worth considering in terms of the possible effect of such stories.

As shown in Chapter 4, newspapers and magazines tend to portray women most often when they are famous in their own right or attached to a famous man, unless they are in some way deeply deviant and/or criminal (though even then descriptions tend to focus on looks, Wykes, 1998, 2001). Such portrayals most often place those women as an adjunct to a man, as mothers or potential mothers or as sexually available and alluring. It is arguable that the star quality of such women adds confirmative weight and promise to narratives that already appear to be consonant with very particular models of femininity. This is a kind of double binding of meaning – in order to be a desirable woman/mother/sex partner first try to look like this famous person or if you try to be a desirable, fertile, heterosexual woman you may achieve public success either individually or via a successful man. Stars depicted outside of the acts that make them famous, that is depicted as individuals with private lives, not performers, may well

articulate what it is to be a human being in contemporary society; that is, they express the particular notion we have of the person, the individual. They do so complexly, variously – they are not straightforward affirmations of individuals. On the contrary, they articulate both the promise and the difficulty that the notion of individuality presents for all of us who live by it. (Dyer in Hollows et al., 2000: 128)

Stars very often role-play publicly and fictionally the embodiment of extremes of human emotion, passion, privacy, pain and pleasure, and they do so in intense and contracted episodes. Hence their iconographic status; they symbolize our lives back to us on fast forward – even soaps do not operate in real-time – but they also offer us aspects of human life that we personally do not experience, hence their larger-than-life quality. Stars appear to live fuller and faster lives than their audiences in their performances and moreover these lives appear most usually to be happily resolved. Unhappy endings remain a scarcity in the popular media wherein only villains and *femmes fatales* suffer. Further, women stars do not only cross media boundaries – a pop star like Madonna might appear on television, in the press, on video, on film and on stage – but they also cross performance boundaries. Hence, actresses sell cosmetics (Liz Hurley), singers model clothes (Victoria Beckham), and soap opera stars sing (Martine McCutcheon). Thus, stardom is at once diverse in form and condensed in content and newsworthy. News loves a star because *elitism* is an important news criterion (Galtung and Ruge, 1965). The conjunction of diversity and concentration and newsworthiness exaggerate the cultural value of fame and associate it with a very narrow model of femininity that is about display, sexuality, beauty, youth and the structure about which these hang – the slender body.

This model, literally cat-walk and photographic model shape of femininity, presents the print media with a conflict that it has unilaterally failed to resolve: anorexia kills yet slender sells everything, from magazines to motor cars. Nowhere is the schizophrenic nature of the resulting reporting more evident than in the UK middle-brow tabloid the *Daily Mail*. In May 1999, a year before a so-called 'summit meeting' about the body convened by the government in June 2000, the *Daily Mail* was arguing that 'feminine charm' and the 'glamorous, pin-up image of Russian Anna Kournikova' on the tennis courts were much preferable to 'mighty shoulders' and 'beefcakes' and 'brawn' (13 May 1999), as if looks have anything to do with women's ability to play tennis. A year later, the same newspaper claimed 'impossibly thin models and actresses are fuelling an alarming increase in the number of patients with eating disorders' (31 May 2000). By October of the same year, it had the headline 'Big is not Beautiful … women reject fashion for the voluptuous, says poll' (12 October 2000). Then, in two days in 2002, it managed first to berate ex-Spice Girl Geri Halliwell for her obsession with dieting and over-thin body – '10lb under the recommended weight' (13 May 2002) – and then describe her rounder previous incarnation before diet and exercise, as 'Jessica Rabbit combined with fifties actress' (14 May 2002). This second article featured 12 female stars before and after dieting and was uniformly admiring of their weight loss. Model Sophie Dahl was described as 'a generous size 16 with ample flesh on display', but 9 months on 'a food combining diet … meant she shrank to a size 10'. Liza Minnelli 'ballooned to 14 stone (196 pounds)' then 'lost six stone before her wedding', so she got slim and got her man. Yet, a couple of months later this newspaper published the story of Vicki Carter, whose weight dropped to 4 stone (56 pounds) when she dieted to look 'like a famous actress' and had to be sectioned under the Mental Health Act and force-fed (6 July 2002) without any apparent awareness of the contradictions in its coverage of women's bodies. As Julie Burchill claimed, famous women are being systematically judged in the paper according to their size despite public and professional anxieties about the impact of such commentary on young women's self-image and identity construction. Two women pop stars in particular reached career points when they were in the news for being thin as well as for their singing: Lena Zavarone and 'Posh Spice' (Victoria Beckham).

Lena Zavarone was a child star who gained fame very young after appearing on television's *Opportunity Knocks* in 1974, aged 10. She died in October 1999 aged 34, weighing four and a half stone (60 pounds), from heart failure after a final attempt at brain surgery to relieve her anorexia. As a young singer she had hit records and many television appearances, but by 16 she

> loved wandering around supermarkets, looking at all the bright packets of food. She knew the nutritional and calorific value of every food going. She just could not eat it. Like all anorexics she had a grossly distorted body image. Seeing herself on TV she could see she was thin, but looking in a mirror all she saw was fat. (The *Mail on Sunday*, 3 October 1999)

Zavarone seemed to have been trapped. All the fame, happiness and adulation were for a girl child and she seemed to have needed anorexia as a route to maintaining that image and the associated identity. She, reportedly, desperately craved love and even children but could not allow herself to become a woman who might enjoy and attract that. Her marriage to her only boyfriend ended because she never ate with him. Her image was only valid as a precocious girl-child singing 'Ma, He's Making Eyes at Me' and then having 'failed' as a star, as a wife and as a mother she became 'famous' again as a star-suicide by self-starvation at a time when anorexia was becoming newsworthy. In many ways she personified the impossibility of blending the two fundamentally conflicting aspects of femininity: the youthful, slender girl who was a successful 'star' and the adult, sexual, womanly lover and perhaps mother.

Media depictions of Victoria Beckham or 'Posh Spice' show her in similar ways. She began a singing career later than Lena Zavarone, as a member of all-girl band The Spice Girls. As a highly successful band during the mid-1990s, the 'Spices' promoted 'girl power' and appeared slim but physically strong, and politically and sexually strident on stage and television. By 2003, all ex-members of the band had featured in the news relating to diet, anorexia or fat and the original wholesome and substantial group has disappeared as a band, paralleling the disappearance of flesh apparent amongst its members. The key to the changes seemed to be the gradual drop in popularity and success, first of the band, and then of individual members as they tried to forge solo careers.

The *Daily Mail* documented their changing body shape in THE YOYO SPICES (7 May 2003), again with no apparent awareness of the media's potential role in the struggle to be slim. 'Baby' Spice was described as having 'chubby thighs and a bulging tum' in January 1999 but is 'slim again' by October 2000 only to have a 'fuller figure' by Christmas of that year. Her 'slimmest yet' was noted in May 2003, 'but some claim this image to promote her new single was doctored'. 'Sporty' Spice was obsessed with 'exercise and eating', leaving her 'stick-thin and depressed' only to bulk up from exercise and gain a 'super-butch' body by 2000, earning her the nickname 'Beefy' Spice. The star stood up for herself at this point in her career and launched a searing attack on the media backlash against the 'Spice Girls' that focused on the body shape and size of the band members. Yet by 2003, the UK's *Daily Mail* reported she was 'looking slim and happy'. 'Scary' Spice, the only black band member, receives least critical attention, but the *Mail* still commented that 'pregnancy leaves its mark as do any slight slippages from a ruthlessly controlled food intake'. She looks 'buxom' in 2001, 'lean' in 2002 and by the beginning of 2003, 'she's piled on the pounds'. Like 'Posh', 'Ginger' Spice received intense media attention in relation to her weight. The *Mail* claimed that pre-1998, when she left the band, men liked her 'big curves, tiny dresses and a wicked glint in her eye'. Struggling to go solo she suddenly 'unveils a shockingly boyish figure' in 2001 as a 'yoga-crazed scrawny Geri'. But in 2003 the paper asks: 'Are her curves coming back?' A feature in the *Daily Mail* on 4 September 2003 was headlined, 'After those waif days, Geri looks swell again', making reference in particular to her increasingly voluptuous bust.

'Posh' Spice, Victoria Beckham, blamed Geri Halliwell ('Ginger') for encouraging her to 'slim' in 2001, saying Geri 'encouraged her to do more exercise and whittle down her food intake' (*Guardian*, 3 September 2001). Of all these stars, it is 'Posh' Spice who gets most coverage in the news and particularly, again, in the *Daily Mail*:

> We've all become used to her stick-thin physique, enhanced by surprisingly full – and she swears, natural – breasts that have somehow not shrunk with the rest of her body. Since the Spice Girls started, Victoria has turned herself into a fashion guru. But, by her own admission, she is a frenzied calorie counter. Rumours of anorexia have surrounded her. And the fact that she can still have cellulite suggests that God is not a woman after all. (*Daily Mail*, 7 May 2003)

No longer successful as a singer, she none the less maintained fame as the wife of perhaps the most famous UK sports star of the day, the footballer

David Beckham. While 'Posh' achieved success as a wife and mother, with two small sons, simultaneously she has witnessed her own career and identity shrink behind the global fame of Beckham who, by the time of his transfer from Manchester United to Spanish club Real Madrid, had become heroic-iconic to the point of Christ-like status. Her quest for thinness seemed to coincide with both motherhood and diminished personal fame, as if she was trying to re-identify herself as a 'star', but primarily on looks criteria as her 'talent' was no longer in popular favour. Writing about 'Posh' in the *Daily Mail*, psychiatrist Glenn Wilson suggested: 'The unspoken message is "the thinner you are the more successful you are as a person"' (30 November 1999). And she has appeared successful, as the adored wife of the world's favourite man, mother of his children and as very, very slender – as if that is the measure or means of fame. Of course, Victoria Beckham's relationship and previous pop-fame make her newsworthy, so any story about her will be published to sell newspapers in the first instance, and then to sell products as advertisers and sponsors clamour to cash in on her high profile. Publicity about her has nothing to do with concern about her well-being or distaste for her vanity. It is merely about her cash-value.

It matters that female stars are represented thus because 'stars' are what women see of successful women. In fact stars, or women who are the partners of male stars, are virtually the only non-criminal women who feature in the print media, as described in Chapter 4. If their stardom and therefore place in that public arena seems dependent on their continued slenderness, then it would be surprising if women using the media did not somehow equate success with men or money as co-relating to shape. Moreover, the news features women performers as private women in relationships, as mothers and as interested in the ordinary business of femininity. It is not just that slenderness is linked to the kind of success that brings fame but fame is linked to the kind of success – sexiness, love, marriage and family – that bring happiness. Again, the familiar constituents of the magazine narrative appear. There is a kind of double confirmation here in the press star-stories – real and representational feminine success, both require slenderness. And most of the women who feature in the news are women who also feature in women's magazines, on our televisions and increasingly on-line, so a diversity of discursive sources confirms a uniformity of required femininity.

Serial women

Such uniform discourses of desirable femininity have leaked between and blurred the boundaries of film, advertising, radio, magazines and into the more recent forms of television and the Web. Pop stars act or try to, like

Madonna. Models and actresses advertise, like Kate Moss and Liz Hurley. Singers strut the fashion catwalks, like 'Posh Spice'. Soap opera stars become pop singers, like Kylie Minogue. That blurring, of course, began overtly with soap opera, which was developed by radio programme makers

> as a prelude to product purchase by constructing a fictional world which they [women] (1) would recognize as relating to them, (2) would find pleasurable, and (3) could access while doing house work or caring for children. (Gledhill in Hall, 1997: 366)

Not only did soap opera address women specifically, but it also featured women's lives and did so through what Gledhill termed *continuous serialization*, sometimes daily or several times in a week. Moreover, it did so, and does so, in women's homes requiring no risk, no financial outlay and no childcare. With the advent of televised soaps, women at home could view their lives and families and communities (or the ones to which they might aspire), as parallel universes to their real lives. Women watch soaps in a very particular context. They are often alone, often partially otherwise occupied and more like voyeurs privately peeking at the continuing lives of others than paying, passive, public visitors to a cinema or theatre. The relationship with the small screen, arguably also with the small screen of the personal computer, is remarkably intimate: it is often one to one, private, increasingly pervasive, pleasurable and, with the exception of BBC television and some personal websites, interspersed with advertising.

The serialized story 'offers fictional experience which audiences encounter as part of a routine in which fiction and everyday life intertwine – to such a degree that major events in soap opera characters' lives become national news' (Gledhill in Hall, 1997: 340). Serial women seep into real women's lives not just via the televised narrative within which their character exists but because that character itself is newsworthy, and therefore so is the real actor. Much content of the tabloid newspapers is actually about fictional televisual worlds rather than the real world. In the process, character and actor become blurred, as do the media sites, which variously represent them.

Ang (1985) argued that the volume and familiarity of soaps leads them to gain hold of our imaginations and become part of our reality. Twenty years later that volume continues to proliferate, as do the mass media. But the familiar shape of the soap is more and more tailored towards particular audiences. Traditional soap operas, such as *Coronation Street*, *Brookside* and *EastEnders* in the UK, retain the close engagement with romantic relationships, family, domesticity and community that characterized the early sales pitch of Procter and Gamble's soap advertising on radio. The genre was derived specifically to attract the female viewer (Morley, 1992) who was also increasingly the major consumer in the household. The genre was and is characterized by being female-focused in content, in fact Morley argued that in order to understand soap a viewer would need to be 'culturally constructed through discourses of femininity' (1992: 129), but as gender roles have shifted in the later twentieth century the genre has proved increasingly attractive to male viewers, perhaps 'finding their feminine side' in the shifting space of sexual politics. Soaps are characterized by never-ending storylines, as the serial form demands that after each programme the viewer is left with a hook to hang the next episode on, a reason to keep watching.

Viewing figures for US soaps like *All My Children* and *The Guiding Light* grew rapidly so that 'By the 1980s some fifty million persons in the United States "followed" one or more soap operas, including two-thirds of all women living in homes with televisions' (http://www.museum.tv/ archives/etv/S/htmlS/soapopera/soapopera.htm, accessed 19 August 2003). UK traditional soaps also retain extraordinarily loyal audiences. Even though *Coronation Street*'s working-class community context seems dated and tired and its figures have dropped, in July 2001 'the soap's audience dipped below 10 million twice but rose above 11 million on eight occasions' (http://media.guardian.co.uk/broadcast/story/0,7493,771452,00.html, accessed 19 August 2003). Hart (1991) found that 60 per cent of *Coronation Street*'s viewers were female but 80 per cent were over 25 years old. Its failure to attract young adult women viewers may be because it was not designed for modern young women but had its origins in the model of housewifely consumption and concerns of the 1950s.

A new generation of young women has been differently catered for in contemporary soaps. The generation of women viewers who suffer most from eating disorders is also the generation for whom new soaps such as *Sex and the City*, *Friends* and *Ally McBeal* seem to be designed. Unlike their predecessors, each of these contemporary soaps is dominated by characters who are young, independent, slender, white (almost exclusively), working, heterosexual women in search of or struggling with relationships with men.

Sex and the City features four young, white, single New York women – Carrie, Miranda, Samantha and Charlotte – all of whom clearly make a great deal of money, though it isn't very clear how they afford their flashy apartments and designer fashion wear, as very little is shown of their working life. The first episode in 1997 offered the following scenario:

> At a birthday party for thirty-something Miranda, Carrie and her friends vow to stop worrying about finding the perfect male and start having sex like men. Carrie experiments with an old flame and meets Mr Big; Miranda warms up to Skipper; Samantha has a one night stand with a man Charlotte wouldn't sleep with on the first date. (http://www.hbo. com/city/#, accessed 27 March 2003)

The following synopsis for the most recent episode at the time of writing is typical of the narrative content and shows that it has barely changed over the six-year run. Old flames frequently occur, as does men's fecklessness or fickleness:

> Carrie receives a pleasant surprise when her High School boyfriend, Jeremy, calls her up and asks her to meet for dinner. The pair broke up in High School, but their chemistry leads them to instantly reconnect. Everything seems perfect, until he reveals one fairly shocking bit of information ... he is actually in the area because he's committed himself to a Connecticut mental facility. (http://www.hbo.com/city/#, accessed 27 March 2003)

The show is produced in the United States by HBO and at the time of writing is on its sixth series. It has a copious website and the number of messages on its bulletin board testifies to its popularity, as follows (26 August 2003):

AskHBO	(1461 messages)
Carrie	(4147 messages)
Samantha	(1179 messages)
Charlotte	(1222 messages)
Miranda	(1429 messages)
The Big Board	(7236 messages)
Fashion!	(2049 messages)
Music	(432 messages)
'Boy, Interrupted'	(417 messages)
SATC Cast in the Media	(658 messages)
General Conversation	(3546 messages)
City Cafe	(2764 messages)

The stars are all very slender, very fashionable and very heterosexual, though one episode did feature Samantha, the most promiscuous character, deciding to be lesbian – albeit only briefly. The content is almost entirely about getting, ending or recovering from sexual relationships with men and what you wear to which trendy night-spot while this happens. After six years it was beginning to show its age, as were its actresses. During its evolution the storyline has always emphasized finding 'Mr Right'. Yet, the search for perfect marriages for the heroines cannot be deferred endlessly or viewers will realize that being young, thin and trendy does not necessarily deliver marital fulfilment, nor perhaps – is the covert message – do the rather haphazard sex lives depicted, so gradually the programme is impregnating and marrying off its characters and returning the women characters to their conventional place. Two of the actresses are in well-publicized conventional relationships and have men and babies in 'real' life. An announcement about the current (2003) series presents the dilemma and after the screening of this 'new run', a further series with any credibility seems unlikely:

> The new run will go into production at the end of March, which will give new mums Sarah Jessica Parker and Cynthia Nixon, who have both had children recently, time to get in shape for their ultra glam designer gear.
>
> However, in true 'Friends' style, HBO insiders have not given up hope they can persuade the cast and 'Sex and the City's creator, Darren Star, to make more shows. (http://www.bbc.co.uk/radio1/news/entertainment/030108_sexandthecity.shtml, accessed 28 August 2003)

Friends began as a series about a group of young flat-dwellers: three men (Chandler, Joey and Ross) and three women (Monica, Phoebe and Rachel); all white, all single, all apparently successful, dating and looking for love. A typical story synopsis might be: 'Remember the cliff hanger from the last season? In the eighth season Joey mistakenly found himself engaged to Rachel as a confused Phoebe automatically assumes Ross is the groom-to-be', and its popularity is vast: 'Season eight rejuvenated the Friends franchise with regular viewing figures of more than 24 million' (http://www.ivillage.co.uk/newspol/dilemmas/0,160990_552761,00.html, accessed 26 August 2003). Nine years on there is marriage and a baby, as the characters have grown up with their actors. The soap is produced by US company NBC but plays on satellite and UK terrestrial. In 1999 Channel 4 secured new UK rights to the hit programme:

> The new agreement is a big win for the channel – the comic lives and loves of the six American twenty-somethings in Friends and the hospital drama ER have been among its biggest draws.
>
> Both series have attracted a regular audience of around 2.6 million viewers per episode on Channel 4 – for episodes already seen on Sky. (http://news.bbc.co.uk/1/hi/entertainment/568283.stm, accessed 28 August 2003)

Now in its ninth season since the launch in 1994–95, NBC continues to claim *Friends* is the 'number one TV show' (http://www.nbc.com/Friends/about/index.html).

Many of the actors have gained fame during and because of the series but it is the three women – Jennifer Aniston, Courtney Cox Arquette and Lisa Kudrow – who are best known. Blonde Jennifer Aniston in particular gained a cult following, enhanced when she married heart-throb actor Brad Pitt. This made her, like Victoria Beckham, doubly successful both as a young, famous, sexy woman and a conventional romantic partner of an 'elite' man. Unlike Beckham, Aniston has not yet achieved the final achievement of femininity, motherhood (though both Kudrow and Cox have), but like Victoria Beckham, she is frequently in the news with regard to her weight. Aniston's 'body' image crosses the media outlets with television and film roles, press coverage and website material. An on-line diet site recently conducted a butt-poll:

> We all have our favourite celebrity, so eDiets asked 'Which celebrity do you think has the most attractive butt?' When the final results were tallied, Jennifer Aniston sat in the driver's seat. JLo was the runner-up while Oprah Winfrey received seven per cent and Calista Flockhart, just one per cent. (http://edietsuk.co.uk/news/article.cfm/article_id,1803)

The site went on to advise: 'While celebrity behinds may be something we can aspire to, the most important thing you can do for your body is to consistently follow a **healthy diet** and exercise programme.' Aniston also made news by losing weight on the new-fad 'Atkins Diet'. Writing for the 'TouchLondon' website, Lynne Craney extolled this diet's virtues and detailed its method. 'Jennifer Aniston and Courtney Cox among them, have discovered, along with many thousands of Americans, that there is a way to lose weight or keep yourself trim, without having to starve yourself or spend ten hours a day in the gym' (http://www.touchlondon. co.uk/newspub/story.cfm?ID=97). The health risks of cutting out carbohydrates are only barely acknowledged towards the end of the piece. Curiously, the search threw up another reference – the 'problem' the Atkins Diet was causing the slimming industry, illuminating the very close relationships between the female body, fame and the food/diet industry.

> However the consumer products giant said sales of its low fat Slim Fast foods brand in the US had been disappointing because of the trendy high-fat, low-carbohydrate Atkins diet.
>
> The diet, followed by celebrities such as Jennifer Aniston and Victoria Beckham, has hit Unilever revenues but the group is striking back with a new Slim Fast ice cream. (http://iccheshireonline.icnetwork.co.uk, accessed 28 August 2003)

Like *Sex and the City, Friends* has run the life-course of its stars, who, nearly ten years on, may well have outgrown their designated audience. The most recent episode to be screened in the United States (4 September 2003) features Chandler and Monica visiting a fertility clinic – a far cry from the carefree young New York flat-dwellers of the original series. This year saw the introduction of a black cast member to *Friends* for the first time in an effort to update the storylines and address critics. Actress Aisha Tyler represents a small shift in prime-time US television, with a huge remit for integration. Furthermore, Gary Younge, points out: 'All of this will fall on her slender shoulders – for regardless of your race, all women's shoulders must be slender on prime time' (*Guardian*, 16 April 2003). Despite this innovation, Warner Brothers appear to have failed to persuade the current stars to make another series and a new spin-off production seems the most likely conclusion to the show as the female cast in particular begin to lose credibility as youth icons, however thin they struggle to remain.

Of the contemporary soaps and stars though, it is **Ally McBeal**, and its star Calista Flockhart, that have been the focus of the media 'panic' about skinny stars as opposed to its celebration of slender beauty. *Ally McBeal* is set in a Boston company of, mainly young, lawyers. Another US product, it straddles an awkward space somewhere between drama, soap opera and musical but its long run of over 100 episodes makes it soap-like in duration, as does its focus on femininity in relationship and identity crises. Ally is a 'thirty-something career woman deafened by the gynaecological tick-tock' (Mark Lawson, *Guardian*, 20 May 2003) but often filmed at the office and the courtroom. The series has a strange tendency to plunge into song and dance routines, and depict Ally living through rather disconcerting imaginary states. The very first episode in 1997 is summarized on http://allymcbeal.tktv.net/. The opening sequence is a flashback:

> 'Ally McBeal' begins with a wonderful voice-over by Ally as she stares out a window. She is recounting how she fell in love with a boy named Billy Alan Thomas … Later, Billy decided to transfer to Michigan because he wanted to clerk when he got out, but he didn't think he would make law review at Harvard. 'So basically you're putting your law career between us, Ally says. 'Well, I choose the law, too. But I choose Boston,' she says. We come back to Ally staring out the window. 'So here I am the victim of my own choices. And I'm just starting.'

Much of the remaining storyline, spreading over six years of broadcast but now discontinued, tells a similar tale of a career woman whose commitment to work thwarts her love life and leaves her constantly unfulfilled. An animated dancing baby occasionally floats surreally across the screen symbolizing her yearning for motherhood.

A typical episode includes a court case, office 'relationships' and some development in Ally's quest for love. In 'Blowin in the Wind' (screened US January 2002) the case involves a man who has bankrupted his wife by buying her presents; at work Glenn argues jealously with partner Jenny about her getting sexual pleasure from a vibrating chair; Ally buys a house to make a home and is intrigued by an attractive carpenter; Richard is surprised at Ally spending time on a project that isn't geared towards finding a man.

Ally is always designer-dressed for work, usually in very short-skirted suits, but often filmed wearing girl-child, sheep-speckled pyjamas at home. The emotional fragility of the character is symbolized by the physical fragility of the actress, Calista Flockhart, who is 5ft 5in. and very slight. Towards the end of 1998 this slightness became visibly more skeletal and the press began to feature articles on her as anorexic, coinciding with the concerns raised about the possible influence of over-thin fashion models on young women, as discussed in the previous chapter.

Calista and Ally appear to be almost interchangeable real and represented women. In her private life, Flockhart is infamously single but as needy of motherhood as her character. She has adopted a baby. She has been associated with much older male actor Harrison Ford. By late 1998 the waif-like actress of the first series appeared at an Emmy awards ceremony 'in a skimpy Richard Tyler dress that emphasised her thin arms and bony back' (*Daily Express*, 30 October 2003). And in the second series, she looked emaciated, prompting a plethora of claims that she was anorexic and a poor role model. By late 1999 she seemed to signify all of the issues that subsequently informed the 2000 Body Summit, with demands in the press that she should 'not appear on the small screen' (*Daily Express*, 19 October 1999). Although Flockhart defended herself, claiming over-work and tiny bones, her appearance fuelled the onslaught on the media as causal of eating disorders:

> Get her off our television screens until the woman fattens up. Would TV bosses allow prime-time coverage and the ensuing stardom to a woman who openly mutilated herself? No, they wouldn't. And that's what Calista appears to be doing – only she's doing it from the inside so it's slightly less gory than the version done with razor blades. (*Daily Express*, 19 October 1999)

Now, of course, she is off the screen except for the endless repeats. Whether her 'role' contributed to her thinness or her thinness secured her starring role is impossible to unravel, but fellow actor Robert Downey Jr returned to drug and alcohol addiction whilst working in the series and another character, Nelle Porter, played by Portia de Rossi, also made the news as too diet-thin. It may be that sensibility to the pressure of high performance leads to addictive coping strategies that are gender specific in that 'real' men drink whilst 'real' women diet.

Each of these series offers a gendered narrative similar to that of the magazines and newspapers discussed in Chapter 4. That narrative features the constituents necessary to be a successful woman (famous and/or desired) but in the serial it is not contained within a discreet episode like a single magazine but rather endlessly deferred over months and years. Moreover, these modern comedy drama series are youth-aimed, focused on young characters and all developed a strong fan base for the stars. This has problematized the narrative and character content because the plots and performances were attached to famous people with loyal fans, but famous stars who were ageing. As the ageing happened so the sometimes juvenile or rites of passage events, portrayed in the soaps fitted less and less credibly with the actors. Until eventually, in all three cases, the heroes and heroines have begun to seem to be experiencing rather implausible lives in their late thirties. The wealthy, young consumers sought by advertisers are not going to be attracted to representations of actors nearing forty still struggling with early adult angst and it is perhaps unsurprising that no further series of any seems likely. But these three have dominated the ratings for new soaps for most of the past decade and each has offered a very particular account of femininity both within the representation of the programme and in the publicity surrounding the real lives of the stars.

The programmes not only feature very slender, fashionable, white, heterosexual, young women but those 'looks' act as motifs for very unitary stories. Occasionally a feature may vary but usually only one, hence the occasional 'slender' black actress. Only in comedy is it possible to find a broad range of femininities, and then actresses like Rosanne Barr make themselves the object of humour. Certainly the looks represented in *Sex and the City, Friends* and *Ally McBeal* appear to justify all the worries about there being too many 'thin' actresses. But to argue that such depictions might have an effect it has to be shown that such thinness is presented in a package that both makes sense to audiences and makes thinness appear desirable – otherwise it will simply neither resonate as meaningful nor positive.

These new series each slightly shifted the focus of traditional soaps from the community, family and personal in order to take account of young women's greater role in work and public space. This creates interpretive space for younger audiences to identify with the characters and stories. But in many ways work is depicted as the new community; friends are the new family and the same issues of the personal are simply played out on slightly different stages.

Although dominated by the women actresses, men in these new series also grapple with love and feelings just as the women now work and socialize outside the home. But in many ways these shifts in content are superficial adaptations to social shifts masking the uniformity and conservatism of the meaning structures that support them. As in print, slender women – the real women actresses and the on-screen characters – are depicted as desirable and successful. However, as in the magazines, the ultimate resolution to feminine identity – marriage and children – is for the most part, and certainly for the main characters, the endlessly deferred goal. These are not programmes about marriage and family but about the promise and prize of it and how to be the kind of woman who deserves and achieves it. There is a kind of *double entendre* at work in these series. The characters appear to celebrate and achieve within a modern, working and liberated model of femininity but they still have to look like sexually attractive women and most of the narrative is about love. Also the romantic quest of the heroines is regularly thwarted if they move too far from traditional femininity. Careerism (*Ally McBeal*), promiscuity (*Sex and the City*), being boss (*Friends*) are synonymous with not finding love.

So although equality of activity with men features in the modern TV comedy drama, it is executed by women with very conventional feminine looks and whose career/independence/sexual activity is often blamed for their unhappiness in love. Femininity is modernized and extended to match young male and female audiences' lived experience and changing expectations, but also evident is what Susan Faludi termed the backlash that warns women 'take the rocky road to selfish and lonely independence or the well-paved path to home and flickering hearth' (1992: 106). The message is that feminism has not meant that women can have it all, just that they should work and spend their own money to make themselves slim and beautiful and successful in order to gain husband and home. Thus, the aspirations of newly liberated young women in the workplace and public sphere are addressed, drawing in large audiences and attracting advertising revenue, but at the same moment the needs and interests of traditional and still dominant patriarchy are served. This is evidence of the complex interaction of small but significant feminist gains, the need for capital to recognize and serve new markets and cultural hegemony:

> Media forms and representations constitute major sites for conflict and negotiation, a central goal of which is the definition of what is to be taken as 'real', and the struggle to name and win support for certain kinds of cultural value and identity over others. (Gledhill, 1997: 348)

Changing social sensibilities have forced political and policy change that support new gendered practices but cultural representations drag old connotations with them, subtly and invisibly inhibiting, confusing or even corrupting new potential. In modern television drama, as in print, women's looks remain as a traditional, gender identity motif that drags meanings back towards a conservative construction of desirable femininity. A key ingredient to both those looks and to more traditional feminine identity is the control of, preparation of and consumption of food. In many ways food and looks go hand in hand both in the media and in women's sense of themselves, so the next section moves women's 'looks' back into the kitchen to examine what television tells us about food and femininity.

Cooking the figures: food on television

The press and television drama offer confusingly contradictory representations of the female body. 'Fat' television stars are decried and ridiculed yet too 'thin' stars are pitied and denigrated in the press whilst very slender is the goal for many women. Women (and the men they are assumed to want to be attractive to) are presented with a large range of unacceptable femininity and a very narrow account of beauty – an account that barely changes in its rigorous requirements of looks from pubescence to menopause and even beyond nowadays. That account is itself a simulacrum and increasingly so, as images are electronically manipulated to remove wrinkles, lengthen legs and make waists narrower. Much of the production of that impossible femininity relates to food, which occupies the terrible space in our lives of being utterly pleasurable and essential but also potentially a source of great misery and obsession. Nowhere is that dichotomy more evident than in the contradictory television genres of the cookery programme and the diet programme. Or in the very persona of television cook Nigella Lawson, feted as the deeply sensual 'Goddess of the stainless steel hob' (Nicci Gerrard, *Observer*, 10 June 2003) but also featuring in the *Daily Mail* as egg-shaped when she 'suddenly favoured baggy dresses and over-sized jogging trousers in an attempt to deflect attention from the extra pounds' (*Daily Mail*, 13 May 2002).

Cookery programmes tend to be hosted by either glamorous or maternal female 'cooks' or either macho or laddish male 'chefs'. Even that distinction in naming indicates something of the different values placed on men and women who cook. In the UK, male TV cooks also tend to be restaurateurs like Rick Stein and Jamie Oliver, and are therefore professionals. Women on television appear to cook to nurture, as Delia Smith, or to seduce, as Nigella Lawson. Male chefs, on the other hand, are depicted as creative, sometimes volatile and usually catering professionally rather than for family. Even in the kitchen traditional gender differences are evident on our television screens. This is evidenced by the lack of a male equivalent to the cookery programme, 'Two Fat Ladies'. This features plump, post-menopausal, eccentric, sisterly spinsters, a gender stereotype unique to femininity.

Feeding and femininity are inexorably linked yet food and femininity are also deeply oppositional in our contemporary culture. Gerrard (2003) commented that women learn to provide food and it has many powerful meanings and associations: 'Food as an offering and a welcome; food as social intimacy; food as ritual and gesture; food as an act of nurture; food as memory … Food as appetite, sex, intimacy' (*Observer*, 10 June 2003). But however much food symbolizes these positive experiences it might also *put weight on your hips*. Food is not only hedonistic, sociable, creative, satisfying and freely available but perhaps the only possibly destructively addictive substance that is essential for human life. For women its preparation and consumption are irrevocably linked to identity: mothers feed; lovers share sensual meals; carers tempt the sick with tasty, nutritious morsels; chocolates say 'thank you' or 'I love you', whilst to be late for dinner, or to refuse a prepared meal symbolizes rejection.

So powerfully does food nurture our selves and society – physically, psychologically, economically and culturally – that not complying with the socio-cultural norms of feeding and eating

> is a provocation; not just to the family with whom the anorexic is at odds, but to society itself, daring as anorexics do to spurn its well fed complacency. To attempt to survive without food is an affront; an affront that is constantly in view. The skeletal body of an anorexic is both pathetic and defiant, arousing sympathy and hostility. (Chisholm, 2002: 100)

Orbach (1986: 82) argued that the anorexic, like the hunger-striker, is in 'protest at her conditions' and seeking a solution. One solution is to refuse to be a woman and take on the burden of sexuality, maternity and, in modern times, a career as well. Young girls may well feel doubly excluded from femininities: that of their mothers may seem unattractive (and for many girls their mother's lot in life may well be experienced as downright miserable within their own families), with its burden of child-rearing, 'man' managing and career juggling, yet the only alternative 'attractive' role models many girls come across are celebrities, with their fame, wealth and attentive consorts. These stars comply with a very narrow ideal physique and so much comment is made on their looks that young women might well feel they should aspire to a similar model in order to achieve approval. At the very least they may feel dissatisfied with what they are.

That sense of disenfranchisement, of having so little value as you are or seeing what is on offer for most women as valueless, may well relate to a perception of self as needing to change to succeed in love and life (or end up like your mother). This is not an issue for anorexics alone but for all women. It is not possible to be a woman in the Western world and not be body-conscious and body-critical:

> The anorexic's attempts to change her body are in essence an exaggeration of the activities of all women who must enter a society in which they are told that not only is their role specifically delineated, but success in that role relates in large part to the physical image they can create and project. (Orbach, 1993: 85)

And there to help women in that quest are not only the magazines, newspapers and television series, but a whole range of other programmes, including the contradictory pairings of diet programmes with cookery programmes which epitomize the incompatible oppositions of feminine identities that dominate Western representation.

Diet programmes are there to undo the problem caused by foods in a culture where eating has in many ways become a leisure activity rather than a necessity for survival. They also provide the anorexic with methods of self-starvation and a justification for the effort at slenderness. Many are not even overtly diet-oriented but supposedly focus on health, fitness and self-confidence. Typical was BBC3's *Body Image* (24 August 2003), which argued 'let's be honest, the media try to sell us things they know we like in the first place'. The programme explained this 'like' of the slender body as biologically based, and relating to waist/hip ratios that indicate fertility rather than cultural norms and values. It argued that media representations merely focus on beauty that all of us desire. It then proceeded to put a taxi-driver on a carbohydrate-free diet and showed how his wife found him attractive again once he had begun to lose weight. Carefully detailed and explained, the diet was not named but was clearly the Atkin's Diet that has featured in the press linked to celebrity weight loss. His wife, significantly, was a very slender 'fitness instructor'. Sexual attractiveness not health was the motivation assigned to dieting. Curiously, the programme again featured a 'male' weight-watcher in the following item on extreme exercise – a weight-watcher who had previously controlled his weight through bulimia. There was no criticism of this practice in the programme. Although surprising, the focus on men in this programme does fit within a slight paradigm shift in advertising and mass media features that seems to be increasingly recognizing representations of the slim/fit male body as culturally relevant.

In 1999, *Weight of the Nation* (BBC1, 5 January 1999) offered us '50 ways to lose blubber', including calorie-reduced recipes, the cabbage soup diet, high protein diet, advice from the British Medical Association, free leaflets and celebrity role models. In the same year, *Fat Files* (BBC2, 14 January 1999) suggested that fat was nothing to do with greed but all about body chemistry. The hormone lectin was the focus for blame, with its levels set higher in fat people, thus absolving them from responsibility for their obesity. A surgeon commented that the obese 'can't limit their food intake' and suggested surgery as the solution. The patient had an intestine bypass and suffered from diarrhoea and scurvy but would 'rather die than be fat' – not so very different from the sentiment of many anorexics. In these pre-body summit programmes, thin is assumed to be a totally acceptable goal.

After Lena Zavarone's death in 1999, the UK's Channel 4 broadcast a programme called *Trouble with Food* (21 February 2000), which focused on eating disorders including anorexia and bulimia but with little attempt to·explain them and with graphic detail on calorie intake, vomiting techniques, extreme exercise and purging as weight control mechanisms. Obesity remained the major concern of the programme, but by 2000 the Downing Street Body Summit had firmly switched concerns to extreme thinness as a problem, rather than extreme fatness, at least for young girls. By October 2001, *Skinny Women,* another Channel 4 broadcast, featured a very thin, young girl on anti-depressants who claimed 'the ultimate target is death', bringing into the discussion of self-starvation not a goal of the sexy, slimness of the models but self-annihilation of the body to match perhaps the lack of psychological sense of valid self-worth. However, on television just as in the print media, the newsworthiness of self-starving slipped as quickly as celebrity starvers and political intervention had raised its threshold. By 2003, there were few programmes of a similar kind to *Skinny Women* and the focus had swung back to obesity as the problem and diet as the solution, as evidenced in BBC3's *Body Image.*

The very contradiction and volume of cooking and dieting programmes is key, perhaps, to describing women's inscribed socio-cultural identity. That contradiction also identifies the discourses that influence such representations: capital's requirement for a market place in 'looks' that must be malleable to serve diet, exercise and fashion sales to women career-consumers, and patriarchy's ongoing interest in the contrasting femininity of fecundity, domesticity and sensuality. 'Post' feminism, women remain trapped in these discursive spaces across the range of the mass media with their deep dependence on audience figures and advertising, and the remaining domination of masculinist ideology, ownership and control (Christmas, 1997; Tunstall, 1996). Yet the past ten years has witnessed the burgeoning of a new media space that is both less regulated, less conglomerate and more interactive than its predecessors. The World Wide Web has been heralded as a new medium: interactive, global, easily accessible and relatively free of conglomerate or political control. This final section of Part One considers whether the information technology revolution can in any sense offer a different site of representation of the feminine.

Info-thin technology

Stars, magazines, soap operas and newspapers also have websites reproducing, globally and repeatedly, on-line much of the same representation as is featured in 'local' print and on television. As such, the Web is another medium, in many ways not substantially different in content than earlier media forms: albeit much wider in distribution, in many ways more readily accessible and more multi-layered in representation – sound, graphics, video, image and text are possible in one message, which might also integrate advertising with entertainment and information more seamlessly than is technically possible in other forms. The Web also appears to be ahistorical, as many sites are not clearly dated, and apolitical, in that there is no control or ownership or ideological line apparent. Each of these differences arguably compounds any potential other individual media forms may have to construct *ways of seeing* (Berger, 1972) for audiences. The Web is both composite and continuous; it is also cheap.

The female body on-line complies with the representation of the body in other media. Electronic magazines look very similar to those on the shop shelves, but of course are 'free'. Some are little more than advertising for the real thing, others offer substantial content. *Vogue* (http://www.vogue.co.uk/, accessed 2 September 2003) had a scantily clad young blonde woman on the 'front' page, Jennifer Aniston, Calista Flockhart, Kate Moss, Liz Hurley and Victoria Beckham all featured 'inside', there were links to fashion pages and celebrity weddings. New technology not only informs young women in many of the same ways as conventional media as to how they should look, but computers readily generate perfect bodies whether from real or animated sources.

Electronic manipulation of images has long been possible, but the extent of its use in magazine images was revealed when men's magazine *GQ* placed an electronically slimmed actress, Kate Winslet, often criticized for her tendency to gain weight, on its front cover (Figure 5.1).

> The editor of a UK men's magazine has admitted its cover photograph of actress Kate Winslet was airbrushed to improve the image. GQ editor Dylan Jones said the 27-year-old Titanic actress had approved the photographs, but that they had been 'digitally altered'. (http://news.bbc.co.uk/1/hi/entertainment/showbiz/2643777.stm, accessed 2 September 2003)

GQ editor Dylan Jones claimed: 'Practically every photo you see in a magazine will have been digitally altered in this way', as if that is simply normal. The problem may be that practically every photograph is normalizing an illusion of desirable bodies that are not actually possible bodies. The image presented of Winslet recalled to memory an e-mail circulated to celebrate Women's History Month some years ago that reminded mail-base members '[i]f shop mannequins were real women they'd be too thin to menstruate and if Barbie were a real woman, she'd have to walk on all fours due to her proportions'.

In 1999, *elite* model agency of New York took this artifice to the limit when it launched the virtually perfect model on-line.

> She will never age, gain weight, develop cellulite or throw a tantrum. Six feet tall with 34B-24-35 statistics, leggy supermodel Webbie Tookay is about as perfect as they come. (The *Mail on Sunday*, 25 July 1999)

Figure 5.1   GQ

Webbie is still 'working' and available at http://www.illusion2k.com. Other animated women on-line also include 'adult' screen-savers – crude and rude but still very slender.

A search for body+image through *Yahoo* came out with a sponsored diet site at the top www.weightwatchers.co.uk. Clicking on, I was offered: 'It's time to lose weight – it's **Time To Eat at Weight Watchers** with our new seasonally inspired diet. It's all about real food, real life and real results for real people – just like you.' Just in case 'I' can't get to meetings, 'I' am reassured that 'I' can follow the diet in private, whether of course 'I' am obese or anorexic, by signing up on-line:

Weight Watchers Online. Can't go to Meetings? Do the Points® diet online … The idea is simple! All foods have a Points value based on their calorie and saturated fat content. All you have to do is stay within your Points range and lose weight!

Diet links and sales seem to characterize on-line space as much as other media space. They appeared as information or advertising in searches relating to health, beauty, sexuality, stars, food, fashion, body, image, relationships and anorexia. The subtlety and complexity of the marketing is both intriguing and disturbing.

When checking the Web for information on Jennifer Aniston from *Friends*, surfers are directed to 'ediets' site, which features her body. The site invited visitors to fill in a questionnaire and sign up for an e-diet. Our 'visitor', at 5ft 4in. and 120 lb, was told, accurately and responsibly: 'Your BMI is currently 20 or less. We do not recommend further weight loss. We have assigned you with a healthy eating programme which will maintain your current weight and help balance your eating' (http://edietsuk.co.uk/dietprofile/results.cfm?dietchoice=1). This advice was followed by an unsolicited eating plan on credit.

9-Week Diet Membership NOW ONLY £25!! Save £10! Less than £3 per week! That's right – we're offering 9 weeks of personalised diet plans for just £25! Commit to 9 weeks of healthy living and get yourself in Super shape! Pay £9.00 a month starting in week 10, which for convenience will be automatically renewed at the end of your payment plan (cancel anytime after 9 weeks).

A 'diet plan' was being sold as a commodity regardless of the fact that the visitor didn't need such a plan.

This 'surfing' showed clearly how different the Web is as a medium. In fact, the Web is not just a single medium providing representation, it also offers a very different representational context in its interactivity and encouragement to visitors to participate and create representation. This participatory quality transcends constraints of time, place and identity and provides 'a locus for creative authorship of the self' (Jewkes and Sharp, 2003: 3). *Vogue* offers inter-activity in its forum, http://www.vogue.co.uk/forum/. Typical of the communications posted are [*sic*]:

> **nora 99999:** 31/08/2003 21:26:25 has anyone seen Kate Moss in the new White Stripes video? She hasn't lost that beautiful bod of hers! Even after having a child too!

Polkadot_ princess: 31/08/2003 20:29:51 Hello everyone, I'm 14 and I check out the forum alot but I understand you maque pierre because often I post questions that no one bothers to aknowledge. Recently there has been no talk about fashion it's all about peoples personal lives. I come here because i love fashion and to ask and answer questions about fashion. I know by reading the posts that Skinny, Craig etc are passionate about fashion but maybe you could do your personal chatting on MSN messenger? Fairy + Angel I totally agree, Kate Moss is THE most stylish person in the world. How cool would it be to be her friend! [sic]

Interactivity is evident via searches and links throughout the Web. A *Yahoo* search airbrushed+magazines listed: 'Pieces of You'. The link is to a page hosted by the Eating Distress Media Awareness Group, Marino Therapy Centre, Dublin, Ireland. Their aim is: 'To dissolve the misconceptions of eating distress that the media help to fuel and to promote positive messages about healthy images and diversity'. The group is perceptive and aware of media values, criticizing not just body image representation coverage of eating disorders – which they claim are often stories featuring stars whom the media know will attract audiences rather than in any sense arising out of genuine concerns about anorexia (or of course the way the media represent women). The site warns that linking anorexia to fame can actually glamorize it:

Not all articles on eating distress are written with the aim to spread awareness … Often magazines or newspapers sensationalize eating distress to gain readership. Often there are tell tale signs to indicate that the article has been written to sensationalize eating distress. Look out for the use of famous people's names on the title or in the introduction.

It also encourages users to respond to the media, has links to further information, reproduces substantial and well-informed articles and offers space for contributions, including:

Open any best-selling magazine and you can read an article on dieting and weight-loss followed by recipes for 'sinful' chocolate fudge cake, followed by 10 steps for healthy eating followed by an advertisement for low fat crisps followed by a fashion spread portraying ultra slim models followed by an article definitively declaring that people prefer curvy lovers followed by an advertisement for the 'must-have' perfume showing two scantily clad ultra slim bodies erotically entwined and all this topped off by an up-to-the-minute 'news' article sensationalising the 'inexplicable' rise in eating distress! I am well aware that my view of food and body shape is distorted but, is society's view any less distorted? And is it any wonder given the constant bombardment of such danger-ously conflicting messages? (irishamethyst41@hotmail.com, accessed 02 September 2003)

Perceptive and critical, this submission from an anorexic illustrates the positive interactive potential of the Web for support, information and dissemination.

This Dublin-based site is not unique. *About-face* (http:// www.aboutface. org/) is based in San Francisco and offers a very similar site. It offers a list of 'offending' companies who advertise in a way that promotes extreme slenderness and/or links that to sexual attraction. Top in September 2003 was fashion house Diesel, who insisted on slenderness by showing images of crude lipo-suction titled 'No pain, no gain' in an advertisement for their 'slim-fit' jackets. *About-face* includes the company's e-mail address and asks site-users to write and complain.

About-Face was born in August 1995 when hundreds of copies of this poster [Figure 5.2] were plastered on temporary structures around San Francisco. The poster is not a statement against thin women, rather it is a protest against the limiting ways that women are depicted in our culture. The image of supermodel Kate Moss was taken directly from an adver-tisement for perfume. In the actual ad, Moss' natural thinness was exag-gerated to skeletal proportions by design. Her pose, her facial expression and the way she was lit all collaborate to make the final image one of incredible vulnerability. (http://www.about-face.org/aau/our-story. html, accessed 2 September 2003)

About-Face publishes letters readers have written to companies com-plaining about their advertising imagery of women, offers links and infor-mation and space for readers' writing. It is also political and seeks change with empowering and supportive advice such as this:

Stop Talking About Your Weight (especially in front of young girls). Young girls listen to the way women talk about themselves and each other and learn the language of womanhood. Young women can only learn to love or even accept their bodies if they see women who love and accept their own. Every discussion we have about weight, or fat, or being too this or that, leaves an impression on the people around us. We are encouraging an unattainable quest for perfection.

Always remember that the main objective of the fashion, cosmetic, diet, fitness and plastic surgery industries is to make money, not to make you the best person you can possibly be. The ultra thin ideal is working for them. But is it working for you? If every season your parent

Figure 5.2 *About-Face* **poster**

or partner told you to change who you are or how you dress wouldn't you question their motives? (http://www.about-face.org/mc/empower/, accessed 2 september 2003)

But that potential of the Web for interactivity to change and challenge the endorsement of thin as sexy and beautiful and successful has also been explored by anorexics desperate to defend, extend, explain and celebrate their condition:

> Anonymity, disembodiment, outreach and speed are the hallmarks of Internet communication and, combined, they can make us feel daring, liberated, infallible ... providing us with the opportunity both to *present* and to *invent* ourselves. (Jewkes and Sharp, 2003: 2)

These web-orexia sites offer 'thinspirations' to would-be slimmers alongside tips on how to 'starve and binge' in an 'underground movement united against persecution in a unique quest for perfection' (*Guardian*, 27 March 2002). On-line pro-Ana sites are very easy to find and offer would-be self-starvers everything they need to know to reduce. One link provides comprehensive links and begins with a warning and disclaimer from the anorexic who runs it:

I love Ana and wouldn't give her up for the world ... NOW. But, if I could go back and start over, I never would have started any of this in the first place. It is not fun or glamourous. SO ... PLEASE ... if you don't have an eating disorder, turn back. Don't start now. Don't go looking for a 'miracle'. Do it the healthy way, with moderation and exercise. Don't let your life become a constant pattern of starving, bingeing, purging, calorie counting, depression, and guilt. Be NORMAL and healthy.

If you feel like you want to stop, but don't know how, go back to the top of the page and click on the apple icon. It will take you to the Something Fishy website. It's a recovery site and you can find a lot of help there. For those of you that are already Ana or Mia and are in it for the long haul, continue on and check out the site. I am constantly updating, so check back often! I love you all and please ... please take care of yourselves! Cuz like I said before ... GOOD ANA'S DON'T DIE!! :) (http://myweb.ecomplanet.com/NAVA9212/mycustompage0006.htm, accessed, 2 September 2003).

One link is to a list of the lowest calorie carbohydrates with the advice:

In order to lose weight as fast as possible you have to cut out as many carbohydrates from your diet as possible, because they stimulate the production of insulin, which makes you fat. (http://fanatasy.esmartweb. com/safe.html, accessed 2 September 2003)

This information mimics the Atkins Diet currently very popular with many of the stars who feature throughout the media as ideal bodies, including Jennifer Aniston. Another link offers tips on how to deal with hunger:

Get outside! Go for a walk, jog, whatever! You are getting fresh air, and burning cals! You are on your way to the thinnish line!!!!

Get a haircut. Hair has to weigh something doesn't it?

Use Crest white strips. After all you have to leave them on for a while and you have to do the top and the bottom, so you won't be able to eat! And on top of that you will have pretty, white teeth!

(http://myweb.ecomplanet.com/NAVA9212/mycustompage0008.htm, accessed 2 September 2003)

Thorough advice is given on diet supplements designed to increase energy and suppress appetite. The producer for this page has 'tested' all the products listed. An example is:

Twin Lab Diet Fuel – I started taking these because after awhile, your body builds up a tolerance ... and well, they just weren't working anymore.

These work great, although you have to be careful. 3 capsules with each meal is the recommended dosage. 2 capsules at a time was all it took for me (at first), so figure out what works for you. Just don't take more than what is recommended! They aren't very expensive, so that is a bonus!! And I do recommend that you eat a little something w/them or you may get slightly nauseated. That may be a plus for some though. (http:// myweb.ecomplanet.com/NAVA9212/mycustompage0001.htm, accessed 2 September 2003)

Anorexics defend and legitimate their sites by claiming that they are about survival as anorexics and safe practices. Anorexia is seen as a lifestyle not an illness. AnnaGrrl's site is called 'Good Anas don't die'. A posting in defence of the site on a university website (http://cim.ucdavis. edu/users/mcmyang/archives/000399.html) argued:

If you consider anorexia a disorder then logic that follows is that sites promoting safety in dealing with a DISORDER would be good, even encouraged. I have known people that are Mia, (Bulimic, if you know absolutely nothing of which you are speaking) That were told by one person that if you brush your teeth after binging it makes your teeth worse. Her teeth are now rotting out. She told me that had she known of Pro-ED sites and read some of their safety tips, she would never have waited an hour before brushing her teeth. Sites that have tips, can be life-savers, like ones that say, don't take ipecac, laxities or diuretics. The majority of Anas, Mias, or Ed-Nos that die are usually from bad advice, or not knowing how to keep safe. I think Ana and the rest are lifestyles, but if you want to believe that they are disorders, feel free. Safety is the whole issue. (Posted by Aingeal at 12 July 2003 07:53 PM link http:// jewelofpain.diaryland.com/)

The participatory and interactive nature of the net is very evident in the pro-Ana world. It would be hard to self-publicize and self-justify to the extent these girls do in any other medium. But it is easy for an ema-ciated young girl to place pictures of herself semi-clothed in a public forum on-line: 'rachael leigh cook's stats: Height:5'2, weight:100lbs, BMI:18.3' (normal Body Mass Index is around 25) (http://princessana.4t. com/photo4. html, accessed 2 September 2003).

A similar personalized web page run by 'Katt' offers support to co-anas by publishing their weight as current and goal on a monthly basis so they can chart their progress. Her slogan is: 'Life is a scale: live it your weigh' (http://myweb.ecomplanet.com/SYLV4264/, accessed 2 September 2003).

Calls to ban and close the sites simply highlight the problem – ethical and technical – of control on-line; a problem that features in pornographic sites, paedophiliac sites, hate sites and terrorist sites. The very character of the Net both enables the freedom to challenge the mainstream legitimately and illegitimately and raises the question of what is legitimate in a zone beyond physical boundaries and legislative reach. In relation to body image there are many resources on-line that take issue with mainstream images of femininity but these certainly do not dominate the body image representations on the Web nor do these subversive sites present themselves easily to girls seeking to diet to death and defend themselves while they do it. Rather most of the new media, whether as adjunct to its more conventional media sources in the televisual and print industries, or as space for chat-rooms and interactivity, seems to repeat the mantra that 'thin is in'. Ironically, it may well only be those women already equipped to resist and challenge the domination of thin who access or use the alternative sites whilst most will just repeat on-line the media habits that prevail off-line.

Summary: Media, mothers and 'me'

The media messages on our small screens seem to be a continuum of the kind of specific body representation identified by the earlier studies referred to at the beginning of this chapter (Downs and Harrison, 1985; Garner and Garfinkel, 1980; Gonzalez-Lavin and Smolak, 1995; Kaufman 1980; Silverstein, Perdue et al., 1986), but they also replicate the fascination with 'stars' found in the print media and reproduce their written narratives of femininity. The associations and narrative are identical: slender is beautiful, slender is sexy and slender is successful. Moreover, being slender, sexy and successful is the route to love. Anorexia begins with dieting in order to comply with these dominant discourses of femininity but whereas most dieters fail completely or lose weight only to gain it again, the anorexic diets to the point of disease and even death. The initial project though is one and the same – to lose weight and appear more slender because that shape is deemed more beautiful.

Orbach (1986) offered a psycho-analytic model of explanation for what shifts the anorexic into a danger area where most women remain hovering on the boundaries. She argued that although women share to some extent feelings about their bodies 'of insecurity and discomfort to some extent or another' (1986: 85) and take up advertisers' advice on how they might improve and change, the anorexic's psyche impels those feelings of not having a good-enough image towards the extreme of 'hunger-strike'. The difference between most women and self-starvers, for Orbach, was that although both struggle with the expectations of society and feel failure and worthlessness, most women experience these struggles on top of some inner sense of themselves. Image pressure may damage these women's self-confidence but they are able to overcome that by purchase, beautifying practice or perhaps politics.

Anorexics, Orbach argued, have no inner sense of self to fall back on so their engagement with the image-makers is a desperate search for a whole self rather than an effort at changing or improving an already existent self. Such young women have been made to feel nothing about them is of value and, for Orbach, the root of that terrible emptiness is in the family and particularly in the relationship with the mother. Seeing mediated all around her that slenderness is associated with love, sexual attraction and happiness the anorexic sees positive rewards associated with the denial and control of diet and that becomes her route to a 'place in the world' (Orbach, 1986: 87). This may well be reinforced when early in the process she is praised for her new slim shape and self-control. Such comment may impel stricter routines and practices as she moves away from the unvalued 'body' and tries to create a valuable self, but as it is a project doomed to fail, she becomes enmeshed in trying harder and harder to gain the self-esteem she lacks. The anger and despair of those around as she literally starves serve only to impel her efforts to become better by the only route she can perceive that has positive attributions, slenderness. Each failure to feel better becomes a spur to diet harder. Orbach sees the desperation of such self-denial as originating in the care-taking environment during childhood. If a mother is:

Unable to provide a reasonably nurturing environment or respond unambiguously to the child's initiatives, the developing ego, and hence the child's sense of itself, will be truncated in one way or another. (1986: 90)

So a psycho-therapeautic explanation for anorexia is that although all girls are bombarded with the same messages about their looks and femininity, and most feel they measure up badly, those who are already compromised by over-demanding, critical or undemonstrative familial relationships will be particularly vulnerable because they have not got the baseline security that many do of feeling loved and valued *at home*, regardless of their looks and actions. It may be hard to move from being a loved child to the contradictory and constricting demands of adult femininity; to move from feeling not good enough as a child to being a not beautiful enough or successful enough woman in the public world ironically makes starvation a means of survival. One obvious problem with that model is why would a young woman choose to try to stay in an unhappy childhood state where she would maintain *ad infinitum* the dystopia of a nihilistic never-never land. In a way the opposite hypothesis makes more sense – perhaps it is girls who are well loved, nurtured and valued who see the adult female world and decide to stay where they are.

So there are really several issues in the representation of the female body in the mass media: first, it presents all women with an illusory, contradictory and limited model of acceptable femininity that any young woman might not rush towards with enthusiasm; second, some already vulnerable young women (perhaps over-loved at home as often as under-loved) may be deeply susceptible to and needy of positive representations of 'public' femininity; third, the body and mind have tended to be 'under-stood' and 'treated' within the narrow confines of the medico-psycho spectrum and, fourth, contemporary Western society has produced conditions that support all these issues: capitalism, patriarchy and 'post' feminism.

But in many ways women's lives have changed. There are both more expectations but also more choice and more autonomy. The media lags behind, dragging women back into the kitchen and the bedroom, as if only then can they succeed in the boardroom. The images presented to women are for most perhaps demeaning and tiresome and amusing and confusing and challenging but they are not real and may only impact when women's real self is already vulnerable and particularly when that self has never been positively experienced, even as a child.

Some evidence of change may well be the perceptible increase in representations of the male body, male beauty and male 'shape'. This may relate to a genuine gender blending in sexual politics, with men beginning to aspire to previously feminine concerns for 'looks'. More cynically, it may be partially resulting from the constant search for new markets within the leisure and pleasure industries, which have increasingly targeted male beauty and body consumers through advertising and associated features.

It may be that, optimistically, in many ways current representations merely serve masculinity as it trundles to the end of its late patriarchal phase but do not deeply shape most women's sense of themselves. As journalist Katherine Viner wrote, many feminist women (post or not) may well see the media model of their world as

> fun but ultimately empty – celebrity and image simply do not leave you with sense of purpose in the way that more rooted, 'useful' forms of identity do. The Internet cannot offer a community; celebrity leads nowhere fulfilling and the television cannot talk back. The ornamental culture may dazzle but its promises are empty. (*Guardian Weekend*, 4 September 1999)

But older contemporary women did not grow to adulthood in today's a media-saturated culture nor in one where their sense of themselves depended on such conflicting and demanding models of femininity. Also, most mature women benefited, either directly or indirectly, from an empowering and supportive feminist politics. The anorexic woman is young and Western and grew up with 24-hour television, the Net and post-feminism. Depressingly, the media have become more and more our world, our community, friend, lover, teacher and even mirror of the self and the point at which we may be most vulnerable to the power of representation is that point at which our sense of self is balanced precariously on the threshold of adulthood. Orbach (1978, 1993) has always argued that the media affects young women's self-perception negatively because it presents very limited and unachievable representations of femininity. At the millennium the apparent rise in eating disorders resulted in something of a media frenzy of accusation and counter-accusation as to their role in creating the thin tyranny. The British Medical Association (2000) joined in the debate and finally the UK government held the Body Summit in 2001. But in effect little has changed. There is no evidence from the media representations analysed for this part of the book of either a broader or more realistic range of feminine imagery. If anything the 'stars' portrayed have become even fewer in number, more limited in type and ever-more frequently accounted for in relation to their body size and shape. More, these representations are not limited to glossy magazines but occupy the newspapers, television and Web as well. For young women entering the world of adult femininity the 'looks' she encounters in the media-represented world reflect:

The mammoth power of the diet/fashion/beauty/cosmetic industries. These industries have both material and ideological thrusts ... their profits are sustained on the enormity of the body insecurity that they both identify and allege to ameliorate while simultaneously reinforcing and amplifying this insecurity. (Orbach, 1993: 52)

Certainly there is evidence in the material detailed in this part of the book that the media is complicit in the selling of slenderness – it could hardly be otherwise given its dependence on corporate advertising and sponsorship – but it also seems to be more implicitly selling sexual identity in its constant repetition of conservative gender roles and narratives. These familiar stories of love and loss are hung around the narrow shoulders of 'slender' stars who become signifiers of success as they slide seamlessly from media form to media form. These representations are worrying enough if they reflect the norms and values of our culture back to us because they depict a culture that appears to ignore or devalue a very large proportion of its female population on the basis of their looks alone. It is also a culture that appears to provide women with a very limited route to any sense of self-worth or success. These serials are even more worrying if they don't merely reflect but actively reproduce feelings of negativity, invisibility and dissatisfaction amongst real women. The second section of this book shifts the focus of analysis to the audience to try to elicit the ways in which young women make sense of the mediated feminine discourses discussed in Part One.

Notes

1   Advertising messages to consumers that make references to body shape represent one aspect of a socialization process that conditions people, especially teenagers, to regard certain physical attributes as desirable (Thompson and Hirschmann, 1995). It has been argued that advertisers carry this process to extremes and promote standards of physical beauty that are potentially harmful (Wolf, 1992). Despite this warning, the belief that the use of physically attractive models as product endorsers can enhance product image encourages advertisers to continue associating their commodities with certain beauty ideals (Belch et al., 1987; Benoy, 1982). Certainly, young people have been found to exhibit greater sensitivity to advertisements that feature physically attractive models (Martin and Gentry, 1997; Martin and Kennedy, 1993).

2   *Daily Mail*, 14 May 2002.

PART TWO FROM MEDIA REPRESENTATIONS TO AUDIENCE IMPACT

Part Two moves the focus of the book from representation to audiences. In the chapters that follow we review empirical research into the impact of the media upon the body self-perceptions of audiences and, in particular, on the body image ideals adopted by women. In addition, we examine evidence for links between the media and the onset or maintenance of disordered eating habits. One convenient methodological distinction that can be applied to this research is between surveys and experiments. Surveys have explored degrees of association between reported media exposure and body self-perception and disordered eating and experimental research has used controlled media exposure conditions in an attempt to demonstrate cause–effect connections between media representations of body image and the body self-image and esteem of media consumers. Each of these methodologies is characterized by idiosyncratic advantages and disadvantages that need to be borne in mind when interpreting the research evidence.

A further important distinction can be made between the types of populations investigated. Most attention has been devoted to the study of female body image. This emphasis is not too surprising given that women tend to be more figure- and diet-conscious than men. Furthermore, serious, health-threatening eating disorders are much more likely to occur among women – especially young women. Nevertheless, men are not without their concerns about physical appearance. While the body shape ideal for women is a slender one, for men it tends to be a muscular one. Of course, the focus on women's body image concerns is related not only to their self-perceptions but also to their perceptions of how others – particularly men – might respond to them.

The research literature is therefore characterized by the types of individuals studied. Most of the research to date has been conducted with 'normal' women. In this context, normal means women who have not been clinically diagnosed as suffering from an eating disorder. Some research, however, has been carried out with women clinically diagnosed as anorexic or bulimic. Comparisons can be made between the results of research with clinical and non-clinical populations and these have value in that they may indicate the degree to which the media may contribute towards the development of serious disorders. If non-clinical populations exhibit similar patterns of relationship between media exposure and body image perceptions as clinical populations, then this strengthens the case for a hypothesized media influence. If, however, these two populations exhibit quite distinct patterns of behaviour and different patterns of relationship between media exposure and body image percepts, this would weaken the case for assuming that the media *per se* may be involved in the genesis of serious eating disorders.

In examining the research in this field, it is also important to distinguish different measures of 'effect'. Among the psychological phenomena that may potentially be influenced by the media are perceptions of one's own weight (thinking of oneself as 'underweight' or 'overweight'), perceptions of one's body shape (thin, average, fat), feelings about one's body (satisfied or dissatisfied with it), attitudes towards eating and actual eating habits. Each of these variables may be differentially ingrained in the individual's psyche and therefore amenable to change. Each, in turn, may be differentially sensitive to media or other cultural influences. Further definition can be given to media effects on body image through consideration of what might be called 'controlling' or 'mediating' factors. Individuals may vary in their existing body weight, their self-confidence or self-esteem, the centrality of body matters to their existence, and the extent to which they tend to compare themselves (favourably or unfavourably) with others. Some studies have explored some of these measures and not others. Some researchers have attempted to define media effects in relation to controlling variables, while others have not.

Finally, the 'media' cover a number of different forms of communication. Within the context of research into media influences on body image, most studies have investigated the impact of either print media (usually glossy magazines) or broadcast media (usually television programmes). Thus, in surveys, respondents are classified in terms of the types of magazines they reportedly read and the types of television programmes they reportedly watch. Respondents are usually offered a choice of magazines and programmes by the researcher that have been selected because they are known or believed to present examples of thin or fat body shapes.

In experimental studies, participants may be presented with media images of bodies (for example, fashion photographs from magazines or clips from television programmes) and their post-exposure reactions are then measured via questionnaires containing verbal and non-verbal ratings scales. In some studies, participants are tested both before and after exposure to media body images, while in others they are tested only after exposure. Comparisons are then made between groups of participants who were shown different types of body image.

Hence, in the chapters that follow these various measures and the relationships between them will be examined. The discussion will not be restricted to a descriptive account of the published research, but will also provide a critical examination of the evidence in order to judge how much confidence we can have in what has been found out so far. The survey and experimental research literature has been supplemented by a small number of qualitative studies in which participants have been questioned in depth, usually with other individuals, for their opinions about media representations of body image and media campaigns designed to promote a slender physique. These studies have offered a different perspective on the issue of the media and body image by giving young people an opportunity to express their beliefs and their feelings freely in their own words.

Before turning to this review and assessment of the empirical literature, however, the next chapter will consider the various theoretical reasons why we might expect body image to be influenced by the mass media and the social, cultural and most especially psychological mechanisms through which such effects are likely to occur. By combining what is known about the psychological factors underpinning body image perceptions and the way they develop with a review of some of the key features of media representations of human body shape, the potential of the media to influence body-related perceptions should become apparent. This chapter will also reinforce this case by examining what is known about the way media consumers respond directly to media representations of body image. Do such media representations have significance for media consumers? Is their significance particularly pronounced among those population sub-groups generally regarded as 'at risk' of developing distorted body self-perceptions and disordered eating habits?

6 From Representation to Effects

This chapter explores the psychological mechanisms through which media representations of body shape could influence public conceptions. A number of writers have postulated that the mass media play a key role in creating and exacerbating the phenomenon of body dissatisfaction (Silverstein, Perdue et al., 1986; Silverstein, Peterson et al., 1986; Silverstein et al., 1988) and, in consequence, contributing to the increase in prevalence of eating disorders (Garner et al., 1980). The value of slimness represents a relatively recent shift in the beauty ideals of the West (Polivy and Herman, 1987). Being fat has been found to be associated with a range of negative attributes, including self-indulgence, lethargy and slovenliness (Glassner, 1988; Ogden, 1992). Thinness, in contrast, is presented as being associated with self-control, success and attractiveness and competency (Glassner, 1988). Concern about physical attractiveness has traditionally been found to be strongest among females for whom weight and body shape are a far more important priority than is usually found among males (Collins, 1991; Wadden et al., 1991).

The first part of this book has examined evidence for the representation of body image in the media. Although such research has been centred on the appearance of body shapes in the media, inferences have been drawn from this work about possible influences of these media representations on public perceptions of the body, with such images believed to play a significant role in setting the standards of feminine and masculine physical beauty.

A number of psychological mechanisms have been identified as underpinning the influences of media representations of body image. Women may identify with fashion models from magazines or celebrities on television or film as body image role models (Garner and Garfinkel, 1980). The media may display fashions that women already covet (Streigel-Moore, Silverstein et al., 1986). The media may cultivate norms that set long-lasting standards to which individuals aspire. Alternatively, the media may provide a number of exemplars of body shape that invoke different reactions among media consumers according to pre-existing 'schema' they have established in their own minds about their own body shape (Myers and Biocca, 1992). What then is the potential of media representations of body image to influence public perceptions of physical attractiveness, body self-esteem, personal body dissatisfaction and, in turn, the onset of health-threatening disordered eating syndromes? A review of the important psychological mechanisms through which media effects have been thought to occur in this context will be presented to consider the potential of the media to impact directly upon body self-perceptions and societal standards of physical attractiveness.

Theories of media influence

Before we consider the empirical evidence for media effects upon body image perceptions and associated eating patterns, are there any theoretical reasons to believe that media representations of a thin ideal body shape as a primary exemplar of beauty and attractiveness condition distorted self-perceptions? If such theories do exist, might they lead us to expect especially powerful effects upon media consumers that take on a particular form, or that are felt more strongly among certain sub-groups of the population, or that follow from particular categories of media representation? Furthermore, are media effects on body image perceptions, if they do occur, derived purely from the media, or do the media interact with or reinforce other social, cultural or physical causes of body self-esteem and related disordered eating patterns? This consideration of theoretical bases for concern is important because it may indicate not simply that media effects on body image can be expected to occur, but also forms a useful backdrop to a critical evaluation of the empirical research conducted on this subject so far.

Attractiveness of body types

Psychologists have observed for at least half a century that body shapes can be classified into three principal types and that these types of physical build are associated with stereotyped behavioural and personality traits (Sheldon and Stevens, 1942; Staffieri, 1967; Walker, 1962; Wells and Siegel, 1961; Yates and Taylor, 1978). Sheldon and Stevens distinguished between ectomorphic (thin build), endomorphic (fat build) and mesomorphic (muscular build) types. The most favourable traits have customarily been assigned to the mesomorphic body build and the least favourable to the ectomorphic and endomorphic builds. Mesomorphic individuals have been associated with strength, happiness and dominance, whereas the endomorphic type has been characterized as socially aggressive, lazy and unattractive. The ectomorphic type has been characterized as being nervous, submissive and socially withdrawn (Dibiase and Hjelle, 1968). More recently, while the endomorph has continued to be seen in a negative light and the mesomorph in a highly positive way, the ectomorph has also attracted positive comments. Both men and women have been found to prefer moderate-sized bodies more than either extremely thin or fat body shapes (Beck et al., 1976).

By the early 1980s, research among student samples found that young men and young women preferred a muscular, well-toned masculine physique for men over one that was paunchy and out of condition (Gitter et al., 1982). Women generally have been found to prefer a tapering 'V' physique in men (Lavrakas, 1975; Wiggins et al., 1968). In judging feminine body shapes, young people of both genders were found to prefer an 'hourglass' figure to one that was either thin or fat. Good posture, with shoulders back and well-developed breasts, were other popular features of the female physique (Gitter et al., 1983). While the mesomorphic physique has consistently emerged as the most preferred body type, there were emergent signs during the 1970s and 1980s that the thin or ectomorphic body type was gaining in popularity, especially among teenage girls and young women (Spillman and Everington, 1989; Staffieri, 1972b; Yates and Taylor, 1978). Whatever the current cultural standards, one consistent pattern has been the greater importance of physical appearance to the way women are judged than to the way men are judged. Women have more to lose by not meeting societal standards (Bar-Tel and Saxe, 1976).

Body shape and size have been found to have important implications for sexual attractiveness. Among young people especially different aspects of physical build are weighed up in the case of each gender in judging an individual's attractiveness (Franzoi and Herzog, 1987). There has been some debate, however, about the significance of build for sexual allure. Many psychologists believe that sexual preferences are learned. They are influenced to some extent by cultural values and norms relating to body shape. There are differences between cultures in the body shape features that are most closely associated with attractiveness. There are other factors linked to sexual orientation of individuals that also come into play in the determination of the body shape deemed to be most attractive.

Evolutionary psychologists have linked body shape and attractiveness to more fundamental factors concerned with the continuation of the species. The selection of a potential mate is guided by identification of whether it is biologically fit to reproduce and to fulfil certain social roles subsequently (Buss, 1989). A coupling with a healthy genetic specimen offers a greater probability that the offspring will be fit enough to survive. Males therefore look for female partners with a body shape that indicates fertility. Females consider male partners whose build not only indicates that they are genetically fit, but also physically capable of providing both for them and for any offspring. Buss believed that men, regardless of culture, are more concerned about body shape and size in women than women are in men.

According to Buss, there are cultural universals in desired body shape and size for man–woman sexual attraction, and that these derive from the division of labour between men and women during the course of evolution, where males specialized in hunting activities and women in food-gathering and child-rearing. As Grogan (1999) observed: 'Natural selection was believed to have operated so that men and women whose bodies were best suited to these roles (normal weight, muscles for men, fat layers around the hips for women) were more attractive to potential mates and so were more likely to reproduce'. Thus, women's attractiveness is important because it signals to potential male sexual partners cues about their health and fecundity (Buss, 1989; Kenrick, 1989).

The significance of body shape resides, however, not only in its influence upon the way other people judge our attractiveness, but also in relation to the way we perceive ourselves. The degree to which we are satisfied with our weight and body build is a significant determinant of self-esteem. As a general rule, women have been found to be more dissatisfied with their bodies than are men (Berscheid et al., 1973; Clifford, 1971; Lerner et al., 1976). Research among heterosexual women has indicated a prominent desire to conform to a slim ideal, since this is regarded as the female body shape most admired and preferred by men (Charles and Kerr, 1986). In this British study, female interviewees wanted to be thinner because they felt this would make them more sexy. Indeed, this feeling is confirmed by women who have lost weight who report experiencing an increase in sexual desire alongside a more positive body image (Werlinger et al., 1997).

The thin ideal as a sign of physical attractiveness has been recorded in other research. Fallon and Rozin (1985) asked samples of more than 200 men and 200 women to indicate their current figure, their ideal figure, the figure that they felt would be most attractive to the opposite sex, and the opposite sex figure to which they would be most attracted, using line drawings. For women, the scale position they chose for their current figure was heavier than their ideal figure, with the body shape expected to be most attractive to men coming in between. For men, there were virtually no differences between these perceptions. It was found that both men and women miscalculated which body shape ideal the opposite sex would find attractive. Men thought that women preferred a heavier figure than they actually chose, and women thought that men would like a thinner figure than they chose in reality. The authors concluded that men's perceptions served to keep them satisfied with their bodies while women's perceptions served to keep them dissatisfied.

Elsewhere it has been found that women tended to believe that men preferred much thinner body shapes than the men themselves actually chose. Women's own ideal is thinner than the size they think men prefer. While women may be sensitive to pressures from men to be thin, there are other more general cultural pressures that seem to influence their ideal body shape beyond the perceived preferences of the opposite sex (Lamb et al., 1993).

The importance of belief in one's own body shape is underpinned by findings that show that dissatisfaction with it is linked to dissatisfaction with self (Berscheid et al., 1973; Lerner et al., 1973; Mahoney and Finch, 1976a, 1976b). Indeed, the correlation between body satisfaction and holding positive views about oneself becomes established during childhood (Mendelson and White, 1982). A further important gender difference has also been found. Body self-esteem appears to be determined by satisfaction with a greater number of body parts for females than for males. With males, satisfaction with the nose and face have emerged as the principal correlates of overall body satisfaction. Among females, however, body satisfaction is dependent on feelings about thighs, shape of legs, waist, ankle, profile and neck (Lerner and Karabenick, 1974).

A number of theoretical models have been proposed to account for body image problems, but social factors especially have been observed to exert a powerful influence on the development and maintenance of body image disturbance in Western societies (Fallon, 1990; Heinberg, 1996). A socio-cultural theory purports that current societal standards for beauty inordinately stress the importance of thinness as well as other difficult-to-achieve standards of beauty (Tiggeman and Pickering, 1996). A socio-cultural model emphasizes that the current societal standard for thinness in women is omnipresent and unfortunately often out of reach of the average woman. Indeed, although the average woman has become larger over the years, evidence suggests that the ideal has become progressively thinner (Wiseman et al., 1993).

Social comparison theory

A theoretical model using social comparison processes can be offered to explain how exposure to the socio-cultural thin and attractive ideal leads to increased body dissatisfaction (Heinberg and Thompson, 1992b; Smolak et al., 1993; Thompson et al., 1991). Social comparison theory posits that individuals establish their personal identity, through making comparisons between themselves and others who possess specific, valued attributes (Festinger, 1954).

The theory assumes there are individual differences in the tendency to compare oneself with others, to engage in upward comparisons or to choose inappropriate comparison targets, whereby some individuals are more vulnerable than others to socio-cultural appearance pressures. For example, women who exhibited a higher level of comparing their own weight with other people tended also to display greater dissatisfaction with their own bodies (Streigel-Moore et al., 1986).

One important individual difference in mode of responding to media models is gender. Boys and men do not face the same volume of attractiveness-related messages as do girls and women (Ogletree et al., 1990). Idealized images of men in advertising have been found to differ from those of women, and men's reactions to these images are dissimilar to those of women (Fischer and Halpenny, 1993). There is some indication that men are less likely to make upward comparisons with male models as their bodies have less socio-cultural importance than do females' bodies.

Another important individual difference factor in relation to the social comparison process is current level of body self-esteem. Women with lower body self-esteem may be regarded by advertisers as more vulnerable targets (Stephens et al., 1994). This belief is underscored by research that showed that female college students who were dissatisfied with their bodies were more likely to agree that being attractive – in the stereotyped way so frequently featured in the media – brought with it certain social advantages (Mintz and Betz, 1988). It is understandable that advertisers use attractive and slender models in commercial messages because these icons serve as an aspirational reference group (Richins, 1991). Indeed, American research indicated that many pre-teenage and teenage girls wanted to become models (Martin and Kennedy, 1994).

Studies examining social comparison theory on body image generally fall into one of two types: descriptive correlational studies and controlled experiments. Correlational studies generally measure the relationship between body satisfaction and individual differences in the tendency to compare one's body with others'. These studies have consistently reported an association between social comparison tendencies and body satisfaction, suggesting that higher levels of comparison are linked to greater dissatisfaction (Heinberg and Thompson, 1992a, 1992b; Thompson et al., 1991).

Social comparisons can be made with a number of role model types from the individual's own life as well as from the mass media. Comparisons with family members, for example, can be significant sources of influence. Girls may make comparisons with their mothers or sisters. The way women feel about themselves as adults may have been shaped by comparisons they made between themselves and siblings as children and adolescents. Having a sibling who was perceived as more attractive than oneself could lead to the development of a negative self-image (Rieves and Cash, 1996).

A related aspect of social comparison involves the perception of other individuals' concerns doubt their appearance and weight. It was assumed, for a long time, that although women with eating disorders are preoccupied with weight and shape, they do not place prime importance on these aspects of physique when evaluating others. Beebe, Hornbeck, Schober, Lane and Rosa (1996) showed female undergraduates a series of photographs of women and asked what aspects of the photo they first noticed as well as how the women in the photographs felt about themselves. Next, participants read scenarios in which women either over-ate or dieted and were asked to assess the women's feelings and likely weight fluctuation. Results showed that women who placed a strong emphasis on their own body weight and shape also emphasized these aspects when evaluating others. Further, women with concerns about their own body image engaged in more social comparisons with others and believed that other people were equally preoccupied with body matters. Making regular social comparisons may not only perpetuate low body self-esteem (see Stormer and Thompson, 1995), but also encourage such women to believe that their degree of concern about their physical shape is a normal preoccupation common to lots of people (Beebe et al., 1996).

In making comparisons between self and others, further evidence has indicated how perceptual judgements can vary depending upon the baseline self-concept with which individuals begin. Undergraduate female students aged between 17 and 34 years were presented with photographs of celebrities in a number of different versions and asked to indicate which was that individual's true body shape. One photograph among a set of seven pictures was accurate, while the other six had been progressively digitally distorted, to render the celebrity thinner or larger than their real body shape. The women who were concerned about their own body shape (that is, exhibited body shape dissatisfaction) tended to be more likely to judge the celebrity as being thinner than actuality, whereas women who were satisfied with their bodies judged celebrity body shapes more accurately. Interestingly, both groups of women judged heavy celebrities to be heavier than they really were (King et al., 2000).

Self-ideal discrepancy

This model also assumes that individuals make comparisons between their own body shape and size and another source. Unlike the notion of social comparison, upward comparisons are not made with another person in the individual's social environment, but with an 'ideal' the individual has formulated in her or his own mind. Thus, individuals compare their real selves with an idealized self that may be a composite of attributes gleaned from many different sources. This theory purports that individuals are motivated to attain a match between their actual self-concept and an internalized ideal (Cash and Szymanski, 1995).

One writer has argued that the self-discrepancy model may embrace a number of discrete self-concepts, including actual self, ideal self and self as preferred by certain significant others (for example, parents). If all these different 'selves' are perceptually close together, then the individual's overall self-esteem would be high, whereas when they are discrepant, body image dissatisfaction and related anxieties are more likely to be present (Higgins, 1987; Strauman and Higgins, 1987).

The discrepancy between an idealized body shape and an actual one has been measured by a number of researchers. Researchers have used assessment measures that consist of a comparison of one's actual perceived size on a schematic drawing compared with a selected ideal size (Fallon and Rozin, 1985; Thompson, 1990). This theory focuses on an individual's tendency to compare his or her perceived appearance with an imagined ideal (Thompson, 1992). The result of such a comparison process may be a discrepancy between the perceived self and the ideal self (Thompson, 1990, 1992). The theory predicts that the greater the discrepancy between the individual's perceived self and perceived ideal, the greater is their dissatisfaction with their own body.

This theory has been supported by a number of studies that have demonstrated that where there is a self–ideal discrepancy, body image dissatisfaction and higher levels of disordered eating, in both genders, are likely to be found (Altabe and Thompson, 1992; Fallon and Rozin, 1985; Jacobi and Cash, 1994; Thompson and Psaltis, 1988). Strauman, Vookles, Berenstein, Chaiken and Higgins (1991) found that general self-discrepancies (between actual self and ideal self) were correlated with body dissatisfaction and eating disorder symptoms. Forston and Stanton (1992) reported that appearance-related actual–ideal discrepancy was associated with bulimic symptoms.

The self-discrepancy model helps explain how situational cues can trigger symptoms. The theory proposes that if an event activates any aspect of an individual's self-discrepancy, then the emotion associated with this discrepancy is aroused. Strauman and Higgins (1987) asked individuals to complete sentences about other people that contained descriptive terms that the participants had previously indicated were discrepant for them (for example, 'intelligent', 'thin'). The act of completing these sentences triggered the emotion associated with that discrepancy. In a similar way, discrepancy-related emotions can be triggered by magazine pictures illustrating different body image characteristics (Altabe and Thompson, 1996). Indeed, self-discrepancy theory would predict that individuals with a hangup about their nose would have negative emotions associated with that feature triggered by watching a news item about noses.

Schema theory

Self-schema theory envisages body image as a mental construction rather than an objective evaluation (Markus, 1977). A self-schema is a person's mental representation of the way they are. This mental representation of the self becomes established over time to a large degree as a reaction to the experience of being labelled in a particular way by others. Thus, an individual who was teased about their weight as a child will continue to label themselves as overweight when grown up. Indeed, if this schema is repeatedly reinforced, it can become deeply ingrained in the individual's psyche so that they also think of themselves in that way.

Schema have been defined 'as cognitive generalizations about the self, derived from past experiences, that organize and guide the processing of self-related information contained in the individual's social experiences' (Markus, 1977: 64). Self-schemata include cognitive representations derived from specific events and situations involving the individual as well as more general representations a person derives from their social environment in which they are classified by others in terms of specific and persisting attributes (for example, 'I am fat', 'I am attractive'). Such attributes are used to evaluate and define our self-concept and determine our self-esteem. Individuals are sensitive to information that confirms their self-schema and are able to recall best of all any past experiences that helped to define or to confirm that schema (Derry and Kuiper, 1981; Markus et al., 1982; Rogers et al., 1977). This was demonstrated in a study that showed that young college adults were better able to recall descriptive terms from a test of sex-role identity that conformed to their self-identity, either as high in masculinity or high in femininity (after Bem, 1977; Spence et al., 1975). Individuals classified by this test as androgynous were equally likely to remember masculine and feminine terms (Markus et al., 1982).

Body image is of interest because it is an example of a schema that is both universal and yet can exert distinctive pressures on individuals. It is universal in that almost everyone develops an elementary organization of knowledge pertaining to their body weight or shape. For some individuals, however, their body image schema becomes a central defining feature of their being. Such individuals are preoccupied with their body shape and size and define most of their everyday experiences in relation to it. People with this preoccupation have been labelled as 'schematic', while those for whom their body shape and size are not central to their concerns have been called 'aschematic' (Markus et al., 1987).

According to Markus et al. (1987: 52):

> schematics consistently evaluate stimuli with respect to their relevance for body weight and consequently develop differentiated knowledge structures in this domain. For schematics, one's own weight has a durable salience, and a wide range of stimuli will be evaluated with reference to body weight (for example, Does she weigh more than I do? Do these pants make me look fat? Will this cookie make me gain weight? I'll never be that thin. There are a lot of chubby people in this restaurant.)

Two individuals could have a similar body shape, but may relate to it, cognitively, in different ways. Their respective schemas of their body shape would therefore be quite distinctive. Schematics will be much more worried about their weight, are more likely to diet and are more attuned to issues associated with body shape and size. Aschematics are less concerned about their weight or shape and are much less likely to evaluate situations in which they find themselves in terms of their body image (Markus et al., 1987). The schema model analyses the influence of media representations of body image in terms of the elements a given individual focuses upon and absorbs into their own self-schema (Myers and Biocca, 1992). Schematic individuals have been shown to be much more attuned to images of body shape and react to them more quickly than do aschematic individuals, when asked to judge to what extent they resemble their own body image (Markus et al., 1987). Although the latter finding occurred in response to drawings of female body shapes, it may have implications for the degree to which readers may respond to photographs of fashion models in magazines or viewers react to actors on screen.

Body image, as a mental construction, is also considered to be 'elastic'. This means that it is subject to change as a function of the individual processing fresh information about body image ideals. A further distinction has been made between four different conceptions of the 'socially represented ideal body' (body shape ideals represented in the media or elsewhere in the individual's social community or cultural environment), 'present body image' (how they currently perceive themselves) the 'objective body' (actual body shape) and the 'internalized ideal body,' a compromise or middle-ground position between the latter two concepts (Myers and Biocca, 1992: 116).

The presence of a dominant body image schema can influence the processing of body-related information or interfere with the processing of other information. For example, individuals with eating disorders or high concern about their own body image were found to be slower on word and number recognition tasks, if the tasks were preceded by the presentation of body shape-related words. The emotional connotations and motivational significance of these words to such individuals occupied mental resources that otherwise would have been available to complete the subsequent task (Newman et al., 1993).

The distinctive information-processing orientations of individuals for whom body size and shape are key defining aspects of their personal identity have obvious implications for the ways such individuals might respond to media representations of body image and any associated me sages. The so-called schematic and aschematic individuals may differ very little from each other in their outward appearance, but their disparate self-identities may lead them to pay attention to media depictions of body shape quite differently.

Cultivation theory

The mass media have been conceived to operate as transmitters of cultural ideals. The media often emphasize specific characteristics of people and provide role models from which the public at large can learn. If the media depict a slim physique as attractive, this body image may attain the status of an ideal that everyone should attempt to achieve. The attachment of social rewards to such an image will render it all the more appealing, especially to young people who seek out role models as part of the process of growing up and learning how to behave. This social learning theory of media influence posits that media 'ideals' can exert powerful effects on media audiences if they are prevalent and provide an incentive to people to emulate them.

External incentives can motivate imitative behaviour if it is anticipated that valued rewards will follow (Bandura, 1977). Individuals can observe the rewards that they believe accrue to others (in the media) as a result of adopting certain physical characteristics or accompanying behaviour patterns. Thus, if maintaining a thin body shape is perceived to produce valued social and material benefits for media models, members of the audience may wish to copy these media representations. If controlled eating is perceived to be an integral part of achieving and maintaining such a body image, then similar behaviour patterns may be adopted by members of the audience (Harrison and Cantor, 1997).

Cultivation theory argues that media representations of social reality tend to be stereotyped and repetitive (see Gerbner et al., 1980; Signorielli and Morgan, 1990). Regular exposure to such images cultivates in the audience's consciousness the idea that certain characteristics of objects are the norm. Under this theory, young women would be expected to adopt a 'mainstream' view of social reality, as displayed on television. In this context, the mainstream view is the socially circulated ideal body shape. Cultivation theory would also predict that young women, who are regular consumers of television, would probably overestimate the percentage of the female population whose body measures up to the ideal. While the effect detected here can be seen as part of the family of cultivation effects, cultivation theory does not yet have a rigorous cognitive theory to explain the cognitive dynamic involved in the construction of a body image or a young woman's self-schema.

The processes involved are psychologically complex. More needs to be known about how media content influences body image perceptions and why this image may fluctuate over time. Cultivation theory would predict a mainstream conception of body image. Yet, research has shown that body image perceptions are elastic and can change as a function of exposure to specific types of body shape representation in the media (Myers and Biocca, 1992). Different outcomes may immediately follow exposure when the ideal-body construct received from the media message is highly accessible (Sanbonmatsu and Fazio, 1991), especially among those prone to use media cues to think about their own body. These immediate outcomes may differ from self-concepts that emerge later, when the message information interacts with non-mediated sources of information and the individual's direct observation of physical and social reality.

Investigations of how people handle information from numerous social situations have indicated that they use heuristics or interpretational biases based on their knowledge and beliefs (Williamson, 1996). Such information processing biases are part of normal thinking. They prejudice our perceptions of the world by encouraging us to think about the world in terms of whatever comes easiest to mind (Kahneman and Tversky, 1973).

Heuristics may play a part in body image disturbance and provide an explanation of cultivation effects. The biased interpretation of social situations in terms of some feature that has a high level of prominence in an individual's life can lead to selective attention to and retention of information from ambiguous scenarios. Jackman, Williamson, Netemeyer and Anderson (1995) compared the interpretations that weight-preoccupied women and women not concerned about their weight placed upon sentences that described appearance-related and health-related matters and tested the women for their recall of the information in the sentences. Weight-preoccupied women showed an information-processing bias that was consistent with their negative view of their own bodies.

Cooper (1997) compared the interpretations of ambiguous interpersonal situations by eating-disordered individuals and those who displayed no such symptoms. Those women who were especially concerned about their own body image were much more inclined to interpret situations as 'weight-related' than were other women, even though the situations themselves may not have contained any explicit mention of 'weight'. For example, a situation in which a fictional person was complimented by another for his or her appearance was rated as a 'weight-related' situation by women with low body self-esteem.

Further evidence has emerged of how a preoccupation with their own weight and body shape can lead individuals to place biased interpretations on verbally described and visually enacted scenarios in which references are made to appearance. Such individuals seem to be ultra-sensitive to any such references. Women who were dissatisfied with their own bodies were found to react negatively towards sentences that described scenarios in which appearance-related comments were made, as compared with sentences with no appearance references (Wood et al., 1998). Similarly, women who scored high in anxiety about their body image formed a stronger negative impression of a female actor in a video scenario in which she appeared with a male actor and remarks were made about weight and appearance, than did women who exhibited little body image anxiety (Tantleff-Dunn and Thompson, 1998).

Perceptions of media representations and attributions of influence

Media content analyses have revealed that media body images in magazines are dominated by thin body shapes (for example, Anderson and DiDomenico, 1992; Cusumano and Thompson, 1997; Levine and Smolak, 1996). How are these images perceived by media consumers? Are these body image representations regarded as attractive? Do readers identify with such images? Do readers regard such images as an ideal for self-attainment?

Research evidence suggests that teen magazines are recognized by their readers as providing ideal body shapes. In one study, girl readers quantified the ideal teenage girl as being 5ft 7in. (1.70m), 100 pounds (45.35kg), US dress size 5 (UK size 8), with long blonde hair and blue eyes. Given that this ideal's body mass index was less than 16, within the anorexic range, this ideal represented a problematic comparison target (Nichter and Nichter, 1991).

One important factor in relation to potential influences of media body image representations is the extent to which girls make comparisons between themselves and role models featured in glossy magazines. An interview study with 15-year-old girls suggested that print media were seen as a major force in the development of body image dissatisfaction (Wertheim et al., 1997). Girls reported making comparisons between themselves and models seen in teen magazines and their initial dieting experiences were triggered by diets found in these magazines. Elsewhere, it was reported that over one in five teenage girls in the United States who regularly read fashion magazines for their age groups also stated they would like to emulate the models in these magazines (Levine et al., 1994).

Some self-attribution evidence has indicated that readers and viewers feel differently about themselves after reading magazines or watching television programmes or advertisements depicting or discussing the thin ideal. In one study, two-thirds of women university students reported feeling worse about their physical appearance after reading women's magazines. One in three of these women also reported that fashion advertisements made them feel less satisfied with their appearance, while one in two wished they looked more like models in cosmetics advertisements (Then, 1992).

In another large American survey, both men and women respondents were asked how fashion models influenced their feelings about their own appearance. More than twice as many women (27%) as men (12%) reportedly always or very often compared themselves to models in magazines, and many more women (28%) than men (19%) carefully studied the shapes of models (Garner, 1997). However, the extent to which women claimed to compare themselves with (43%) or closely study (47%) magazine representations of body shape increased markedly among those respondents dissatisfied with their body shape. Two-thirds (67%) of those women who were dissatisfied with their own body shape reported that studying thin models in magazines made them feel insecure about their weight and made them want to lose weight (Garner, 1997).

Although young women have displayed sensitivity to attractive, physical role models in the media, the capacity of such images to influence body image ideals must operate in a subtle fashion. Any deliberate appeals to slenderness in messages attempting to 'sell' the thin ideal to this market may meet with resistance. In a study of a campaign designed to promote exercise and fitness among teenage girls, messages were used that appealed to health ('Fitness Today: For a Healthier Tomorrow'), activity ('Fitness Today: For a More Active Tomorrow') and slimness ('Fitness Today: For a Slimmer Tomorrow'). Focus group interviews with teenage girls found that although many were concerned about their weight and body shape and were careful about their diet, they did not invariably accept slimness-promoting messages in a poster health campaign. The girls associated being slim with being fit, but the association of slimness with fitness in the campaign did not work well when there was an emphasis on body image and the weight-control benefits of fitness. Instead, being slender was important because it was a defining feature of being attractive, and this was an outcome more important to girls in their mid-teens than being fit (Shaw and Kemeny, 1989: 683). This point was illustrated with remarks made by two of the girls' interviewed:

'We don't think *being* fit is as important as *looking* fit.'

'Girls feel being slim is more important than being physically fit; they just want to be attractive, not actually healthy … Most girls just starve, not exercise, to lose weight.'

Indeed, there was a stigma associated with participating in fitness-promoting activities that conflicted with the projection of an attractive image. Playing sports left you hot and sweaty, which was not consistent with looking good. Furthermore, taking part in sports meant having to wear clothing that often revealed existing body shape. This was a potential embarrassment for those girls who were self-conscious about their bodies.

This research is interesting in so far as it revealed a degree of discrimination among young women, apparently 'at risk' from the influence of exposure to media representations of a slender female body shape or media promotion of that ideal. Promotional campaigns for a slender physique, in particular, would only work with this age group provided the advantages of being slim and the course of action needed to achieve the ideal had positive appeal.

Third-person effects

A further twist in the tale has been the discovery that perceptions of media effects upon body image can vary depending upon whether such effects are attributed to influence self or others. Research into the 'third-person effect' has indicated that people perceive stronger media effects upon others than upon themselves, where socially undesirable or negative effects are concerned (Cohen et al., 1988; Gunther, 1991, 1992, 1995). When the effects are socially desirable, this effect reverses to a first-person effect (Gunther and Mundy, 1993; Gunther and Thorsen, 1992). The attribution of a media effect on the self may also be linked to the person's existing level of self-esteem. Individuals with higher self-esteem are less likely than those with low self-esteem to compare their own body image with others, and to do so unfavourably (Martin and Kennedy, 1993). The degree to which others might be regarded as more vulnerable to media influences, however, depends upon the degree of social distance between self and other comparison groups. The greater the social dissimilarity between others and self, the more likely they will be regarded as vulnerable to media influences (Cohen et al., 1988; Gunther, 1991).

David and Johnson (1998) examined the perceived effect of idealized media images on self and similar others in relation to ideal body weight, self-esteem and likelihood of developing an eating disorder. In an experimental study, college women were allocated to watch or not watch a video that discussed ideal female body images found in the popular media and discussed the potential effects of these images on body weight, self-esteem and eating disorders. The purpose of this video was to heighten the salience and draw attention to standards of thinness and attractiveness portrayed in the media. Participants were asked to indicate the effects of such media images on self-female classmates, women on campus and women in general.

Results showed a social distance effect on strength of perceived media effects, with the third-person effect widening with social distance. The experiment examined in greater detail the perceived effect of the media on self and classmates. As the undesirability of the outcome increased from perception of ideal body weight, through self-esteem to likelihood of disordered eating behaviour, the effects attributed to the media weakened, both for self and others. This decline in perceived media impact was much sharper for self than for others though.

There was an experimental effect of order of questioning about perceived media effects on self and others, especially with regard to the most undesirable media outcomes. If asked to judge the media effect on others first in respect of a highly undesirable outcome such as the development of eating disorders, the participants attributed a stronger media effect on themselves than when they judged media effects on self first. The magnitude of perceived media effects on self also grew with low self-esteem among participants. The third-person effect was greater among high self-esteem than among low self-esteem participants. High self-esteem participants perceived a much greater impact of media on body image to occur among other people than upon themselves.

Summary

This chapter has established that there are theoretical reasons for hypothesizing media effects upon the development of body image distortions and associated patterns of disordered eating. Satisfaction with our bodies is a key aspect of wider self-esteem. Dissatisfaction with own body shape not only produces lower self-regard, but may also motivate behaviour patterns designed to reduce the discomfort that such low esteem can produce. Sometimes, these behaviour patterns may take on extreme and health-threatening forms. The theoretical models that have been invoked to explain the importance of body image to self-identity and the way in which this cognitive construct is influenced by socio-cultural forces, have been reinforced (though not fully substantiated) by empirical evidence from two sectors of enquiry: first, studies of the representation of body shape in the media and second, studies of attributed media effects upon body self-perceptions.

The representation enquiries have indicated that the media have provided role models and established wider socio-cultural standards relating to physical appearance and attractiveness. Furthermore, the media have emphasized certain body forms over others in terms of what may be judged attractive and desirable. The attribution studies have indicated that media consumers, and especially young people, regard media role models as important influences upon their own and other people's body shape aspirations and provide benchmarks against which self and others are judged.

To establish more confidently that the media do have systematic influences upon body image perceptions, a different kind of evidence is needed. Objective scientific data are required based on carefully developed measures of body self-esteem, body satisfaction, disordered eating symptoms and media exposure that provide clear evidence of links between media representations of the human body and media consumers' self-perceptions and standards of physical attractiveness in self and others. It is to this type of enquiry that we turn in the chapters that follow.

7 Media Exposure and Body Image Ideals

One of the principal methodologies applied to the investigation of possible media influences upon public conceptions of body image has been to undertake large-scale surveys designed to uncover broad associational links between reported exposure to relevant media content and body image perceptions, body dissatisfaction levels and disordered eating propensity. Some of these studies have examined links between exposure to print media and these perceptions (for example, Levine et al., 1994) and others have investigated potential television-related effects (Harrison, 2000a; Harrison and Cantor, 1997; Tiggeman and Pickering, 1996). These studies have mostly focused on female respondents but have varied in terms of the age of respondents (that is, usually school-age samples or college samples). While the correlational findings of these studies have indicated significant degrees of association between specific patterns of media exposure and relevant attitudes, perceptions and reported behaviours, they do not prove causal links. Furthermore, question-marks can be raised about the quality of some of the key measures used, particularly those designed to indicate media exposure.

Throughout history, beauty ideals have been projected by the dominant communication forms of the time. Visual art depicted images of voluptuous, even plump, female forms as the epitome of feminine beauty. Such historical icons, however, were romanticized as unattainable. In contrast, today's modern media present role models whom readers and audiences are invited to emulate (Mazur, 1986). Television, films and magazines present realistic representations of role models, disguising the fact that such images have almost invariably been artificially manipulated and developed. Computer technology has provided the capability of enhancing specific attributes and characteristics of models and actors to create an almost perfect, unblemished form, that nevertheless appears natural.

As we saw in the previous chapter, an important psychological mechanism that may underpin mediated influences upon body self-perceptions is the tendency for individuals to make comparisons between themselves and role models. Specific role models may be found in real life among people whom the individual knows in person. Increasingly, though, the mass media provide a prominent source of comparison points. When American college students were asked, in the early 1990s, to indicate the importance of six comparison targets in relation to self assessments in terms of attractiveness, athletic ability, figure-physique, intelligence, confidence, fashion clothes and popularity, friends turned out to be the most important reference group for appearance. After friends came classmates and other university students. Thus, same-age peers emerged as the most significant source of influence in relation to overall perceived self-esteem. Following these real-life points of comparison came celebrities. Members of the individual's own family also received a mention in this context but were far less influential than any of the aforementioned groups (Heinberg and Thompson, 1992b).

The same study found that males and females mentioned the same reference points, but with male college students attaching somewhat more importance to the influence of celebrities than did female college students. More pronounced gender differences emerged, though, when the degrees of importance attached to different reference groups were correlated with levels of body dissatisfaction and eating disorder symptoms. For female students, the importance ratings for comparison groups in relation to judging one's own appearance were significantly correlated with levels of body dissatisfaction, whereas the same was not true for male college students. This finding signalled that the stronger the tendency to make comparisons between self and others – whether real-life others or mass-mediated others – the greater the likelihood that the young women in question were dissatisfied with their own appearance.

Such attributions of influence on the part of some young women are indicative that they do pay attention to others, and make comparisons between themselves and role models. Such evidence does not conclusively demonstrate a causal connection between the examples set by role models and the aspirations and behaviour of young women in relation to their own bodies. To move towards this sort of demonstration, independent evidence is needed which shows systematic relationships to exist between exposure to specified (and relevant) role models and subsequent self-perceptions or behavioural tendencies.

The available evidence is examined in detail in this chapter and the next. The current chapter will review evidence based on demonstrable degrees of association between reported exposure to media and verbal reports of body image and eating habit disturbances. The next chapter will explore the evidence for a causal connection between exposure to body image representations in the media and body self-esteem and disordered eating patterns.

Prevalence of concerns about body image

There is ample evidence that concerns about body image are prevalent within Western societies. A number of large-scale surveys from a wide variety of sources have indicated that a substantial number of individuals are unhappy with how they look. In the United States, the popular psychology magazine *Psychology Today* has conducted several surveys to track, over time, the prevalence of body image satisfaction among men and women. The samples comprised readers of the magazine and, although not representative of the general population, they are indicative of how far-reaching are people's concerns about their physiques and attractiveness. The surveys were carried out in 1972, 1985 and 1996. Respondents were asked to indicate how content they were with different aspects of their body (mid torso, lower torso, upper torso, weight, muscle tone, height, face and overall appearance). Over this time, overall appearance dissatisfaction increased from 23 per cent to 56 per cent for women and from 15 per cent to 43 per cent for men. Women were especially likely to be unhappy with their mid torso, lower torso and weight. Men were also most likely to be concerned about their mid torso and weight. Men were more likely to be unhappy with their chest area than were women with their breasts (Cash, 1997).

Considerable stereotyping of body shapes occurs, especially among children and teenagers. Obese and overweight body shapes tend to be described in more negative terms than other, more slender body shapes by children as young as five (Felker, 1972). Children are also more likely to choose a slim body shape as their ideal and as a signal of attractiveness among members of their own and the opposite sex (Collins, 1991; Maloney et al., 1989; Rolland et al., 1997; Tiggeman and Wilson-Barrett, 1998).

Further surveys in the 1990s among American adults and youth revealed a widespread tendency for young women to be unhappy with their weight and to be actively pursuing one form of diet or another (Serdulla et al., 1993). One survey of more than 60,000 adults found nearly four in ten women (38%) who reported attempting to lose weight. Among a comparison sample of more than 1,000 high school students, more than four in ten females (44%) were trying to lose weight. While it has been observed that there are cultural differences in body image concerns and in the type of body shape that is idealized (Grogan, 1999), US surveys have revealed an evening-out of ethnic differences in prevalence of body image concerns and in the nature of those concerns. Both black and white American women have been found to express concern about their appearance to the point where they want to change it to feel better about themselves (Streigel-Moore et al., 1996). Elsewhere, differences were reported between black and white American women in their satisfaction with their bodies, but no differences of note occurred between Hispanic and white women (Cash and Henry, 1995).

Widespread concerns about body image have been reported in other parts of the world, especially among females. Body image problems and associated eating dysfunction have been found in Norway, China, Italy and Argentina (Davis and Katzman, 1997; Martinez and Spinetti, 1997; Santomastaso et al., 1995; Wichstrom, 1995). Body self-esteem issues were found to be salient among males and females in Hong Kong (Davis and Katzman, 1997). An investigation of nearly 1,000 high school students in Australia found that one in four (25%) of normal weight girls and a much smaller faction (6%) of normal weight boys rated themselves as overweight (Maude et al., 1993). In Britain, more than one in two school girls (56%) surveyed in the south of England said they felt 'too fat' (Button et al., 1997).

While much attention has been focused on the body image concerns of young females and associated eating disturbances, evidence has also emerged that boys and young men are not immune to such preoccupations. With males, the emphasis is placed on the cultural drive towards increased muscularity. Although the manifestation of male body image concerns is therefore somewhat different from that of similar concerns among females, it can none the less have significant health implications associated with dietary habits. While girls may take laxatives, vomit and stop eating, boys may take steroids, dietary supplements and high protein diets that, in their own way, can cause as much harm if carried out to extremes.

Hence, body image disturbances can occur in males just as much as in females. While the cultural ideal body shape popularly promoted for females is one of thinness, for males it is one of exaggerated muscularity (Cohane and Pope, 2001). This cultural trend has been confirmed by research that has shown that young men who were dissatisfied with their body shape wanted usually to be more muscular (Lynch and Zellner, 1999).

The prevalence of concerns about physical appearance and body weight cannot be in any doubt. It is a world-wide phenomenon, being found in Western, industrialized societies and some developing countries. Given the observed differences among cultures in standards of physical beauty and attractiveness (Crandall and Martinez, 1996) and the tradition in some cultures to regard increased body weight in a positive light (Rothblum, 1990; Sobal and Stunckard, 1989), the spread of anxieties about body shape and weight must presumably have been accompanied (and possibly caused in part by) shifting value systems. Such value shifts occur when one culture comes to influence another, either through interpersonal or mediated communication. Thus, immigrants from one culture who settle within another culture, with different values and standards of physical attractiveness, may display values and concerns that reflect those of the culture within which they have set up residence. This cultural shift has been observed to occur in relation to body image (Furnham and Alibhai, 1983).

If such culture shifts do occur, and are responsible for the spread of changing standards of physical beauty or attractiveness, it opens up a real possibility that the mass media are contributing agents. Value shifts may not only occur as a result of individuals settling in new cultures, but also within cultures as a consequence of the infiltration of dominant cultural value systems by values from extraneous cultures. Whilst this 'cultural infiltration' process might occur through immigration, it may also be communicated via the importation of cultural commodities such as media products. In order to find out whether the media are responsible for the cultivation of body image ideals and associated anxieties, appropriate empirical enquiry is necessary to discover whether links do exist between media exposure and body image perceptions and related behaviours. This chapter explores research on this subject.

Reported media exposure, body self-image and disordered eating

Some studies of the possible effects of media images of body shape upon body shape ideals held by the public or upon disordered eating have taken the form of surveys in which correlations between reported patterns of media exposure and eating habits were measured. Correlational studies have been conducted with print and broadcast media. The evidence from much of this work has been interpreted as suggestive of a media influence upon body shape perceptions and related eating behaviours.

Print media links

Quite apart from how attractive readers may rate thin models in fashion magazines and report being made to feel less confident in themselves after exposure to these images, what evidence is there that the degree of exposure to such images is systematically linked to self-perceptions and related behaviour? Research has shown that the reported level of magazine readership (and thus exposure to the images of thin models that typically populate these publications) is correlated with and even predictive of perceived body shape ideal and eating patterns.

Reported exposure to magazine articles and advertisements on body shape and the thin ideal has been found to predict the perceptions of teenage girls (aged 11–14 years) of body shape ideal, weight management behaviours, disordered eating and a drive for thinness (Levine et al., 1994).

Other research has compared magazine exposure, awareness of societal ideals about body image and the degree to which individuals have internalized socio-cultural messages about body shape as indicators of body image impressions held by undergraduate women. It emerged that internalization was by far the most important correlate of body image disturbance. Thus, mere exposure to magazine articles or pictures may not be enough to explain body image disturbance. The ability of magazine copy or pictures to influence readers' self-perceptions of their own shape and attractiveness is mediated by the degree to which they have absorbed the surrounding culture's ideals about body shape and by whatever the cultural ideal may be (Cusumano and Thompson, 1997).

Despite the prevalence of body image disturbance among girls and women, growing recognition has been directed towards understanding similar concerns among boys and men. Content analysis research has indicated that both women's and men's magazines contain many articles concerned with body matters and weight loss. While the prevalence of such material has stabilized or even declined in women's magazines, it has increased in publications aimed at men (Nemeroff et al., 1994).

Evidence has also emerged that magazine consumption is linked to body image perceptions and eating habits among both males and females, though not in exactly the same ways. Botta (2000) reported a study of adolescent boys and girls in which data were collected from them about their reading of magazines on fashion, health and fitness, and sport, and their body image perceptions and incidence of eating disturbances. Both boys and girls were more concerned about their body image the greater their body mass index. For girls, greater reported reading of fashion magazines was related to increased bulimic tendencies; greater reading of health and fitness magazines was associated with increased bulimia, anorexia and drive to be thin; and increased reading of sports magazines was linked with greater desire for muscularity. Among boys, greater reported reading of fashion and health and fitness magazines was linked to desire for greater muscularity and, in the case of fashion magazines only, to lower body satisfaction.

The apparent influence of magazine exposure on girls' and boys' body self-perceptions was mediated by the extent to which they made social comparisons between their own bodies and those of others. Girls who spent time comparing their own bodies to those of magazine models reported feeling less muscular the more they read of these magazines. Girls who made no such comparisons exhibited no association between fashion magazine reading and self-perceptions. A similar finding emerged for boys in relation to reading of sports magazines. Those boys who made comparisons between their own bodies and those of magazine models showed less satisfaction with their own muscle definition the more they read sports magazines, while boys who did not make such comparisons actually displayed greater body satisfaction the more they reportedly read these magazines.

These results do not demonstrate causal connections between magazine exposure and body image perceptions of adolescents. They do indicate associative links between them, however. More significantly, if they do suggest possible causal connections, it is clear that such causality is dependent on the way adolescents use magazines as points of comparison.

Television links

Correlational studies have indicated that reported exposure to television is linked to body image disturbance. Martin and Kennedy (1993) found that in a sample of 9-, 13- and 17-year-olds, a two-item measure assessing their tendency to compare themselves with advertising models was negatively correlated with self-reported physical attractiveness. Gonzalez-Levin and Smolak (1995) found that number of hours of television exposure was unrelated to dieting and disordered eating behaviour in girls of middle-school age (9–13). However, girls who watched more than 8 hours of television per week reported significantly greater body image dissatisfaction than did girls with less television exposure.

A later survey of teenage girls revealed little association between measures of body dissatisfaction and total amount of reported television viewing. More detailed measures of media consumption, however, indicated that exposure to particular types of content may have a bearing on body self-perceptions. In particular, viewing of music videos exhibited a small but significant relationship with body dissatisfaction, suggesting the possibility of an influence derived from self-comparisons with attractive role models among popular music artists (Borzekowski et al., 2000).

A survey of Flemish teenagers in Belgium took a wider view of examining possible links between television viewing, eating habits and obesity amidst growing public concern that young people were snacking on sugar-rich foods while watching excessive amounts of television. There was no indication that watching more television was necessarily associated with a more passive lifestyle, however, nor any link between amount of television viewing and obesity. Viewing was found to be significantly related to teenagers' perceptions of their weight and their appearance. There was suggestive, though not conclusive, evidence that such self-perceptions were sensitive to depictions of attractive role models in programmes where much emphasis was placed on the physical attractiveness of actors (van den Bulck, 2000).

Further findings were produced by Tiggemann and Pickering (1996). Measures of high school girls' (aged 14–16 years) body image dissatisfaction and drive for thinness were examined along with reported television exposure during the previous week. Frequency of television exposure did not correlate with either body dissatisfaction or drive for thinness. However, it is interesting to note that the amount of exposure to specific types of programmes was related to dissatisfaction and drive for thinness. Specifically, exposure to soap operas and movies predicted body image dissatisfaction and exposure to music videos predicted drive for thinness, whereas amount of time spent watching sports was negatively correlated with one's body image dissatisfaction (Tiggeman and Pickering, 1996). It appears then that the type of programme watched may be a more important variable than television exposure *per se* when examining the media influences on body image.

Print and television links

Further research, incorporating measures of television viewing as well as magazine readership, has indicated that the potential influence of the mass media on body image perceptions cannot be considered divorced from other personal factors. Stice, Schupak-Neuberg, Shaw and Stein (1994) tested a structural equation model involving media exposure as an exogenous variable, gender-role endorsement, ideal body stereotype internalization and body dissatisfaction as mediating variables, and eating disorder symptoms as the dependent variable. This study was carried out among female college undergraduates. The path coefficient for the direct link from media exposure to eating disorder symptomatology was significant. In addition, media exposure was found to be indirectly related to eating disorder tendencies through gender-role endorsement, ideal body stereotype internalization and body dissatisfaction.

These findings supported the assertion that exposure to the media-portrayed thin ideal is related to eating pathology and suggested that women may directly model disordered eating behaviour presented in the media (for example, fasting or purging). Additionally, focus on dieting in the media may promote dietary restraint, which appears to increase the risk for binge eating (Polivy and Herman, 1985).

These results were also interpreted to support the hypothesis that internalization of socio-cultural pressures mediates the relation between media exposure and eating pathology. Media exposure predicted increased gender-role endorsement (that is, degree to which respondents agreed with various stereotyped views about women and men). Gender-role endorsement was in turn related to heightened ideal body stereotype internalization. The indirect effect of media exposure on ideal body stereotype internalization through gender-role endorsement was statistically significant. Greater ideal body stereotype internalization increased body dissatisfaction, which was related to heightened eating disorder symptoms.

Furthermore, gender role endorsement showed significant indirect effects on body dissatisfaction (through ideal body stereotype internalization) and on eating pathology (through both ideal body stereotype and body dissatisfaction). A limitation of this study was that it did not distinguish between thinness-depicting media and other media. In a related study, however, Stice and Shaw (1994) found significant links between exposure to thin female magazine models and bulimic symptomatology in a sample of female college undergraduates.

Harrison and Cantor (1997) examined the relationship between college women's media use and disordered eating symptoms, body dissatisfaction and drive for thinness. They also assessed the relationship between college men's media use and their endorsement of thinness for themselves and for women. They regarded the media as sources of social learning. The media present role models whom readers and audiences may decide to emulate in terms of behaviour and image.

Media exposure was distinguished between television viewing and magazine reading. Respondents indicated their overall television viewing in terms of average hours they watched on weekdays and weekends and also indicated the frequency with which they watched six named television shows. These shows were selected not only because they were popular and well watched, but also because they featured characters who had either thin bodies, fat bodies or average bodies. Respondents then indicated how many issues they read of popular magazines each month in each of five categories: health and fitness, beauty and fashion, entertainment and gossip, news and current events, and men's entertainment magazines.

For women, media use predicted disordered eating symptoms, drive for thinness, body dissatisfaction and ineffectiveness. The relationship between media consumption and eating disorder symptoms was stronger for magazine reading than for television viewing. Overall, magazine reading was positively and significantly related to disordered eating symptoms. Fitness magazine reading was linked to eating disorders even when interest in fitness and dieting as magazine topics was controlled. Thus women who read fitness magazines for reasons other than their interest in fitness and dieting scored higher on disordered eating symptoms than women who rarely read such magazines. Selective exposure based on interest, then, could not fully account for the demonstrated relationship between consumption of fitness magazines and eating disorder symptoms.

In contrast, the viewing of television shows that depicted thin people as major characters was not significantly related to disordered eating symptoms. Given the regularity with which these shows were reportedly watched by a majority of respondents, however, there may have been a ceiling effect operating here.

Television viewing was a significant predictor of body dissatisfaction, but magazine reading was not. But only the viewing of fat-depicting shows and the reading of fashion magazines were significantly related to body dissatisfaction. In contrast again, television viewing was not a significant predictor of drive for thinness but magazine reading was.

For men, media use predicted endorsement of personal thinness and dieting, and select attitudes in favour of thinness and dieting for women. Only viewing of television shows with thin leads was a significant predictor of men's endorsement of thinness and dieting, both for themselves and for women. Overall, magazine reading and reading of men's entertainment magazines were related to selected attitudes concerning the importance of thinness for women.

A companion study was reported by Harrison (1997) in which a sample of 232 female college students were questioned about their television viewing and magazine reading habits. Once again, media exposure questions focused on respondents' personal estimates of watching or reading frequency in respect of pre-selected programmes and publications. In fact, the magazine readership measures were based on genres rather than individual named publications (for example, health/fitness, beauty/fashion, entertainment/gossip, news/current affairs). The television viewing measures were derived from endorsed watching of just six television shows, pre-classified as 'thin,' 'heavy' and 'average' on the basis of the judged body shape of lead characters in each case.

This research went beyond simple measures of media exposure however. Respondents were also presented with photographs of six female characters from the listed television shows and three photographs of popular magazine models, representing thin, average and heavy categories. Each photograph was given three ratings: (1) How much do you like this character/model? (2) How similar do you feel to this character/model? (3) How much do you want to be like this character/model? Measures of eating disorder symptoms were then obtained, with sub-scales designed to measure anorexia, bulimia, body dissatisfaction, drive for thinness, perfectionism and ineffectiveness.

A number of simple bivariate relationships were found between reported media exposure measures and scores on eating disorder sub-scales. Reported frequency of watching television shows with thin lead characters was correlated with anorexia tendencies and drive for thinness. Reported frequency of watching television shows with heavy lead characters was correlated with body dissatisfaction and (greater) ineffectiveness. Reported frequency of reading fitness and fashion magazines was also significantly correlated with many eating disorder measures, including anorexia, bulimia, drive for thinness and body dissatisfaction.

These simple correlations may give a misleading impression of the extent of relationships between different types of media exposure and eating disorder symptoms. Some of the media exposure measures may themselves be inter-related, while eating disorder symptoms may have causes other than media exposure, the significance of which correlational analyses are unable to reveal. Harrison therefore conducted a series of multiple regression analyses in which eating disorder symptom was treated, in turn, as a criterion variable and on which the various media exposure measures and measures of identification with thin, average and heavy characters/models were regressed as possible predictors. These analyses revealed fewer significant relationships between media variables and eating disorder variables. Anorexia was predicted by greater reported frequency of reading fitness magazines and by attraction to thin media personalities. Bulimia was predicted primarily by attraction to thin media personalities. Drive for thinness was predicted by reported viewing of television shows with overweight leads. Body dissatisfaction was predicted specifically by attraction to thin media personalities, as were perfectionism and ineffectiveness.

Thus, interpersonal attraction to thin media personalities emerged as the most powerful overall predictor of eating disorder symptoms. It was far more important as a predictor than any of the reported media exposure measures. Interestingly, there was no converse relationship of eating disorder symptoms to a tendency *not* to watch television shows with fat lead characters. However, the absence of the latter relationship may be due to the fact that the illustrative 'fat' shows (*Roseanne, Designing Women*) were very popular and had leads who, though fat, had other attractive qualities.

Harrison (2000b) replicated and extended this earlier work among young adults in a further study with adolescents within the 11–17 years age range. Measures were obtained on interest in body improvement, disordered eating symptoms, degree of interest in different types of programme or magazine, and respondents' self-estimates of their exposure to television programmes and magazines pre-classified to contain relevant thin or fat body imagery. Pre-tests were conducted among college students who were invited to evaluate a list of television programmes and magazine genres, along a seven-point scale, according to whether their main characters (in the case of programmes) or typically featured models or celebrities (in the case of magazine genres) could be deemed to be 'conspicuously thin' (1), through 'average' (4) to 'conspicuously fat' (7). Separate ratings were provided for typical male and female characters/models observed in these media. Eating disorder symptoms included measures of body dissatisfaction, drive for thinness (wanting to be thinner) and anorexic and bulimic tendencies.

Among female respondents, greater reported exposure to television programmes pre-classified as containing conspicuously fat characters was related to increased bulimia, whereas reported exposure to magazines containing thin models was related to increased anorexia, and for girls aged 14–17 years, also to increased bulimia. Greater reported exposure to sports magazines, featuring images of athletic, well-toned bodies, was related to increased body dissatisfaction among 17-year-old girls only. Among male respondents, there was only one significant finding to emerge between a media exposure measure and body image perceptions. Among 11-year-old boys only, greater reported exposure to television programmes classified as featuring conspicuously fat lead characters was related to increased body dissatisfaction. According to Harrison, boys in early adolescence have learned to stigmatize fatness, but have not yet themselves developed a mature athletic physique. They may be more inclined to identify with the rounded features of overweight television characters and exhibit lowered satisfaction with their current physique. This speculation, however, requires empirical evidence showing that fat characters on television are indeed ridiculed, by this age group especially, and that such identification occurs.

In a study by the same author with children aged between 5 and 9 years, Harrison (2000a) found positive correlations between reported television viewing and preferences for leaner body shapes and greater display of eating disorder symptoms, especially among girls. Meanwhile, boys who were greater television viewers were especially likely to display negative stereotypes towards fatness in females. There was no conclusive evidence from this study, however, that young girls' exposure to television increased the extent to which they showed disordered eating symptoms through internalization of the thin ideal from the medium. Girls who were attracted to thin characters on television displayed a tendency to overestimate their own body size. In contrast, finding overweight television characters attractive was associated with a lesser tendency to perceive fatness in negative terms whether in relation to boys or girls.

Other survey data have provided evidence that varying degrees of association can be found to exist between reported consumption of print and broadcast media and body image, satisfaction with own body, drive for thinness and related eating habits. Such evidence has derived from adolescent and young adult populations and usually from among young women, who have been identified as the groups most susceptible to a preoccupation with body image and disordered eating patterns. Where the survey studies discussed so far have been limited is in regard to their measurement of media exposure. Although distinctions have been made between relative levels of exposure to different media, much less attention has been paid to the informational relevance of specific types of media content to the shaping of particular body image perceptions (Botta, 1999).

One significant issue in this context is the degree to which individuals make direct comparisons between themselves and role models they observe in the media. It is not enough to know how much of particular media, or of types of media content, individuals consume. Further information is needed about whether particular body representations strike a special chord with observers. The notion of social comparison is relevant here. Under this model, the media can provide sources of influence of body self-image that operate through incidental learning. This kind of learning can produce powerful effects upon media consumers without the need for them to pay special attention to specific role models. The media may nevertheless present a series of images within a stereotypical mould that encourage the occurrence of automatic comparisons between self and role models on the page or screen. Such comparisons may be especially likely to occur among individuals already pre-occupied with thinness (Goethals, 1986). Botta (2000: 146) made the following observation:

> Social comparison theory makes a crucial link between television viewing, attitudes and behaviour. Viewers who perceive a discrepancy in their comparisons are more motivated to close the gap on that comparison (Wood, 1989; Wood and Taylor, 1991). This link could account for increased motivation to perform eating disorder behaviours and an increased drive to be thin. The comparisons help to confirm their belief in being thin and their need to act on that belief, particularly when they are highly motivated to achieve that goal (Wood and Taylor, 1991).

Heinberg and Thompson (1992a) used social comparison theory as an approach to explaining the effects of others' appearance on body image and eating disorders. They surveyed male and female undergraduate students. Participants were asked to rate the importance of six different groups, ranging from family and friends to celebrities and American citizens in general. The most important reference group was friends. Then came celebrities, classmates and other students. US citizens and family followed behind. Among female respondents, celebrity figures represented an important reference group. The more these young women made comparisons between themselves and attractive media celebrities, the less satisfied they tended to be with their own bodies and the more inclined they were to be preoccupied with being thin and to indulge in disordered eating habits (for example, bulimia).

The significance of this social comparison analysis of the psychological mechanisms through which the mass media could affect body image perceptions and associated eating patterns is that it underlines the need to consider media consumption in more detail than gross measures of generalized media consumption. There is a need to establish whether body image perceptions are particularly vulnerable to specific role models or types of goal attainment that can only be found in certain types of magazines or television programmes. It might also be useful to know whether individuals are consciously aware of making comparisons between themselves and media images or whether they compare people they know with media images. Further, do mass media, such as television shows and films, provide the kinds of role models that viewers regard as ideals? In an extension of surveys of the media and body image, these questions were asked in a study of the significance of specific types of mass media content to comparisons of self and others with media images made by adolescent females (Botta, 1999).

The key dependent measures included endorsement of thin ideal, body image disturbance, body image dissatisfaction, drive for thinness and presence of bulimic behaviours. Television viewing was the principal media predictor variable. A general measure of amount of television watching per week was used along with a measure of amount of viewing of 'thin television dramas', such as *Melrose Place* and *Beverly Hills 90210*. Respondents were also asked about how often they compared themselves or friends to television characters in terms of body shape, and how much they agreed that women in television and movies provide realistic role models in terms of body image.

Reported total television viewing did not emerge as a significant predictor in its own right of any of the dependent variables. Claimed amount of viewing of television drama series featuring slim female actors in prominent roles was a significant negative predictor of bulimic action tendencies, but accounted for just 2 per cent of the variance. The more respondents reported watching 'thin' dramas, the less they reported engaging in bulimic action tendencies.

Of more importance to body image perceptions than mere exposure to television was the perceived realism of media images and their significance as points of comparison with self or others. Greater realism attached to television role models, and the tendency to use them as body image yardsticks predicted stronger endorsement of the thin ideal, and stronger drive for thinness. Making personal comparisons with televised role models also predicted body dissatisfaction and bulimic tendencies. Overall, the results indicated a television impact on the body image perceptions of adolescent girls that acts through encouragement of comparisons between themselves or their friends and attractive television characters, by encouraging endorsement of thinness as an ideal shape and by presenting thin role models in programmes who are regarded as providing realistic attainment targets.

Botta (1999) observed that her results contrasted with those of Harrison and Cantor (1997), who did not find a relationship between television eating disorder behaviours. The latter study, however, did not examine body image processing, which emerged as a key factor linking television to behaviours. While total reported television viewing was found to be associated with viewers' tendency to endorse the thin ideal, there was no evidence of a link with drive for thinness and eating disorder behaviours. Exposure to drama series depicting thin actors, however, was linked to drive for thinness, but not to body dissatisfaction. Botta (1999) reported that exposure to thin dramas was related only to bulimic behaviours, but in the opposite direction. Botta's respondents, however, watched fewer of these programmes than did the women in the Harrison and Cantor study. Those women were also four years older than the girls studied in Botta's study, an age gap that could have given rise to a different perspective in the way such dramas were cognitively processed.

In another survey of American college students and their friends, ranging in age from 16 to 48, respondents were asked to nominate the person they would most like to look like. A content analysis of responses found four dominant categories: actor, model, sports person and family member. Media figures represented significant role models for male and female respondents, and most especially for those aged under 20. Although older respondents still named celebrity figures as reference points, such individuals tended to be in the minority in their age group (Grogan, 1999).

Cultural and ethnicity factors

Most survey studies in this field have been carried out with white females. There has been an implicit assumption – though sometimes openly stated – that the influence of media role models on viewers' body self-perceptions is a distinctly Western phenomenon. African American women, for example, have been reported to display much lower levels of body dissatisfaction and less desire to be thin, despite being on average heavier than white American women (Abrams et al., 1993). While in the past this might have been attributed to differences in body sizes of different ethnic groups in the media, Cusumano and Thompson (1997) reported a parallel increase in the numbers of very thin non-white models and actresses over time to that found for white performers.

Evidence has emerged, however, that media effects on body self-perception can cross cultures. Where body dissatisfaction was observed to occur among African American women, it tended to affect those who identified most strongly with white culture (Makkar and Strube, 1995). This observation would seem to be consistent with social comparison theory, with black adolescents joining their white counterparts in drawing comparisons between themselves and white media role models. Relevant evidence, as we will see, derives from surveys that have included non-Caucasian and non-Western respondents, and also from experimental intervention studies on mixed culture groups. The latter will be examined in the next chapter. Below, some evidence is provided from surveys with cross-cultural samples.

Wilcox and Laird (2000) explained the mediating role of social comparisons by looking at individual differences among viewers and readers to idealized thin imagery in television programmes and magazines. They found differences in the amount of body dissatisfaction between women who relied on 'personal cues' to account for self-perception and those who used 'situational cues'. Cues were elicited by asking participants to smile and then say how happy this made them feel or frown and say how angry this made them feel. Those who used personal cues (that is, felt happiest when smiling) were more negatively affected by thin images; those who relied on situational cues (that is, felt least happy when smiling) actually found that the thin images created more positive feelings about their own bodies. The researchers argued that this finding might explain the mixed results typically obtained in laboratory studies of media effects on body dissatisfaction. However, the methodology they used makes it difficult to establish the extent to which self-perception is really a predictor of body image, except that it might involve a degree of emotional control, which is important for dealing with external media influences.

In one such study, Botta (2000) compared African American and European American girls, aged 15 years, in their body image perceptions and their responses to media images of body shape. African American girls were found to respond differently from European American girls. However, there were also many similarities that suggested a narrowing of the ethnic gap in the development of eating disorders. Black girls were more satisfied with their bodies and had a larger personal ideal size than did white girls. Black girls, however, engaged in fewer behaviours in a drive to be thin. Further, black and white girls were equally likely to make comparisons with television images while viewing. In both cases, the more they idealized television body images, the more dissatisfied they were with their own bodies and the thinner was their personal ideal size. Black and white girls were no different in how much they reportedly watched television shows that depicted thin characters (for example, *Melrose Place* and *Beverly Hills 90210*). They were also equally likely to compare themselves and their friends to these images and the more they made these comparisons, the more they were likely personally to engage in disordered eating behaviours, the stronger was their drive for thinness and the more dissatisfied they were with their own bodies. The only difference was that in making the latter comparisons, white girls were likely to choose a thinner figure size for themselves than were black girls (Botta, 2000: 146).

Confidence in the survey evidence

The evidence for media effects upon body image disturbance and disordered eating derives from a fairly narrow range of survey and experimental methodologies. Survey evidence cannot demonstrate causality, but even as evidence of an association between media exposure and body image, can the existing survey research be believed?

Typical surveys obtain data from respondents via questionnaire-based measures of body self-esteem, body size estimation, body shape satisfaction, motivation to achieve a thinner body and attitudes towards eating. Many of these measures are verbal self-reports, though some (such as body size estimation) use non-verbal measures. While these measures may provide acceptable indicators of self-perception and behavioural dispositions, the measures of media exposure are often more problematic.

Measures of magazine reading have tended to ask respondents to indicate their frequency of exposure to broad genres such as health and fitness, beauty and fashion or sports (Harrison, 1997; Stice et al., 1994). Measures of television viewing have included general estimates of hours of viewing per week (for example, Botta, 1999) or frequency estimates of exposure to programme genres (Stice et al., 1994) or to specific programmes (Botta, 1999, 2000; Harrison, 1997, 2000a). Sometimes, programmes may have been pre-classified as 'thin' or 'heavy' shows on the basis of the body size of lead characters (for example, Botta, 1999; Harrison, 1997). However, frequency estimates of viewing, ranging from 'never' to 'regularly,' or based on numbers of hours for which certain types of programmes are viewed, may represent highly problematic indicators of television consumption.

Furthermore, many of the shows typically selected as 'thin' (for example, *Ally McBeal, Melrose Place, Beverly Hills 90210*) contain characters with varying body shapes, ranging from short to tall, very slender through shapely to voluptuous. There is no indication of the degree of prominence attained by specific characters across a television series or indeed of their relative salience to viewers. Even when base viewing estimates are supplemented with questions about social comparisons with media models or characters, there is a lack of specificity in such measures of identification. An exception to this rule was found in a study by Harrison (1997), in which respondents rated their degree of liking for and wish to be like a number of specific television characters whose photographs they were shown. It is worth looking at the details of this study further.

Harrison (1997) defined 'thin' and 'heavy' shows on the basis that these body types could be considered 'conspicuous' features because the characters were represented in such a way that drew attention to either extreme size or slenderness. A research team classified specific characters as either fat or thin. This study therefore went beyond an examination of mere exposure to media and obtained from each survey respondent an indication of their strength of identification with specific types of media personality. Even so, the study still failed to provide an assessment for each television show of the degree of prominence of characters for viewers. This might not be such a problem in the case of shows such as *Roseanne* where the two lead characters are central to major plot-lines each week and are both clearly overweight. With shows such as *Ally McBeal*, however, in which average-sized characters, who are as attractive as the thin female lead, play significant roles each week, it may be important to establish how important, as role models, these different characters are judged to be.

There is a need for future research, using a survey methodology, to conduct more extensive and detailed preparatory work on the media outputs on which self-report exposure measures are obtained. For example, when asking about magazine reading habits, magazine genres should not just be clarified with the names of exemplars, but those exemplars should be separately content analysed over a number of editions to establish the degree to which specific types of body images are presented. The same point applies to the classification of so-called 'thin' and 'fat' television programmes. To what extent do particular characters, with thin and overweight body shapes, appear on screen as central to the action?

Even taking into account the need to deploy tighter measures of reported exposure to relevant media images of the body, there remains the fundamental weakness of survey evidence that correlation coefficients do not demonstrate causality. Strong degrees of association between reported exposure to media representations of body image and body self-perceptions or eating disorder symptoms merely indicate the possibility of a causal connection; they do not conclusively demonstrate this link.

To explore the possibility that media representations of body image can directly affect media consumers' own body image or wider attitudes towards body shape and attractiveness, researchers have used experimental designs in which exposure to media images is controlled systematically. It is then possible to find out if one type of mediated body image (for example, a magazine photograph of a slim model) has a different post-exposure effect on observers' self-perceptions from another mediated image (for example, a photograph of a fat model). Research of this kind has been carried out with print and broadcast media images of the body. There is evidence that even brief exposure to such images can produce short-term changes in self-percepts, especially among young females who already lack self-confidence in their body shape.

Summary

For many years, research has indicated that concerns about body self-image have been prevalent among women and men, and especially so among the former. Women want to look thinner and men want to be more muscular. Such socio-cultural ideals are reinforced by media images, where much focus is placed on a slender body shape for women and a well-defined musculature for men. When body image becomes a pre-occupation – even an obsession – as it does with some individuals, it can lead to psychological problems and behavioural disorders. The latter take the form of disordered eating habits that may achieve the goal of thinness but may also cause harm to the individual's general health.

In exploring what we know about the possible role of the media in this process, the current chapter has reviewed research that investigated degrees of association between exposure to specific types of media and body self-perceptions and eating habits. Such research has consistently revealed that these variables are inter-correlated – often to a significant degree. Individuals who exhibit greater concern about their body shape do report more frequent reading of magazines that deal with relevant fashion, diet and fitness issues and which often depict models with very slender body shapes more than any other type of body shape. Exposure to films and television shows that starred slender body-shaped lead actresses was also often more prevalent among individuals who exhibited the strongest personal concerns about their body shape.

Links between television viewing and preferences for thin body shapes have been found among young women, female teenagers and pre-teenage girls. There is evidence, therefore, that while certain slender female icons in the media are popular with most women, they may be especially well-liked by women who show the greatest concerns about their own body shape. The latter link may be even more pronounced among young women who profess that they do tend to make regular comparisons between themselves and other women in terms of body shape and general appearance.

While there are cultural differences in body shape norms and ideals, relationships between media exposure and body shape ideals have exhibited consistent patterns across cultures, though they may vary in their absolute degree. In considering all this evidence, however, it is important to acknowledge that the survey approaches used here measured degrees of correlation between variables, and such links do not demonstrate or prove causality. Survey questionnaires request self-report evidence from respondents about their social behaviours – whether related to their consumption of food or media content. Such correlation-based evidence can indicate variables between which causal relations could exist, however, it cannot demonstrate the direction of such causality, even if causality does exist. The next chapter, therefore, turns to the issue of causality and reviews research from studies that deployed methodologies that were equipped to address the causal agency of variables more directly.

8 Media Causation and Body Image Perceptions

The ideal image of feminine attractiveness presented in the media has been accused of being rigid, with a particular emphasis on thinness (Cash and Henry, 1995; Freedman, 1984). A number of writers on the subject have suggested that media images of attractiveness may be responsible for the widespread discontent among young women regarding their own body weight (Jacobi and Cash, 1994; Polivy and Herman, 1985; Silverstein, Perdue et al., 1986; Wolf, 1991). If females perceive a discrepancy between the accepted standard of female attractiveness and their own bodies, they may become concerned that their own weight is not acceptable.

Cause–effect analysis can be directly tackled only through the use of experimental methodologies. A research literature has emerged over the past 20 years based on experimental studies of links between media representations of body shape and readers' or viewers' perceptions of their own body image and associated disordered eating patterns. This research has investigated the effects of photographic images from magazines (Cash et al., 1983; Champion and Furnham, 1999; Irving, 1990; Ogden and Mundray, 1996; Richins, 1991) and television programmes and advertisements (Heinberg and Thompson, 1995; Myers and Biocca, 1992). This research has indicated that short-term effects upon body image satisfaction can be produced following exposure to images of attractive and thin media models, and that such effects are most likely to occur among young women whose body self-esteem is already low.

Causal links between exposure to media representations, body self-image and disordered eating

To test for possible cause–effect relationships between media content and body image perceptions, it is necessary to move beyond a survey approach. Experimental methodologies enable researchers to manipulate the content to which individuals are exposed, the conditions under which exposure takes place, and to implement other controls that minimize the potential influences of other social factors.

When evaluated in the context of more attractive, same-sex individuals, an otherwise average-looking person may be perceived as less attractive (Geiselman et al., 1984; Kenrick and Guttieres, 1980). This attractiveness contrast effect has also been observed in self-evaluations of one's own appearance (Brown et al., 1992; Cash et al., 1983; Thornton and Moore, 1993). Not only may self-perceptions of attractiveness be diminished from such comparisons, but lowered self-esteem and heightened public self-consciousness and anxiety may also result (Thornton and Moore, 1993).

Such comparisons may be particularly relevant for women, considering the social emphasis on physical attractiveness and the perpetuation of a thin ideal body image (Polivy et al., 1986; Wiseman et al., 1993). For instance, increased body dissatisfaction and diminished self-esteem have been reported among women following exposure to photographs of women characterizing this thin ideal (Irving, 1990; Stice and Shaw, 1994). The internalization of an attractiveness ideal and a perception of body dissatisfaction may serve to mediate the relationship between media exposure and disordered eating (Stice et al., 1994).

While the internalization of a cultural ideal of attractiveness may indeed be a consequence of media exposure, Nemeroff (1995) alternatively suggested that the ideal may serve to direct media exposure. She noted that people exert choices when it comes to media consumption and thereby may selectively control their exposure to mediated depictions of an attractiveness ideal. Women who do not adhere to such an ideal would presumably be disinclined to consume media sources emphasizing portrayals of idealized attractiveness and hence would experience little self-denigration as a result.

Judgements of physical attractiveness may be subject to a perceptual contrast effect in which an individual who is moderately attractive may be rated as very attractive when evaluated alongside someone else who is unattractive. Equally, that same moderately attractive person may be regarded as lacking in attractiveness when judged against someone who is extremely attractive (Geiselman et al., 1984). This effect has been observed to occur when moderately attractive women were judged against highly attractive media celebrities such as actresses (for example, *Charlie's Angels*) or models (Kenrick and Gutierres, 1980) and centrefolds from soft-porn magazines (Kenrick, 1989).

In the remainder of this chapter, we examine studies conducted within an experimental paradigm that attempted to measure cause–effect relationships between controlled exposure to selected media representations of the body and observers' immediate reactions in terms of body self-esteem. The studies reported here were carried out mostly with young women and focused on the impact of media depictions of female body shapes. In some instances, the reactions of men were obtained as well.

Research with magazines

Experimental studies have been used to investigate the impact of magazine and television content on body image perceptions. Such studies have also varied in terms of whether they have examined the potential impact of role models in advertising messages or in programmes. In some experiments, comparisons have been made between the relative impact of magazine and television content, while in others, the effects of television programmes and advertisements have been measured independently and in combination. In the typical experiment of this kind, participants are shown images (for example, photographs of fashion models, videotape advertisements) and measures are taken before and afterwards concerning body self-perceptions and eating habits. If pre- and post-exposure measures of body image show a significant downturn following the presentation of attractive media images, a social comparison process is inferred to have occurred.

In one of the first experimental studies of print media influence on body shape perceptions, Cash, Cash and Butters (1983) showed 51 women participants pictures of female models from magazine advertisements and features articles. The photographs were pre-tested for the attractiveness level of models. Participants were then allocated to three exposure conditions: pictures of physically attractive women; pictures of physically attractive women labelled as professional models; and pictures of women judged to be not physically attractive. After viewing the photographs, participants provide physical attractiveness and body satisfaction. The experimental groups did not differ in terms of the body satisfaction measure, but participants exposed to pictures of attractive women rated themselves lower on physical attractiveness than did those women exposed to pictures of less physically attractive females. The effect occurred, however, primarily in response to pictures of attractive women not labelled as professional models. This result suggested that women contrasted themselves in a negative way against attractive women featured in magazines. The professional model stimuli had no such effect but these women were not regarded as appropriate role models or points of comparison.

The research conducted by Cash et al. (1983) implies that women (and perhaps also men) are selective in whom they choose as role models. Only those role models present in the mass media who are regarded as realistic comparisons may therefore be influential in relation to media consumers' own body image perceptions. As noted in Chapter 7, young women and men tend to regard same-age peer groups as more significant points of comparison in relation to their own appearance than celebrity figures (Heinberg and Thompson, 1992b).

Richins (1991) showed advertisements to female participants that featured thin, well-proportioned models. Such images did not significantly affect viewers' own body satisfaction. In this case, however, body satisfaction was measured via a single-item, seven-point scale which may have lacked the sensitivity to pick up all the relevant perceptual changes that might have occurred.

Irving (1990) was interested in the effects that media images of thinness could have upon women with eating disorders. She showed women college students slides of thin, average and oversized models and then measured the women's self-evaluations. The women were further differentiated in terms of their responses to a scale designed to measure bulimic symptoms (Smith and Thelen, 1984). Regardless of the severity of disordered eating symptoms, those women who were shown slides of thin models displayed subsequently lowered self-esteem and weight satisfaction, though no effect was observed upon their satisfaction with their current weight. The validity of the results was undermined by the absence of pre-exposure measurements of self-evaluation. A post-test-only design such as this one is vulnerable to the criticism that post-exposure differences in self-perceptions could have already existed before or may be accountable in terms of other pre-exposure differences among respondents that had not been controlled, either in the allocation of participants to experimental conditions or through post-hoc statistical tests.

Many experimental studies have investigated the impact upon body image perceptions of specific types of media image, where the latter have been manipulated one at a time. If media output is characterized by a predominance of thinness-promoting body images, however, it could be important to find out what effect combinations of messages depicting consistent or inconsistent messages about body image can have on media consumers. The significance of this point is underlined by the observation that media consumers usually watch more than one programme or one commercial during the course of a single viewing session.

A few experiments have focused exclusively on the impact of magazine representations of thinness on normal women who exhibit no evidence of eating disorders. In one study, female respondents were shown 12 photographs of models taken from popular magazines, over a 3 minute exposure period. Subsequently, higher levels of depression, stress, guilt, shame, insecurity and body image dissatisfaction emerged when compared with prior exposure to photographs of average size models (Stice and Shaw, 1994).

A later experiment examined the influence of photographs of thin models in a non-eating-disordered population of college men and women. College women exposed to photographs of thin models from *Cosmopolitan* and *Vogue* magazines reported significantly higher levels of private body self-consciousness, body competence, and state anxiety (Kalodner, 1997). No effect was found for men.

Thornton and Maurice (1997) exposed undergraduate women to 50 photographs of models for 8 seconds each. The women were aged between 17 and 28 years. Measurements were taken from the women of the importance to them of being attractive, their self-confidence in social situations, anxieties about their own figure, body self-esteem and eating habits. In comparison to a control condition, women who saw photos depicting idealized physiques subsequently expressed lowered self-esteem and heightened self-consciousness, body dissatisfaction and anxiety about their own body shape. Although women who displayed lower adherence to an attractiveness ideal had generally higher body self-esteem than women who had greater adherence to such an ideal, they did not show any greater resistance to the effects of attractive photographic images (Thornton and Maurice, 1997). It is not clear from any of this work, however, whether there is a lasting effect of media exposure on body image.

Ogden and Mundray (1996) attempted to establish effects of acute exposure to media images with a non-clinical adult population. In this study, the effect of showing experimental participants (40 medical students) media images of stereotypically attractive individuals (thin models) was compared to the effect of presenting images of overweight individuals. Male and female participants completed measures of body satisfaction before and after viewing the images of thin or overweight individuals, matched for gender. It was found that participants of both genders revealed greater dissatisfaction with their bodies – as measured by rating scales, body silhouettes and body size estimations – after viewing the stereotypically attractive pictures and improved body satisfaction after viewing the overweight pictures. Indeed, viewing pictures of overweight or obese models resulted in improved esteem on some measures. This response was found to be greater in female than in male participants. Thus, acute exposure to magazine-type pictures of physically attractive models can produce short-term changes in satisfaction with own body shape. The important finding of this study was that even though men exhibit generally higher body satisfaction than do women, even they are not insensitive to media images.

Champion and Furnham (1999) replicated Ogden and Mundray's study with adolescent girls aged 12–13, 14–15 and 16–17 years. All participants provided data on their weight and height, self-assessments of body image using a verbal scale and body silhouette scale, and other data on body image. They were then invited to examine and rate one of three sets of pictures in terms of attractiveness, thinness, health of depicted person and extent to which the picture represented a body image ideal. The three sets of pictures comprised five photographs of thin models taken from teen magazines, five photographs of overweight or obese females, and five photographs of rooms. After viewing the pictures, the participants responded to seven visual analogue scales designed to measure self-worth.

While a main effect of age emerged, with older girls feeling more dissatisfied with their own body than did younger girls, no effects of picture exposure were found on scale scores. There was an interaction between satisfaction with own body and type of picture to which the girls were exposed. Being dissatisfied with their own body and exposure to photographs of slim models were together significantly related to the extent that the girls reported thinking about their weight. This finding suggests that girls who were already dissatisfied with their own body were inclined to think more often about their weight, and that exposure to pictures of thin models only added to this concern. In contrast, viewing pictures of overweight models led girls who were relatively satisfied with their body image to think less often about their weight. While indicative of a role of magazine-style photographs of models as part of a more complex array of causal factors that might influence body image perceptions, this study is limited by its failure to conduct a more comprehensive multivariate analysis of potential contributors to girls' body image perceptions from among the wide range of measures on which data were collected.

Evidence has emerged elsewhere that not all young women are equally affected by media exposure when tested for their body self-esteem and satisfaction with their own bodies. Posavac, Posavac and Posavac (1998: 188) argued that, 'Women may experience stable satisfaction with their bodies if (a) their body shape is not markedly different than models pictured in media images (a rarity) or (b) body weight is not an important determinant of their self-worth because they are confident in skills and abilities unrelated to physical attractiveness'. The former category are unlikely to perceive a discrepancy between their own bodies and the media ideal. In the latter category, any physical discrepancies may hold little importance because their self-confidence stems from other aspects of their lives.

Posavac et al. (1998) conducted three experiments to explore these matters further. In the first experiment, female undergraduates completed a measure of trait body dissatisfaction prior to being shown slides of either fashion models from popular magazines or neutral images of motor vehicles. Weight concern was also measured following exposure to the slides. The slides themselves were rated by participants using a 'Fashion Preference Questionnaire' (five statements about each slide: for example, 'This is something I would wear in public', 'This outfit would be flattering to my figure'). Women dissatisfied with their bodies at the outset displayed greater weight concern when exposed to fashion model slides than when exposed to slides showing cars. Women initially satisfied with their bodies did not differ by condition and showed no tendency to become more concerned about their weight.

The second experiment was a repeat of the first, with a further condition added in the form of pictures of attractive women who were not fashion models. Indeed, the third set of pictures were of other college women. The results replicated those of the first experiment for fashion models and the control condition. Dissatisfied women displayed some increase in weight concern following exposure to photos of attractive women who were not fashion models as compared to women who were satisfied with their bodies. Thus, images of realistic beauty were not as likely to induce women to become concerned with their weight as were images of glamorous models.

The third experiment repeated the previous design, but with a change of photographic ratings to a scale that did not prompt social comparisons. The question did not focus on the photos but asked more generally about shopping habits. The idea was to distract participants from the true purpose of the study. However, even with this distraction, women who were dissatisfied with their bodies exhibited enhanced weight concern as a function of exposure to pictures of attractive fashion models.

In conclusion, Posavac et al. believed that exposure to media representations of body image could affect women's personal weight concerns through a process of social comparison. The women readers of a magazine containing pictures of glamorous fashion models make comparisons between their own bodies and the bodies of attractive models who can be regarded as representing societal standards of beauty. Not all women are susceptible to this effect, however. Women who are broadly satisfied with their own figures are much less likely to express concern about their own weight after seeing pictures of attractive fashion models.

Further corroborative evidence concerning the more powerful impact of body shape stereotyping in the media on women than on men has been produced in an American study of pre-teenage and teenage boys' and girls' reactions to magazine advertisements with attractive same-sex models endorsing the advertised products. While reactions to these advertisements did not differ much between these young people when the commercial messages were shown without models, when models were present, significant differences in reaction occurred between girls and boys and among girls with high versus low body self-esteem. Girls were more sensitive to same-sex models than were boys. Furthermore, girls with lower body self-esteem perceived advertisements with same-sex models as more appealing than did girls with higher body self-esteem. This effect also rubbed off on the products being advertised. For boys, the presence of male endorsers rendered the advertisements more attractive overall, but there was no link between body self-esteem among boys and the way they evaluated the advertisements or the products being advertised (Martin et al., 1999).

Wagner, Hartmann and Geist (2000) assessed the immediate effects of brief exposure to images taken from print media on the general self-consciousness and body self-consciousness of American female undergraduates in their late teens and twenties. After viewing photographs of either thin female models or control photographs not concerned with physical appearance, the women completed questionnaire scales designed to measure self-perceptions. Those young women who had looked at the pictures of thin female models were found to produce higher self-consciousness ratings – especially body self-consciousness – than their counterparts who viewed the control pictures.

Television effects

In addition to studies of the potential causal role of magazine representations of body image in conditioning body shape perceptions of readers, experimental research has also involved the use of televised images as stimulus materials. Despite its prevalence as a mass medium, however, there have been only a few experimental studies of television's influences on body image so far. Most attention has been directed at measuring the potential effects of advertising images on television.

In one study, Strauss, Doyle and Kriepe (1994) examined the effects of television advertisements on dietary restraint level. Dietary restraint theory (Herman and Polivy, 1975, 1980) can account for a number of eating-related phenomena, such as binge eating among chronic dieters (Heatherton et al., 1988). Pre-tests were used to divide participants into those who exhibited high restraint and low restraint in their eating patterns. Participants were given a high calorie, nutritionally balanced banana drink at the outset. They were then invited to watch a film that was interrupted by advertisements. The advertisements promoted either diet-related or non-diet-related products. Both low and high restraint participants watched this material and were provided with nuts and confectionery to eat during the movie. A third group saw the movie without any interruption by advertisements. The results indicated that participants high in restraint level who viewed the movie with diet-related advertisements ate more while viewing than did other participants.

Although most of the research on the media's influence on body image and eating disturbance has examined effects that follow mere exposure to relevant magazine content, some writers have indicated that it is important to consider the individual's awareness and acceptance of socio-cultural pressures to conform to certain physical standards. Heinberg, Thompson and Stormer (1995) developed the Sociocultural Attitudes Towards Appearance Questionnaire (SATAQ) as an index of both awareness and internalization of cultural pressures regarding appearance. Each factor was strongly related to multiple measures of body image and eating disturbance. In regression analyses, however, the Internalization scale accounted for roughly six times the variance associated with measures of body image and eating dysfunction as the Awareness scale.

Heinberg and Thompson (1995) explored the role of awareness and internalization of societal standards of appearance by examining the effect of television commercials on body image. College-age women viewed 10-minute videotapes of commercials that either contained stimuli emphasizing societal ideals of thinness and attractiveness or contained neutral, non-appearance-related stimuli. Results indicated that participants who viewed the videotape stressing the importance of thinness and attractiveness reported greater depression, anger, weight dissatisfaction and overall appearance dissatisfaction than those given the neutral manipulation. Furthermore, participants who possessed high dispositional levels of body image dissatisfaction showed increases in dissatisfaction with both weight and overall appearance following exposure to the experimental tape, whereas participants who had low levels of dispositional body image dissatisfaction either showed improved or unchanged body image self-perceptions following the exposure to the appearance-related video. All participants exposed to the neutral control video, regardless of their original self-perceptions, demonstrated decreases in both weight and appearance dissatisfaction (Heinberg and Thompson, 1995).

The interaction between type of stimulus exposed to and pre-existing dispositional status (high versus low body image esteem) found by Heinberg and Thompson contrasts with the results of Irving (1990). The reason for this may be found in the way effects of media stimuli were measured. Heinberg and Thompson chose a measure of body size estimation that may be sensitive to immediate changes in the environment, while Irving used a questionnaire-based measure of disordered eating tendencies that may measure a more permanent trait that is less amenable to change.

Perhaps the most sophisticated experiment to date is one that systematically manipulated participants' exposure to television programming and advertising materials, depicting either thin or obese models. Myers and Biocca (1992) adopted an experimental paradigm to investigate the impact on college women's estimations of their own bodies of exposure to programmes and advertisements depicting thin and non-thin bodies. They hypothesized that the mass media, specifically through 'ideal body' advertising and programming play an indirect role in the promotion of body image distortions. This process starts with the media's influence on young women's development of an internalized ideal body concept.

Changes in the internalized ideal body concept may lead to changes in the individual's present body image. This effect has been observed in very young women. In adolescence, when young women are strongly focused on developing a sense of self-identity, they may be highly sensitive to social cues. According to Myers and Biocca, '... in adolescence young people are particularly narcissistic, that is, they are in a literal sense preoccupied with their own physical attributes' (1995: 117).

Myers and Biocca (1992) compiled four videotapes of material that comprised a combination of programming and advertising with body image messages or no body-image-messages. Programmes and adverts had been pre-coded by an independent panel of judges in terms of whether they were body-image-oriented or not. Four conditions were created: body image programme with body image advertisements; body image programme with neutral advertisements; neutral image programme with body image advertisements; neutral programme with neutral advertisements.

A body image detection device (BIDD) was deployed to measure participants' impressions of their own body image. The BIDD used three projected bands of light which were supposed to represent the size of the chest, waist and hips of the individual. The individual could manipulate the widths of the bands of light from an overhead projector to produce a projected image that matched her perception of her body shape.

In general, body image overestimations were the most common form of distortion. Body image commercials produced a distortion in body image perceptions, but in the opposite direction to that hypothesized – namely, overestimations were less frequent among participants' in the body image commercials conditions than among those in the neutral commercials conditions.

Body image commercials did not affect estimations of chest measurements, but did affect estimated size of waist and hips. Body image programmes did not significantly affect short-term body image perceptions of the subjects' chests, waist or hips. However, when paired with body image commercials, body image programming resulted in lower estimates of waist measurement.

Effects of body image commercials and body image programming on mood were also measured. Presence of body image commercials led to lower levels of depression. Body image programming had no effect on this measure. There were no effects of commercial type or programme type on participant hostility levels nor participant anxiety levels. This study confirmed that young women tend to overestimate their body size – in line with previous studies (For example, Birtchnell et al., 1987; Garner et al., 1976; Thompson, 1986). However, it also showed that a young woman's body image of her own body is elastic. According to Myers and Biocca (1999: 126) 'body shape perception can be changed by watching less than 30 minutes of television. If the mental construct of a woman's body image is responsive to cues, television appears to be a significant carrier of those cues'. Evidence emerged that fluctuations in a woman's body image can occur after brief exposures to advertising and programming that depict the 'ideal body'.

Myers and Biocca originally thought that young women would tend to reject their present bodies upon exposure to media depictions of an ideal body shape. Faced with this image young women would see their own body as larger than it really was. Such persistent rejection of their own body might result in enhanced anxiety, depression and hostility. Instead, the opposite effect occurred. They suggested that body image advertising may have a therapeutic value – and might help to bring young women's body images closer to their objective body shapes. However, Myers and Biocca acknowledged that this argument lacks face validity. Advertisements more often aim to change rather than to confirm a person's image through the purchase of the advertised product. Hence, the young women studied by Myers and Biocca may have identified with the ideal body in the advertisement. As a result, they may have seen the ideal as more attainable. They may have seen their own body as closer to the ideal and internalized that new body image of themselves – hence feeling better about themselves in the process.

Seddon and Berry (1996) compared the responses of women to video-taped sequences of television advertisements to assess their impact on the women's self-esteem and eating preferences. One set of advertisements contained stereotypically thin and attractive females, while a second set did not contain any such images. The women, in turn, were differentiated via a psychological test in terms of whether they exhibited controlled or 'restrained' eating patterns. Self-esteem measures were taken before and after exposure to the advertisements. In addition, a further post-exposure task was administered, described by the authors as a taste task. Participants were presented with three ice cream containers with lids labelled as 'salty,' 'sweet' and 'sour'. They tasted each ice cream and gave it a series of ratings for taste. The real intent, however, was to find out how much ice cream the women would eat.

The findings revealed no overall changes in self-esteem from before to after exposure to the advertisements. This was true for women participants regardless of their long-term eating predispositions. On the post-exposure eating test, there were no main effects of women's eating habit type or of the type of advertisement seen. There was, however, an interaction between these two variables. Restrained eaters ate significantly more than unrestrained eaters in the condition in which both were shown television advertisements with stereotypically thin female actors and models. In fact, although not quite significant, the restrained eaters ate more after seeing the advertisements with thin actors and models than after seeing the other advertisements, which was the *reverse* of what happened for unrestrained eaters.

The researchers concluded that stereotyped images of thin women had disinhibitory effects on the behaviour of restrained eaters. Seeing thin women on screen – especially in advertisements in which they were depicted eating – could have given justification to women respondents to eat more themselves. Not surprisingly, this effect might be expected to be more pronounced among women who would normally restrict how much they eat. There was no evidence, however, that any variations in eating ice cream emerged as a function of changes in self-esteem. One confounding factor was that the scale used to measure restrained eating habits was not administered until the end of the study, so as to avoid priming participants of the purpose of the experiment at an earlier stage. However, prior eating of ice cream could have affected participants' responses to the scale, perhaps causing restrained eaters to deny that they are restrained in their eating. They might then have been grouped during analysis with true non-restrained eaters, hence reducing differences between those groups categorized as restrained and unrestrained eaters.

Lavine, Sweeney and Wagner (1999) examined whether exposure to television advertisements that portray women as sex objects can cause increased body dissatisfaction among women and men. This research was carried out among students aged 18 to 35 years. Participants in this experiment were exposed to sexist advertisements, or non-sexist advertisements, or no advertisements at all. The results revealed that women exposed to sexist advertisements judged their current body size as larger and revealed a larger discrepancy between their actual and ideal body sizes (preferring a thinner body) than did women exposed only to non-sexist advertisements or to no advertisements at all.

Lavine et al. also examined what effects exposure to advertisements with female sex object depictions would have on male viewers. Their reasoning was as follows: 'If the female sex object subtype heightens men's beliefs that women are flirtatious and seductive, this may increase the salience of their perceived characteristics of men (e.g., a muscular physique) to which women are attracted. Thus, such ads may increase men's awareness of and concerns about their own bodies and thus increase body dissatisfaction among men' (1999: 151). Where such advertisements also depict muscular men, then there might be an even more direct effect on men in the audience at home who compare themselves with such models unfavourably.

Men exposed to the sexist advertisements judged their current body size as thinner, revealed a larger discrepancy between their actual and ideal body size (preferring a larger body), and exhibited a larger discrepancy between their own ideal body size and their perceptions of others' male body size preferences (believing that others preferred a larger ideal) than did men exposed only to non-sexist advertisements or no advertisements at all.

As we have seen already, social comparison theory has been offered as a form of explanation for the effects of media images on media consumers' body image perceptions. Media images of thinness are purported to reflect socially sanctioned standards of physical attractiveness. While social comparison is often invoked as a post hoc explanation, it has only rarely been directly manipulated in advance by researchers.

One such study was reported by Cattarin, Thompson, Thomas and Williams (2000). Social comparison was manipulated by creating three instructional conditions that either encouraged participants to make comparisons between themselves and media images (comparison condition) or distracted their attention from doing so (distraction condition), or did neither of these things (neutral condition). All participants were young women, with an average age of 23 years. These women were shown advertisements and video material that either made a point of emphasizing the physiques and physical attractiveness of models and actors on screen or made no such point. No overall difference in participants responding after exposure was found as a function of the type of screen material shown to them. There was an effect upon subsequent self-perceptions of being in the condition in which participants' attention was drawn specifically to the physical attractiveness of on-screen actors. In this condition, the women reported a greater degree of comparison-making than did women in the other two instructional conditions. Further evidence emerged that the stronger such social comparisons were, the less favourable were the judgements the women made about themselves as compared to the media models.

Many of the studies reviewed in this chapter so far have used television advertisements as stimulus materials. While there is no doubt that this aspect of television's output represents a potential source of influence on viewers' self-perceptions, because many products are promoted by physically attractive models and actors and these icons appear in a selling context, can more subtle effects upon body image occur following exposure to programmes? Myers and Biocca (1992) studied programme-related and advertisement-related effects together. But what impact can non-commercial material have in the absence of any commercial material?

Harrison (1999) reported an experiment designed to test the impact of television characterizations of thinness and fatness upon adolescent males' and females' subsequent mood. This study investigated whether this effect was mediated by self-discrepancies in perceptions of own body (actual body), the kind of body they regard as the ideal (ideal body) and the kind of body they believe significant others (that is, parents) think they should have (ought body). Participants were aged 12, 15 and 18 years and were randomly assigned to watch one of three videos. The control film depicted a teenage girl camping with her stepbrother and father. One experimental film depicted a teenage girl being socially rewarded for her thinness. A second experimental film saw a teenage girl being socially punished for her fatness. The fatness-depicting video produced the greatest agitation and dejection of the three videos among both male and female adolescents. However, the thin-rewarded film caused particular dejection and agitation among adolescent girls who exhibited dissatisfaction with their own body. In contrast, body-dissatisfied adolescent boys were soothed by watching this video.

Confidence in the experimental research evidence

This chapter has reviewed experimental evidence for effects of media representations of body image on observers' body self-esteem and associated eating disorder symptoms. Experimental methodology enables researchers to tackle directly the issue of causality. While experimental studies are therefore capable of going beyond surveys in their investigation of links between media depictions of the body and media consumers' body image perceptions, even with these studies there have been limitations. In evaluating this part of the literature, it is useful to examine specific methodological elements where problems have arisen. There are two areas that deserve closer inspection in this context. The first of these concerns the measures used operationally to define body shape judgements and self-perceptions. The second concerns the types of media stimuli used in these studies.

Body shape measures

A number of techniques have been used to measure body size, shape and satisfaction. The crucial measures here have centred on experimental participants' personal estimates of their own body size and shape and their feelings of satisfaction or dissatisfaction with their body. These measures have also been used when participants have been invited to make judgements about the physiques of other people, including people depicted in the media. Four basic techniques have been used by most researchers working in this field: (1) the linear method; (2) the configurational method; (3) the pictorial technique; and (4) verbal questionnaires (Fisher, 1970; Shontz, 1969).

The linear method has been widely used and invites individuals to convert their perceptions of a body (whether their own or somebody else's) into estimates on a linear scale. This works by getting the individual to take a distance indicated between two points on a body (for example, the width of the chest, waist or hips) and two points on a line drawn on a piece of paper, or on a rod with sliding markers attached to it. This technique can be used to produce estimates of a person's actual size as they perceive it, as compared with their preferred or ideal size (or the size they would like to be), or the size of a media model on those same physical dimensions.

The configurational method invites experimental participants to select a body shape from a range of pictured options (either a range of photographic models, line drawings of same-gender body shapes, or silhouettes of body shapes of their own gender), that most closely matches their perception of their own body shape.

The pictorial technique asks participants to draw pictures of their bodies or body parts. The verbal questionnaire approach elicits verbal judgements about whether the body or any part of it feels unusually large or small.

Each of these measures has been used independently and sometimes in combination, but little is known about how comparable they are. There was some early indication, for instance, that individuals would register smaller estimates of body sizes using verbal measures in a questionnaire than when using linear judgements by setting markers (Shontz, 1969). Methodological experiments have indicated, however, that body size judgements based on linear measures seem to be largely unaffected by the posture of the model being assessed (that is, whether depicted in a standing or sitting position). Furthermore, such judgements did not seem to vary with repetition or as a function of practice in using the technique (Shontz, 1969). However, certain body parts are more likely than others to be under- or overestimated. Hence, head width and forearm length are the parts of the body most often overestimated, while hand and foot lengths are the most likely to be underestimated. Further, women are more likely than men to over estimate the width of their waist (Fuhrer and Cowan, 1967). When women made verbal assessments of body size, however, by stating a body dimension in inches, they more often *under-*estimated physical dimensions than did men (Shontz, 1969). Over time, women are likely to change the estimates of their body size more than men will (Furlong, 1977).

As we will see in the next chapter, body size estimates also vary with the personality of the individual. Those individuals who display symptoms of anorexia nervosa, for example, exhibit body self-perceptions that differ from most non-clinical populations. What this evidence indicates is that the measures of body size and shape that are often used as operational dependent variables, hypothesized to be influenced by exposure to selected media stimuli, may give rise to judgements of body dimensions that vary independently of supposed media influences. The degree to which these measures are expected to produce stable judgements over time and across populations may differ from one measure to another. This is an important point to bear in mind when interpreting the results of media effects experiments in which these measures have been used.

Media stimuli

Some experiments have used still photographs as stimulus materials (for example, Champion and Furnham, 1999; Grogan et al., 1996; Ogden and Mundray, 1996; Waller et al., 1992), others used moving video footage (for example, Harrison, 1999; Heinberg and Thompson, 1995; Myers and Biocca, 1992). Studies have varied also in the intensity of the dose of media images presented: a single video sequence (Harrison, 1999); 5 still pictures (Champion and Furnham, 1999; Ogden and Mundray, 1996); 16 still pictures (Grogan et al., 1996); 20 TV adverts (Heinberg and Thompson, 1995; Waller et al., 1992). Some studies compared the impact of 'thin' images with neutral images (Grogan et al., 1996; Heinberg and Thompson, 1995; Myers and Biocca, 1992; Waller et al., 1992), others compared 'thin' images with 'fat' images (Champion and Furnham, 1999; Harrison, 1999; Ogden and Mundray, 1996).

Experimental studies varied in the 'effects' they measured. Thus, effects of exposure to the thin ideal in the media have included altered perceptions of own body size (Champion and Furnham 1999; Ogden and Mundray, 1996), non-verbal estimates of body shape (Heinberg and Thompson, 1995; Myers and Biocca, 1992), verbal estimates of whether underweight or overweight (Champion and Furnham, 1999), body dissatisfaction (Harrison, 1999; Ogden and Mundray, 1996), and disordered eating symptoms (Grogan et al., 1996; Heinberg and Thompson, 1995). Fairly consistent findings have emerged indicating that exposure to pictures (whether still or moving) of thin models or actors leads to a short-term over-estimation of own body size (for example, Myers and Biocca, 1992; Ogden and Mundray, 1996) and lowering of body self-esteem and satisfaction (for example, Grogan et al., 1996). The latter reactions were especially likely to occur among individuals already low in body self-esteem or high in disordered eating symptoms (for example, Harrison, 1999; Heinberg and Thompson, 1995; Waller et al., 1992). In contrast, however, when exposed to pictures of overweight models, young women and teenage girls may perceive themselves in more favourable terms (Ogden and Mundray, 1996).

The results of these experiments are indicative of short-term changes in some areas of subjective judgement about body size and shape that suggest that some individuals make comparisons between themselves and attractive models they see pictured in magazines or popular actors or characters on television. It is also clear that some individuals are more sensitive than others to the thin ideal represented by fashion models. Hence, not all readers and viewers react in the same way to body image representations in the media. Furthermore, most experimental studies examined reactions to pictures of thin models or actors, which were compared with the responses of control participants who saw images with no emphasis on human body shape.

Since one study indicated that exposure to pictures of overweight models could make female observers feel better about themselves (Ogden and Mundray, 1996), it is possible that one type of body shape could balance out another in terms of its impact upon observers' body self-image. As yet, no research has been conducted to establish whether this counterbalancing effect occurs in practice and whether it is more or less likely to occur in individuals who already suffer low body self-esteem. To understand both the nature of long-term effects of media representations of body image and the probable efficacy of editorial or production policies to use a wider range of body types in fashion photography and leading dramatic roles, this sort of comparison is important.

Even when comparisons have been made between observers' reactions to pictures of thin and fat models, the pictures have comprised different models. This means that differences in attractiveness of thin and over-weight models might be accounted for by factors other than their relative body size, such as facial attractiveness, style of garment or attire, pose, scenery in the background, and so on. One way of circumventing this problem is to use the same models in all conditions and, through a process of digitization, to use computer technology to produce different sized versions of the same models. Thus, a photograph of a thin fashion model can be digitally altered to make her look bigger in systematically varying degrees. In this way, the only feature that would vary across conditions would be the overall body size of the model.

Summary

This chapter has examined research into media and body image based on experimental cause–effect analysis. This research has investigated the possible role of magazine and television stimuli upon readers' and audiences' body image perceptions and related attitudes to eating. In so doing, test paradigms were deployed under controlled conditions to assess changes in individuals' perceptions of their own body size and shape that could be triggered by exposure to specific media representations of human body forms. Much of this research focused on the impact of media stimuli upon female observers and found that at least some females are sensitive to these media images and, in the short term, may alter their perceptions of their own body shape and size upon comparing themselves with more attractive media role models.

While the research on this subject has certainly not yet produced conclusive evidence of how significant such media representations of body image are, as compared with other influences, in shaping body self-perceptions and self-esteem, the findings are indicative. The work reviewed in this chapter, however, was conducted among non-clinical populations. Concern about media depictions of body shape has largely stemmed from a belief that they may contribute towards not only lowered self-esteem, but also the onset of health-threatening disordered eating habits. In their extreme form, such behaviours can become established into clinical syndromes that have the status of an illness. In the next chapter, we review research conducted among clinical populations into the role of the media in the development of eating disorders.

9 The Media and Clinical Problems with Body Image

Many studies have indicated that young women today see models, actors and centrefolds who are thinner and far less curvaceous than those seen by their mothers and grandmothers. This trend has been illustrated by research showing that the body measurements of models and even beauty contest finalists, for the past several decades, have gradually become less hour-glass like, more boyish or more androgynous (Garner et al., 1980; Levine et al., 1994; Silverstein et al., 1986).

Women's beauty and fashion magazines may be among the most influential media formats in perpetuating and reinforcing the socio-cultural preference for thinness and in creating a sense of dissatisfaction with one's body (Harrison and Cantor, 1997). Given the popularity of teen beauty and fashion magazines – at least three in four white females in the United States between the ages of 12 and 14 read at least one on a regular basis – it should not be surprising that they might play a major role in socialization and identity formation (Klein et al., 1993).

The previous two chapters reviewed research among non-clinical populations. However, some research has been undertaken with women who were clinically diagnosed as suffering from eating disorders. This chapter will look at what evidence has emerged suggesting that media imagery contributes to problems such as anorexia and bulimia among clinical populations. While non-clinical populations may display some degree of sensitivity to media images of thin role models, resulting in lowered body self-esteem, it is less clear as to whether this reaction represents the first step towards the development of a more health-threatening behavioural syndrome of disordered eating. We ask whether it is possible to reveal a contribution that the media may have made to the behaviour of young women who are known sufferers of eating disorders via clinical diagnosis or the application of cause–effect methodology.

A small amount of experimental research with anorexics and bulimia has indicated that these young women do exhibit stronger reactions to media images of thin body shapes than do non-clinical populations (Hamilton and Waller, 1993; Waller et al., 1992). This early evidence is indicative, but not yet conclusive. This chapter will consider the strengths and weaknesses of the evidence so far.

Stereotypes associated with body size

Before turning to the evidence for possible media effects upon women with eating disorders, it may be helpful to consider more generally the aetiology of clinically diagnosed eating-related problems and their implications for those who experience them. The significance of body shape for most people is captured in the social stereotypes that are associated with fat and thin physiques. A person's physique is often used by others to judge their character and abilities. Being overweight is associated with negative stereotypes, such as self-indulgence and laziness. Thinness is associated with people of a nervous and shy disposition (Brodsky, 1954; Lawson, 1980; Lerner, 1969a, 1969b; Sleet, 1969; Staffieri, 1967, 1972a). Such stereotypes, however, can change over time. While being fat has continued to be seen in a negative light, being thin is linked to ambivalent views.

Boys and men have consistently been found to rate figures of average-sized or mesomorphic physiques most favourably and fat or endomorphic physiques most negatively. Thin or ectomorphic physiques were rated as intermediate, though generally more negative than positive, especially with regard to supposed submissive or nervous qualities. Girls and women have also shown a preference for average-sized bodies and an aversion to fat physiques (Lawson, 1980; Lerner, 1969b; Lerner and Gellert, 1969; Staffieri, 1972a). Females, however, exhibit a different opinion about thin physiques from males. When boys were asked which body type they themselves would like to have, few chose a fat body type, while most chose a lean, muscular frame (mesomorphic type) (Lerner and Gellert, 1969; Staffieri, 1972a). A few chose the thin body type. Girls, making the same choice, *never* chose the fat physique and were about half as likely to choose the thin body as the average one (Lerner & Gellert, 1969; Stafieri, 1972a).

In sum, girls exhibit more favourable attitudes than do boys towards a thin body type. For instance, while thin people were rated as submissive by both boys and girls, for girls this attribute was seen in positive terms, associated with characteristics such as being quiet, clean, honest and unworried, whereas for boys, it was seen in more negative terms as associated with being more afraid, sneaky, worried and unpopular. When evaluating job applicants, whose weight, height and sex were included in an application form, young men and women regarded fat applicants in less flattering terms, but thin applicants in positive terms (Roberts and Herman, 1980).

Social pressure for thinness

Growing social pressures for a slim body shape have resulted in a greater prevalence of restrained eating (Herman and Polivy, 1975, 1980). Restrained eaters are individuals who are concerned about their weight and eating and are preoccupied with limiting their diet. Research with restrained eaters has revealed that excessive dieting can have dramatic effects beyond slenderness.

Restrained eaters may even overeat under conditions that, with normal individuals, would produce reduced food intake. This pattern was illustrated by the following report from Polivy et al.:

> Herman and Mack (1975) found that giving two milkshakes to restrained college co-eds led them to eat more ice cream afterwards than did giving them only one or even none. Non-dieters naturally ate less ice cream after one milkshake and much less after two. The restrained eaters, in keeping with their attempt to lose weight, ate less than normal eaters when not forced to consume anything first (that is, in the 'no milkshake' condition). College men showed a similar response whether they were overweight, average weight or underweight, those who were dieters ate significantly more after two (as compared to zero) milkshakes, whereas non-dieters significantly reduced their intake. (Hibscher and Herman, 1977) (1986: 100)

Thus, chronic dieters do not feel sated after a certain calorific intake in the same way as do normal individuals. Restrained eaters may adopt cognitive strategies to convince themselves that they have consumed less than they actually have. (Polivy, 1976; Ruderman and Wilson, 1979; Woody et al., 1980).

Anorexia nervosa

Another serious consequence of the socio-cultural emphasis on thinness in women, according to some writers, is the increased prevalence of anorexia nervosa among young women. As Polivy et al. noted: 'Anorexia nervosa is a syndrome of self-imposed starvation and relentless pursuit of thinness to the point of emaciation' (1986: 102). The causes of this syndrome are still not fully understood, though a number of explanations have been attempted. Psychoanalysts have regarded anorexia nervosa as representing a regression to a more primitive stage of development among individuals who cannot cope with the demands of growing up (Sours, 1974; Szyrynski, 1973). Symptoms frequently occur in adolescents who feel uncomfortable with the onset of puberty and the physical changes it brings. By dieting, the individual hangs on to a pre-pubertal body shape and, in a sense, withdraws from the physical maturation that accompanies puberty (Crisp, 1965, 1970, 1980).

Other psychodynamic explanations of anorexia nervosa (Ehrensing and Weitzman, 1970; Goodsitt, 1977; Masterson, 1977; Story, 1976) have identified disturbances in early mother–child relations that vitiated the child's ability to establish her own identity. Exaggerated efforts to control weight represents a part of the young person's struggle to establish some kind of distinctive identity – even if it may be unhealthy for them (Bruch, 1973, 1978; Palazzoli, 1978; Vigersky, 1977).

Much of the theorizing about possible causes of anorexia nervosa has focused on physiological explanations. One of the critical findings behind this mode of thinking was that menstruation appears to stop in some anorexics before they lose the percentage of their body weight that is deemed necessary for menstruation to cease (Fries, 1977). One hypothesis is that problematic functioning of the hypothalamus may be a causal factor. Indeed, evidence has emerged that anorexics do display abnormal functioning in this part of the brain (Mecklenburg et al., 1974).

The question remains whether this abnormal functioning is a cause or an effect of the lack of eating. Most of the hypothalamic functions are known to return to normal once eating is resumed and weight regained. Hence these abnormalities may be an 'effect', rather than a 'cause', of the anorexia nervosa (Garfinkel and Garner, 1982).

It should be kept in mind that starvation and weight loss, which are what anorexics undergo, result in many profound physiological changes (Leibowitz, 1987; Pirk and Ploog, 1986). Failure to finish meals, taking a long time to eat, obsession with food, and hyperactivity, all symptoms of anorexia nervosa, have also been observed in humans and non-humans who have been deprived of food either in the laboratory or under natural conditions (Epling et al., 1983). Some of the psychological and physiological symptoms may therefore be due to the effects of lack of food. It is hard to tease apart what is cause and what is effect in anorexia nervosa because experimental simulation of the disorder in humans is unlikely to be approved by human subjects' ethics committees. Results from clinical observational studies are often the only data available.

Evidence has emerged over several decades that the incidence of anorexia nervosa has increased (Crisp et al., 1976; Duddle, 1973; Halmi, 1974). In research in England, Crisp et al. (1976) reported one serious case of anorexia for every 100 high social class girls aged 16 to 18 years. This finding confirmed earlier data on the prevalence of anorexia in girls from more affluent homes (Bruch, 1973; Crisp, 1965).

Accompanying this increase in the prevalence of anorexia nervosa has been a cultural preference for thinness in women (Bruch, 1978). The changing trend towards a thinner ideal shape for women, observed even during the 1970s, was regarded as a cultural phenomenon, reinforced by the mass media and other purveyors of cultural values and ideals (Garner et al., 1980). The impact of this thin idealized shape is evidenced in the pervasiveness of dieting among women.

The media, however, do not operate in a vacuum. Other social and cultural factors have been identified that have probably contributed towards the establishment of a thin ideal. For instance, it has been observed that friends and relatives of anorexic patients may, in some cases, actually provide reinforcement of their behaviour by expressing admiration for their slender figure (Bruch and Eurman, 1980). Changes in the role of women in Western societies have opened up fresh opportunities for women, vocationally as well as domestically, but also brought new pressures that may begin to be felt in adolescence (Selvini and Palazzoli, 1974). Such contemporary socio-cultural pressures on women must also be considered alongside other genetic and early background factors that might underpin this disorder (Garfinkel and Garner, 1982; Garner and Garfinkel, 1980).

Research with Swedish teenagers by Nylander (1971) found that serious cases of anorexia nervosa numbered less than one per cent. Nevertheless, most of the girls surveyed perceived themselves to be too big or ove weight. This perception could create a psychological climate that encou ages active dieting. This pattern was not generally observed among teenage boys. Prolonged dieting could eventually give rise to the emergence of anorexic symptoms.

If the development of serious eating disorders arises from these social pressures to be thin, there may be certain groups who are especially likely to develop such tendencies. In this respect, research with professional ballet dancers has revealed that distorted perceptions of body shape, excessive dieting, vomiting to control weight and anorexic symptoms can occur (Druss and Silverman, 1979; Vincent, 1979).

Garner and Garfinkel (1980) confirmed these earlier observations and found that highly competitive vocations such as dance and modelling, in which pressures to adhere to a preferred body shape exist, were often susceptible to the development of distorted body images and controlled eating patterns.

In relation to possible media effects upon anorexics, of course, the assumption made is that young, eating-disordered women have their perceptions of themselves influenced by the representations of slender female body shapes in magazines, films and television programmes and advertisements. Anorexics, however, by definition, have a different perception of their body size, compared with the impression that other people may have of them. Anorexics tend to see themselves as being heavier than they really are.

Anorexic women tend to overestimate the width of their bodies to a greater extent than do women without such problems (Slade and Russell, 1973).

This tendency has been demonstrated under controlled conditions using a method called the distorting photograph technique. With this technique, a participant can adjust someone's photograph to between +20 per cent and −20 per cent of the actual photograph's normal width. When this technique has been used with both anorexic and normal females, the anorexics have been found to show a greater tendency to adjust pictures of themselves so that the adjusted version is bigger than their actual size. However, this tendency did not emerge when anorexics were invited to adjust pictures of people other than themselves. Apparently, the anorexic's tendency to distort body self-image is limited to herself (Garfinkel and Garner, 1976, 1982). While an anorexic woman may define her own body as bigger than it really is, she does not exhibit similar distorted judgements about the body sizes of other women (Slade and Russell, 1973).

Further evidence has indicated that although anorexic women have a tendency to overestimate their body weight and size, this phenomenon is not unique to this clinical group. Non-anorexic women who have lost a lot of weight and women of normal size and stable weight have been found to exhibit a similar tendency (Fries, 1977; Slade, 1977; Wingate and Christie, 1978). Indeed, the evidence for differences between anorexic and non-anorexic women in their propensity to overestimate their body size and weight has been mixed. While there is evidence that anorexics supply distorted body size estimates for themselves more frequently than do non-anorexic women (Pierloot and Houben, 1978), there is other evidence that contradicts this finding (Ben-Tovim et al., 1979; Strober et al., 1979; Toutz et al., 1984).

Even when faced with a projected photographic image of themselves, which they could manipulate using specialized equipment, anorexics were found to be more likely than non-anorexic women to produce a revised image of themselves that overestimated their actual body size. Anorexic women were also less satisfied with and obtained less enjoy-ment from their own body than did non-anorexic comparisons (Garfinkel et al., 1983). In another study, groups of anorexic women, bulimic women, women of normal weight with no clinical symptoms and non-eating-disordered psychiatric patients were asked to judge the point at which a television image of themselves wearing a bathing suit accurately repre-sented their own physical shape. Judgements were made first after par-ticipants had abstained from eating for 12 hours and then again after eating a meal. Although some overestimation occurred in all groups, the anorexic and bulimic groups overestimated their body size significantly more than did the other two groups. Fasting or eating a meal made little difference to these judgements (Freeman et al., 1983).

Bulimia

While overeating has been observed to occur in the general population, it can occur to an extreme degree in clinical populations suffering from disordered eating. As a disorder, bulimia (Russell, 1979), bulimarexia (Boskind-Lodahl, 1976; Boskind-Lodahl and Sirlin, 1977) or the dietary chaos syndrome (Palmer, 1979), is behaviourally manifest in terms of consumption of large amounts of food, often in eating 'binges', frequently followed by attempts to get rid of the food by self-induced vomiting, the use of laxatives or diuretics, over-exercising or fasting. Such behaviour occurs repeatedly (American Psychiatric Association, 1987: 68). These episodes might average at least two or three per week for periods of up to 3 months. According to Russell (1979), bulimia nervosa is accompanied by a marked fear of becoming fat. By the mid-1980s, in the United States, the prevalence of bulimia nervosa was estimated at about 2–4 per cent of the population (Johnson and Connors, 1987).

Bulimia is often preceded by dieting (Boskind-Lodahl and Sirlin, 1977) or anorexic symptoms (Boskind-Loblahl, 1976; Palmer, 1979; Russell, 1979). The causes comprise a mixture of biological factors, including brain disease, and social and cultural pressures on women to be thin.

One major problem with the criteria outlined above is that they fail to distinguish between those individuals who purge after eating and those who do not. The former have been found to be more disturbed than the latter on measures of eating behaviour, psychological stability, body image, depression and attitudes towards eating (Willmuth et al., 1988).

Body image disturbance and eating disorders

Eating disorders involve a body image disturbance. However, the degree and form of body image disturbance can vary among women who display disordered eating syndromes. Indeed, body image disturbance can take on a multidimensional character that involves perceptual, attitudinal and behavioural features (Cash and Brown, 1989; Garfinkel and Garner, 1982; Rosin et al., 1989; Thompson, 1990). Bruch (1962: 189) was first to postulate that body image disturbance was a pathological feature of anorexia nervosa, which she referred to as 'the absence of concern about emaciation, even when advanced, and the vigor and stubbornness with which the often gruesome appearance is defended as normal and right'.

In essence, patients with eating disorders tend to perceive themselves as unrealistically big or fat and as being grossly out of proportion or protruding at certain body regions, such as having excessively wide hips or a stomach that sticks out too far. No matter what objective evidence may be placed before the patient to show that she is normal, she relies primarily on her own feelings about and perceptions of her size.

Despite widespread clinical agreement that individuals with eating disorders are remarkable for their belief in being abnormally fat, the measurement of these perceptions has often been difficult in standardized size perception tests, casting some doubt on the validity of perceptual distortion as a fundamental feature of eating disorders. One controversy stems from reports of inconsistent intercorrelations between the size distortion of different body parts (Cash and Brown, 1989). One argument is that if those with an eating disorder possess a perceptual abnormality, it should be manifested consistently in body image. But why? Different body parts can vary in salience and importance. It is possible that an individual can be unhappy with one aspect of their body – their thighs, for instance – and nothing else.

Another difficulty stems from the finding that non-eating-disorder individuals often overestimate their size as much as do women with anorexia nervosa (Cash and Brown, 1989). This has led some investigators to argue that size distortion is not unique to this clinical population. Thus, perceptual body image disturbance might not be a criterion for eating disorders (Hsu, 1982). However, there are reasons to reject this view. First, many studies have reported greater overestimation of body size perception in eating disordered people (Cash and Brown, 1987; Cooper and Taylor, 1987). Second, size distortion can be remarkably stable, even after the patient has been partially rehabilitated (Garfinkel and Garner, 1982). Third, it is not surprising that 'normal' women also overestimate their size given the widespread concern with weight in Western cultures. Fourth, body size distortion is only one symptom of body image disturbance in patients with eating disorders and because it is a multidimensional problem, the absence of one type of disturbance is not sufficient evidence to rule out any kind of clinically disturbed orientation.

Body dissatisfaction can often be traced to particular body areas, such as the width of the hips or thighs, the protrusion of the abdomen, or the dimpled flesh on the back of the legs. Dissatisfaction is expressed in terms of dislike for the body part, thoughts that that part of the body appears unattractive, and beliefs that the part is too fat or lacking muscle tone (Cash et al., 1986; Garner et al., 1983).

Cooper and Fairburn (1987) argued that women with eating disorders feel that other people evaluate them mainly on their appearance and that other personal attributes do not mean as much. Thus, adolescent girls who displayed bulimic behaviours had lower body self-esteem and were more concerned than other girls of their age about their appearance (Brown et al., 1988; 1989; Cash et al., 1987). Indeed, it appears that individuals with eating disorders cannot be distinguished from other weight preoccupied women on ratings of body dissatisfaction alone (Garner et al., 1983; Wilson and Smith, 1989). They are distinguished, however, by the importance they place on weight and shape for their self-worth (Wilson and Smith, 1989).

The Role of the Media

Body image disturbances in women with eating disorders have been attributed to cultural standards for beauty, learning within the family, disturbances in development of self-identity and disturbances in psychosexual development. Body satisfaction and physical self-esteem are closely associated with more global self-esteem (Cash et al., 1986; Rosen and Ross, 1968). Women with eating disorders have extremely low self-esteem and generally feel bad about themselves (Garfinkel and Garner, 1982; Johnson and Conners, 1987). Drive towards thinness in adolescence, at a time when they would otherwise be developing physically, raises the possibility of an underlying fear of emerging sexuality (Crisp, 1980). However, direct comparisons of anorexic and normal populations have revealed no significant differences in sexual attitudes, behaviour or experiences (Haimes and Katz, 1988; Mizes, 1988; Scott, 1987).

Families with domineering, intrusive and over-protective parents, who make it difficult for the developing adolescent to become autonomous of parental control, may produce young women with no clear sense of self-identity (Bruch, 1973). Pursuit of thinness may represent an effort on the part of such young women to exert personal control over at least one aspect of their life, despite the lack of freedom she may be afforded elsewhere by her parents. Losing weight may therefore serve to enhance perceptions of self-efficacy (Cattanach and Rodin, 1988).

It is clear that a number of causal agents may influence the onset and determine the severity and manifestation of disordered eating. Accompanying and forming an aspect of this syndrome is a distorted perception of the individual's physical self. Although not likely to represent the sole causal agent, there is growing empirical evidence that the media may contribute to the development of body image disturbance. Some studies have been carried out within a clinical sphere demonstrating that acute exposure to media images can increase body dissatisfaction in anorexics and bulimics (Hamilton and Waller, 1993; Waller et al., 1992). Waller, Hamilton and Shaw (1992) found that participants with eating disorders (anorexia and bulimia) demonstrated a significant increase in body size overestimation following exposure to photographs of models from popular fashion magazines. In this study, photographs displayed individual women in three-quarters to full-length shots (from the head down). In a control condition, participants were shown photographs depicting home interiors. While the effects of seeing pictures of slim models were most pronounced among women with clinically diagnosed anorexic or bulimic disorders, even a control group of non-clinically diagnosed women, those who displayed eating attitudes in the same direction as those typically found among disordered eating populations, exhibited greater sensitivity to photographs of slim models than other women from the control group who showed no eating-disordered attitudes.

Hamilton and Waller (1993) measured the effect of exposure to photographs taken from women's fashion magazines on 24 women meeting the DSM-III-R criteria (American Psychiatric Association, 1987) for anorexia nervosa or bulimia nervosa. Participants' self-perceived size of waist, chest and hips was measured using callipers and used to obtain an average body perception index for each woman. Comparing these measurements to participants' actual size revealed that overestimation of body size was found to be significantly greater when participants had been exposed to, and rated, such images of fashion models, as opposed to neutral images of rooms. Indeed, anorexic and bulimic women in this study overestimated their actual body size by 25 per cent after watching slides of pictures of slim women.

Thomsen, McCoy and Williams (1997) adopted a 'uses and gratifications' approach to understand media effects in the context of body image. The approach emphasized the role of social and psychological factors in mediating an individual's media choices. This model proposes that media consumers make active choices based on their belief that the media can fulfil specific needs and produce desired gratifications. Further, the effects of these messages are the result of the selective interpretation and use of media by consumers. In other words, individuals often use the media to induce the effects they desire (Arnett, 1995).

Using a qualitative, ethnographic approach, Thomsen et al. interviewed anorexic participants to find out how 'at-risk' women use women's beauty and fashion magazines. Does the use of these magazines serve to moderate the development and continuation of their eating-disordered thinking and behaviour?

Anorexia most often occurs in adolescence, which is an important period of socialization and identity development in young women (Arnett, 1995). The images and messages presented by the media leave an important impression on these young women, particularly those who are vulnerable because of affective and cognitive needs (Arnett, 1995).

In the Thomsen et al. study (1997), women were invited to attend sessions at which they talked about their use of beauty and fashion magazines, the needs these publications may have satisfied for them, and whether there were specific factors, within their social and family lives, that could be identified as giving rise to these needs. Twenty-eight women outpatients at an eating disorder treatment facility participated in this study, aged between 18 and 43 years. The interviews revealed a social comparison dimension with magazine consumption reinforcing a process that had already begun before reading of the magazines in question had started. Some of these women reported that fashion and beauty magazines did provide a source of roles models and that they would restrict their consumption of food or exercise a great deal to maintain a slender physique. Many of the women interviewed here reportedly cut out photographs of models from these magazines and pinned them on their bedroom walls and kept them in folders or scrapbooks. Women's magazines also provided a source of information on dietary, health and fitness issues which this clinical population would actively seek out.

While anorexia has been regarded as an attempt by women to starve themselves back to a pre-pubescent state, there was evidence that magazines with pictures of thin models made such readers feel more mature, rather than less so. By modelling themselves on well-known fashion models, it gave these women a sense of being more mature. There were also signs of dysfunctional use of beauty and fashion magazines. Articles written to scare women away from eating disorders were used by some of the women interviewed in this study to support eating-disordered behaviour. The articles were turned around and re-interpreted to reinforce the behaviour they had attempted to discourage.

There was evidence that fashion and beauty magazines, with a reputation of containing a multitude of pictures of thin models, started to be noticed by these women once their eating disorder had got under way. Such media may have a cognitive dissonance-reducing function. Anorexic women may use pictures of slender models and celebrities not only to motivate themselves to lose weight, but also to reduce cognitive dissonance created by having a life-threatening disorder. Seeing successful, famous women who are portrayed as extremely thin makes it easier to distort the painful reality of having a psychological disorder.

Summary

Body image disturbances have been associated with clinical disturbance. It is not uncommon to find dissatisfaction with body shape among general populations, especially among young people in adolescence who are most sensitive to how they appear. When such concerns are carried to an extreme, however, individuals may alter their eating patterns and dietary habits to control their appearance. At this point, the pressure to be thinner can result in health-threatening behaviour. This can take the form of binge eating followed by purging of ingested food through enforced vomiting or food avoidance. Such behaviours are attempts by the individual to gain control over themselves and to create a self-image with which they are satisfied, even though it may cause serious harm to their health. While various psychological and psycho-physiological factors have been identified as contributing to bulimic and anorexic behavioural syndromes, there remains a public concern that mediated images also play a part in encouraging or shaping such behaviour patterns.

Anorexic women tend to overestimate their weight and body size. This is not unique to these women. Anorexic women may strive harder than other women, however, to make harsher comparisons of themselves against mediated images than do non-anorexic women. Eating-disordered women also believe that other women judge them more on their appearance than may actually be the case. Such clinically diagnosed women hold distorted perceptions of themselves and their body shape. According to some experts on this subject, images of thinness in the media may contribute towards this self-distortion. As the small body of evidence among clinical populations reviewed in this chapter has indicated, anorexic and bulimic women do seem to be more likely to overestimate their own body size than do other women after exposure to media images of thin models. Furthermore, media images may be used by anorexic and bulimic women to convince themselves that being excessively thin is normal. Such findings are indicative but need further confirmation with research among wider clinical populations, before such research could be drawn upon to trigger media editorial policy or regulatory recommendations.

10 Conclusion: Body Messages and Body Meanings

> Each one of us has a complex lifelong relationship – with our body. We exult in it, feel betrayed by it and, given the chance, would change some aspect of it.
>
> (T. Adams, *Observer*, 26 October 2003: 4)

In the sixth of its 'uncovered' series the *Observer* Sunday newspaper in the UK featured, in its supplement, the British obsession with the body – their own and other people's. Tim Adams' piece was titled 'The skin we're in' and recounted 50 years of bodies from 1953 to 2003. He commented, 'we can in the spirit of our age go shopping for bodily transformation' (*Observer*, 26 October 2003: 7), adding that whereas Wolf (1992) 'seemed a little hysterical' in her predictions that 'personal insecurity' and 'international capitalism' would support an upsurge in plastic surgery, in practice in 2003 'the overwhelming theme of our times … is self-transformation' and the possibility and promise of it is sold to us – as the media analyses undertaken here have shown in this book – everywhere and often.

The magazine included articles on tattooing, designer babies, piercing, contortion, transplants and several short body-focused fictional stories but around two-thirds of the material was directly about the relationship between size, shape and sex. The newspaper conducted a confidential poll about body perception amongst 1,074 UK adults in September 2003. The results included some interesting data in terms of the remit of this book:

- We judge our own bodies more harshly than those of others. 29 per cent rated their own bodies between 7 and 10 but 57 per cent rated their partners between 7 and 10.
- Men prefer short (62%), slim-waisted (73%), long-haired (75%), tanned (77%) women.

- 74 per cent of both men and women felt they had better sex when they felt good about their bodies.
- 61 per cent felt obese people were responsible for their own predicament.
- 41 per cent felt the media was responsible for dictating public perceptions of the ideal body shape. Fifty-one per cent felt the media was one of many factors.

(*Observer* Supplement, 26 October 2003: 14–22)

Also curious was the very obvious orientation of this 'special' supplement towards male bodies. The reason for this may be that there has been a genuine upsurge in male body sensibility, both from men and women, making the male physique 'newsworthy'; or that journalists are still unsure about how to focus on the female body after the accusations made about the role of magazines, particularly, in 'nurturing' eating disorders; or perhaps, the beauty industries are now overtly targeting sales to males, having saturated the female market, and are placing pressure on media producers to file suitable supporting copy for their product advertising placements. A cynic might expect the latter explanation to be evident but the supplement had only three advertisements: one for the very 'sexy' underwear of 'Agent Provocateur', featuring two women in a slightly sado-masochistic pose; a second was for a charity offering male impotence advice; the third was for a gender-neutral slimming club. Yet some 14 pages featured males and male bodies almost exclusively with the slender but muscular footballer David Beckham as the preferred male body-ideal of 33 per cent of all interviewees (*Observer* Supplement, 26 October 2003: 18). As if to confirm this, British independent television screened a documentary entitled 'Beckham's Body Parts' on ITV and ITV2 in November 2003.

This media emphasis on the 'fit' male body may be in part an effect of feminism turning the tables on objectification and in part a fear of focusing on the thin feminine body in the media after the furore of accusations linked to waif-like depictions causing extreme dieting, both of these explanations relate to the beauty industry's need to generate new markets in less contentious areas. On 4 November 2003 GMTV, independent television's breakfast show in the UK, featured a discussion in Los Angeles that alluded to very thin actresses now 'not working' in Hollywood because media producers are anxious about the audience and critical backlash to representations of skeletal femininity. None the less GMTV's website home page featured an advertisement for Weight-Watchers (http://gm.tv/index.cfm?articleID=52).

Recent research on situation comedies in the United States indicated some rejection of overweight male body types among television audiences suggesting perhaps a groundswell shift towards the masculine body as an object both of desire and criticism. Although audiences did not appear to support overweight men being criticized on screen by female characters, they did accept obese male characters' humorous self-criticisms (Fouts and Vaughan, 2002). Although in the programmes analysed only some 13 per cent of men were above average weight (compared to 30 per cent in US reality), the figure for women in situation comedies was 7 per cent obese compared to 25 per cent in the US population (Fouts and Vaughan, 2002: 441). So this research suggested that women remain significantly undersized on television. Even though men do seem to be featuring occasionally as critically evaluated bodies there is no obvious media presence of the full range of women's size, shape and age either in this recent US research or in the media texts that are discussed in this book.

It was that undersized portrayal which inspired the millennial panic about media representation of thin women affecting eating and possibly even leading to disease and death. A panic that seemed to be legitimated by the large numbers of cases of self-starvation in various forms: 'There are 60,000 eating disorder sufferers in the UK at any one time' (Ryan, 1998: 28) and by authoritative sources such as the medical establishment, government and journalists targeting the media as causal: 'Certain sections of the media provide images of extremely thin or underweight in contexts which suggest that these weights are healthy or desirable' (BMA, 2000: 44). This book has attempted to explore that hypothesized relationship by analysing two constituents: textual data and audience responses. It has also focused on women because despite some evidence of body dissatisfaction among men (Hill, 2003) and the objectifying of the idealized male body in some media sources (Nixon, 1997), it remains overwhelmingly women who display self-harming starvation:

> Accurate figures are not easy to establish but a useful estimation assumes that in the age range 15–30 years around 1% of the UK female population are affected. ... Men also suffer from the eating disorders but in much smaller numbers. The ratio of woman to men is around 10–1 but there is growing evidence that figures for men are also rising. (http://www.maryhart.co.uk/index/who, accessed 14 November 2003)

A further reason for the focus on women was that it is women's *bodies*, rather than any other attributes, which appear to make them worthy of being represented. Women feature in culture more often than not because of how they look and the preferred look is young, slender, sexual and white. The female body is spectacle, both something to be looked at, whether real or mediated, and to be looked through in the search for feminine identity. The argument that the media causes eating disorders assumes not merely that media representations misrepresent but that they also inscribe, directing women to 'train, shape and modify their bodies to conform to what, very clearly, are impossible ideals' (Woodward, 1997: 141).

Mediated bodies

The first part of this book examined how the media have come to be linked to theories of eating disorders, how culture represents women and how the history of representation and theories of discursive power can inform an analysis of contemporary media texts of the sort deemed harmful by the UK Labour government's Body Summit of 2000.

Anorexia has a long history but until the second half of this century it was an activity associated with either religious piety or nervous sensibility. The later-twentieth-century notion of diet, rather than self-denial or delicacy as reasons to reject food, indicates that slenderness is now the goal of food restriction rather than a symptom. This coincided with the burgeoning of the mass media and the political impetus of second-wave feminism from the 1960s and the drive for capital to find new markets during post-industrialization.

These developments impacted on the prevalent but neither preventative nor curative psycho-medical explanations for eating disorders, explaining the focus on media as causal. The turn to media studies saw femininity explored as a cultural construct not a natural phenomenon, while feminist theory introduced psychoanalytical and political accounts of gendered identity focusing on both patriarchy and capitalism. What emerged was an influential set of ideas that linked patriarchal dominance of the family, the media industries and international capital to the representation of a very male ideal of female roles and looks. Women were seen as subject to these discourses, always struggling to 'fit' the required shape or die in the effort, sometimes literally through self-harm but also subjectively in a kind of self-denial.

This would seem ludicrous if it were simply that women were suddenly told thin is desirable by the mass media but 'a well adjusted woman does not starve herself to death just because she sees a picture of a skinny model' (*Guardian*, 31 May 2000). The thin message is neither singular nor sudden. Nor is it merely a modern mass media construction. Rather, the mass media reinforce and reproduce thinness within a whole history of cultural constructions of femininity which make it acceptable to audiences and so sellable to advertisers. The long history of representation made the post-World War Two shift to slender beauty acceptable because it fitted into a long history of imagery wherein women were the objects of male desire and used to being presented as men would like them to be. Moreover, it was not only the diet industry that described women's bodies but fashion, beauty, fiction, fitness and even, in the post-feminist phase, finance, all of which are aspects of 'the dominant capitalist culture in its para-national phase' (Williams, 1981: 143).

The power of body images is not just a legacy of a vertical history of depicting femininity that pre-empts readings and acceptances but the cumulative impact of horizontal intertextuality. Each representation is placed in conjunction with others to form a feminine syntagm, composite, compliant woman, who when meeting the cultural ideal is then placed in the romantic gendered narrative of love, family, financial security and perhaps even fame. If not ideal, she is placed in a situation of tutelage very often involving buying a better version of herself. And, of course, she is encouraged to work hard in order to earn the money to self-improve whilst 'incidentally' serving the interests of a multi-billion dollar industry in remodelling bodies (Orbach, 1978). This happens within texts across genres – so a magazine composes a whole woman from adverts, features, letters, fashion and lifestyle and between texts, factual and fictional, whilst newspaper narratives mimic those on television and/or vice-versa.

Such discourses are part of the technology of power – capitalist and patri-archal but also heterosexual, white and Western and also part of subjective consciousness. We only know who we are through language, yet for women language represents them according to the interests of those who 'represent' rather than according to women themselves. At the outset of the twenty-first century those representations are also discontinuous – frail but fertile; sexual and maternal; career-girl and geisha; independent but arm-candy; flirtatious but faithful. With the demise of a feminist critique during the Thatcher/Reagan years in the 1980s, it is unsurprising that some, perhaps in some ways most, women simply try to comply until they die – sometimes early and tragically when the effort ends in self-harm and disease – whilst others reach the threshold of womanhood, say 'no' to what is on offer and simply self-starve themselves back to childhood. Thirty years ago Berger argued that 'capitalism survives by forcing the majority, whom it exploits, to define their own interests as narrowly as possible' (1972: 154) and that it per-vades that definition through 'publicity'. Publicity is not just advertising but all means by which information and ideas are made public.

In the twenty-first century we live in a publicity saturated culture that is arguably subject to what Baudrillard (1983) termed an information bliz-zard wherein the images and messages refer to each other rather than to any external reality. He even claimed that so great is the gap between rep-resentation and reality: 'We are living in a society of excrescence, meaning that which incessantly develops without being measurable against its own objectives' (Baudrillard, 1989: 29). He goes on to say that, 'So many messages and signals have been produced and transmitted that they will never find the time to acquire any meaning. ... The tiny amount that we nevertheless absorb already subjects us to perpetual electrocution' (Baudrillard, 1989: 30). It is interesting that this by Baudrillard is entitled 'The anorexic ruins'. The modern mass media bombards audiences with images that increasingly self-refer, either historically or contemporane-ously, in cultural and political conditions that minimize the radical pessimism Baudrillard calls for as resistance.

Theoretically it seems likely that such media representations in such conditions might in some way 'electrocute' either to stimulate, shock, stun or even kill but to claim this in relation to any aspect of attitudes and behaviour requires some careful analysis both of the messages themselves and of audience reactions to them. In relation to an effect of self-starvation, texts must be shown not just to depict waif-like and frail femininity but to depict such images in contexts that give them positive connotation and credibility. Images, for example, of starving Ethiopian women feature often in the Western news but would never be attributed with anorexic causation. Yet, since the 1990s, media images of often equally skeletal young white women were and are systematically deemed as suicidally inspirational by a range of authoritative institutions. The analysis of print media newspapers and magazines revealed a range of possible reasons for attributing representations of thin femininity with powerful resonances but also highlighted the poverty of explaining self-starvation by blaming a few photographs of skinny girls in designer clothes – a poverty best articulated by the already cited accusation (*Guardian*, 8 July 2000).

The British print media sell themselves by selling sex and slenderness. Women largely either barely feature at all or feature promoting those twinned aspects of femininity. Newspapers are narratives simply written, repetitive, habitual, culturally relative and purporting to tell the truth. Those constituents alone suggest they may be more powerfully meaningful than the dislocated stills of emaciated fashion models that pepper magazine pages. The newspapers sampled in 2000 and 2002 showed little evidence of progression from the early 1980s when Gaye Tuchman (1981) argued that they 'symbolically annihilated' women. Nor was there much evidence of changed representation in the light of the recommendations of the June 2000 Body Summit in Britain which charged the mass media with responsibility to present healthy and various images of women. Women rarely featured in the British press unless sexually attractive, linked to a famous man or more rarely were deeply deviant or the victim of a deeply deviant 'dangerous stranger'. Even when they were featured in their own right, usually because of 'star' status, it was their bodies and their sexual status in relation to a man that formed the image and the story. Further, those deemed newsworthy fell within a narrow category of femininity: young, slender, white, blonde, famous, often long-haired and small rather than tall and revealingly dressed or undressed, apparently confirming the *Observer* poll (26 October 2003). This was evidenced by the tendency for journalists to present women-stories visually rather than verbally. The underlying story anchoring and explaining the image (Barthes, 1977) corroborates Burchill's point and resonates with a very traditional pattern of gender relations and roles wherein women's success is measured by the man they catch and the man they catch depends on how they look. The modern twist in this tale is that women must still comply to be desired, but now that they are liberated career women, they are expected to pay for that expensive effort at compliance themselves. This post-feminist shift is even more clearly evident in the glossy magazines.

Macdonald (1995) argued that from the late 1960s women's magazines reflected the impact of feminism by focusing on careers and sexual liberation. With an audience of young, politicized, ambitious and sexually active women to attract and retain this was arguably as much or more about business acumen in the industry than about deep commitment to sexual equality and women's rights. By the turn of the century the sample of glossies analysed for this book appeared to retain that focus on independence and liberation but *Glamour, Cosmopolitan* and *Marie-Claire* also offered a much less modern myth. Each magazine worked as a complete narrative in structural terms with apparently discontinuous and discreet sections actually combining into a full story – a story replicated monthly but also across magazines and a story very similar to that on offer in the newspaper coverage of femininity. Yes, women do appear to be represented as career-successful and sexually free but these representations are confusingly embedded in the much more traditional gender narrative of 'finding the right man'. The heroine (represented model and real reader) is on a quest for love; the journey is arduous; villains must be identified and heroes seduced; the body must be tamed and adorned for each encounter; the means is beauty and the goal is 'marriage'. Stars feature as women who have made the journey and won the prize. All of this is infiltrated by often barely detectable advertising of products, which for the large part make the heroine the preferred size, shape and style for the hero and, of course, require a large proportion of her income. The most common size, shape and style of woman in the glossies is very slender, young, white and also often blonde and long-haired.

Young women are prepared for this adult journey by very similar heroines in the teen-magazines such as *Sugar, Bliss* and *J17*, so by the age they are buying the glossies they are well primed and anticipatory of the formula: thus the adult narrative makes sense of the preparatory work in the teen texts. These are less coherently narrative as whole products than the glossies but almost more titillating and tempting because the promise of sexual love and fulfilment is withheld but the means of attracting it – 'looks' and the mystery of it are abundantly featured. Young girls are dressed like vamps and taught to flirt. Again they are, usually, blonde, white and very slender. There are less advertisements in these, unsurprisingly as schoolgirls have less money, and more lessons about love and life. These chart the rite of passage to adult femininity as if only a very limited kind of woman exists there. Many of the products featured as desirable and the ideals represented for desirable women are also associated with a thin aesthetic.

The print media in the UK in the twenty-first century are writing a version of their bodies for women readers. They rarely explicitly argue that women should comply with a very slender look but they show little else that has any positive association. This was a subtle and complex representation but performed very similarly across newspapers and magazines of arguably different genre and audience appeal. The shifts wrought by feminism have been very effectively harnessed into contradictory discourses that are so pervasive and repeated that they seem to make sense. Women have the right to work and to be sexual, but ultimately in order to construct themselves as desirable to men by using their earnings to buy the beauty and bodies represented in the texts. But the model of woman featured and the manner of her featuring is consistent with quite conservative masculine ideals of feminine desirability. So women's sexuality and earning power are extolled, satisfying the liberated sensibilities of the female audience, but they are harnessed to the twin interests of patriarchy and capital. Women are buying their gender identity but it remains described in accordance with the masculinity at the heart of patriarchy and the corporate power of the beauty industry.

Screened images do little to ameliorate that inscription. Most quantifying content analysis of televised body images shows an alignment of beauty with thinness (Downs and Harrison, 1985) of thin characters in relation to food and of a greater proportion of underweight women than men (Kaufman, 1980). The intertextuality of the mass media supports a repetitive pattern of body shape representation. There are mutually reinforcing body messages as the press prints stories about film stars, television follows up news in the morning papers and the World Wide Web has sites for print news, broadcasting and celebrities. So the media comprise an almost closed circle endlessly referring to the media as if media texts were themselves real events worthy of reportage and representation making them empty in relation to actuality and only meaningful in relation to each other (Baudrillard, 1983, 1989). This process is best exemplified by the way celebrities have become a kind of cross-media currency when stars are in themselves 'performers' on a public stage – that is, they are already mediated – and their real lives as 'people' are largely hidden from public view.

Female stars also have added news value as 'elite' personalities and, as the work on print representations in Chapter 4 showed, they also 'represent' femininity as a whole in that they dominate news and features and images about women. Famous women of the film and television screen smile sexily and skinnily from our magazines and newspapers, often attached to a man, just married or even pregnant or 'temporarily' unattached but alluringly, desirably available. Again these rich women – Kylie Minogue, Kate Winslet, Victoria Beckham, Geri Halliwell, Anna Kournikova, Kate Moss, Sarah Jessica Parker, Calista Flockhart, Jennifer Aniston and others – are of a type: very slender, sometimes electronically aided, white, blonde (except for Victoria Beckham), heterosexual and young. There is a twin message here: to be a famous, independent, attractive star necessitates a certain 'look' and that same look will also deliver a man. Sexual success and financial success are both modelled on a certain body image.

Furthermore, these stars from the print media feature on screen in serials that narrate for viewers that very same story mimicking the kind of appeal of the women's magazines to both feminist sensibilities and traditional gender roles. Evidence of actual paid work is little seen, though lifestyle and designer clothes suggest substantial incomes, but what is clear is that these serial women want men and love. Career is not fulfilling in itself, merely as a means of earning the money needed to buy the body and beauty that men want. As the actresses in the modern soaps like *Sex and the City*, *Friends* and *Ally McBeal* grow older in real-time (and marry and have children) their dreams of love and marriage seem less and less credible in represented time and what started as an optimistic journey for gorgeous girls, jars and deflates as a sad search for anything in trousers before the biological clock stops. Each of these serials is losing audiences and closing but each has sustained the Cinderella story for many years by deferring the princely moment for its slender-aspiring central heroines. Often that lack of a prince charming and the unhappiness caused by it is attributed to the central character's career success or even sexual liberation. Young women's freedom of choice to work, have sex and be independent is depicted and appears glamorous and exciting on the surface but that equality comes with a health warning, a sell-by date and a solution to both – stay young, slim and sexy if you don't want to stay single.

The obsession with food on television, discovered in the content analysis and the evidence that anorexics are also food-obsessed, made food programmes an area of interest for this research. Self-starving girls spend hours shopping for low-calorie drinks but gazing in longing at chocolates, or they pour over cook books to produce sumptuous meals for their families that they don't eat themselves. Recovered anorexic Kate Chisholm confessed:

> I used to have amazingly vivid dreams of bustling kitchens filled with huge tray loads of cakes, steak pies, vats of custard, apple tarts – steaming hot fresh out of the oven, ready to take a bite. Then I would wake up with a start, creep downstairs (it was usually about three in the morning), take an apple out of the bowl, cut it in half, remove the core, slice one half into eight segments (leaving the other half in the fridge), eat each segment painfully slowly, before writing a letter to my mother to confess how much I had eaten. (Chisholm, 2002: 147)

Food is deeply sensual and deeply feminine in the private sexual and domestic context of love and family but in the public world of restaurants it becomes more masculine and professional. This gender split is replicated in cookery programmes where women are featured 'femininely' in their homely kitchens while men occupy and oversee the busy business of restauranteering. Food, as love and nurture, is feminine food; it is a marker of femininity, to reject it is to reject the femininity associated with food, that is, motherhood, family, home, servitude, solace and seductiveness. Television reinforces these associations of food with adult femininity (in the UK most television cooks are either maternal like Delia Smith or curvaceously glamorous like Nigella Lawson, dubbed a 'domestic goddess') while showing frail, skinny, girl-like femininity as the route to love and power. The subtle implication is like food and be like your mother, or reject food and be sexy, successful and maybe even a star. Diet programmes are there to help in the latter quest and diets are often sold by association with stars (with numerous Hollywood stars swearing by the benefits of the Atkins Diet), as are exercise videos – again usually associated with slim-built celebrities.

And the obsession with diet and body size has now spilled over into the ever-expanding space of the Internet. Many of the stars have their own sites and feature on others. Magazines and newspapers also have Web versions, often barely dissimilar to the print output. Each of the serials discussed in Chapter 5 has a website repeating the televised narrative and offering images of the stars and 'inside' information about them. These sites offer alternative, instant and continuous access to the familiar gendered representations of the press, magazines and television. But computing power also offers difference from the other media.

One difference is that computers allow images to be manipulated, as in a ridiculously elongated image of Kate Winslet (*GQ*, February 2003, see Figure 5.1) or even created, as in the emaciated, animated 'Webbie' on-line model at www.illusion2k.com. Computer images of skinny beauty are juxtaposed with and often linked directly to diet-sites, and search engines allow the selection of only material of interest, increasing the topic volume and intensifying the surfer experience. On the Net you only have to look at skinny stars and find out how to be like them if that is your preference. That level of selectivity makes the Web a different medium, so also does the feature of interactivity. Surfers can create their own narratives and representations on the Web; they can also 'chat' to others with similar concerns and interests and many girls and women with eating disorders and other body image preoccupations do just this. Sites celebrate anorexia and offer advice on self-starving and 'thinspirations' to encourage ana-addicts. Like other addicts, the message is about safe practices not recovery. Eating disorders are often promulgated as a life choice with associated sets of rules and beliefs, such as those at *Starving to Perfection*:

Thin commandments:

- If you are not thin you are not attractive.
- Being thin is more important than being healthy.
- You must buy clothes, cut your hair, take laxatives, starve yourself, do anything to make yourself look thinner.
- Thou shall not eat without feeling guilty.
- Thou shall not eat fattening foods without punishing oneself afterwards.
- Thou shall count calories and restrict intake accordingly.
- What the scale says is the most important thing.
- Losing weight is good/Gaining weight is bad.
- You can never be too thin.
- Being thin and not eating are true signs of will power and success.

Quotes:

- Nothing tastes as good as thin feels.
- An imperfect body reflects an imperfect person.
- Food is a hindrance to your progress.
- Don't eat anything today that you'll regret tomorrow.
- I'm not starving myself. I'm perfecting my emptiness.
- Hunger hurts but starving works.
- Thinner is winner.
- Let your bones define the beauty of your body.

(http://realm2-blessedbe.com/StarvingForPerfection/Ana/AnaIndex. html, accessed 12 November 2003)

This site contains images of most of the stars featured in the texts analysed in this book, at their thinnest, in a section called 'Thinspirations'. These sites self-publicize and mutually appreciate self-starving activity; some contributors also admit to the use of drugs and diuretics, others claim that they self-mutilate by cutting or suffer from depressive illness. Most defend their right to be anorexic, as Elizabeth does below:

> I am so mad that people dare lecture us on how we live, eat, exercise, and our goals. All my life I have been raised to see that slim is beautiful, and the only way anyone can really be successful is to be thin. Yet, the same people who put this idea in our head are the ones who lecture us.

And this was posted by Kylie Everrett at 24 July 2003 01:29 pm:

> Fat people are allowed to be fat so why can't the thin be thin. I don't even know if my eating disorder has a name, I like pro-Ana sites. I think anorexics are beautiful. It's a stupid thing to say but I think and feel it. (http://cim.ucdavis.edu/users/mcmyang/archives/000399.html, accessed 12 November 2003)

Although there are sites on-line that warn against self-starving and even embrace 'fat', as in the conventional media, 'thin is in' and the images available merely replicate those off-line. There is less narrative context because the Web is less coherent and more polygeneric by virtue of its cyber-form, but none the less, for those already obsessed with the body, fashion, stars and self the message is clear and rampant – slender is sexy and successful.

The positive associations with slenderness are not entirely a problem in a Western society where obesity is a major killer. For many, being slender means better health, fitness and agility, all attributes that are also socio-economically as well as personally desirable. But slenderness is not sold in those terms anything like as much as it is associated with success and sex-ual desirability. Moreover, even, in those terms women are free agents who can choose to accept, negotiate or reject such imagery – or move between those positions at different times or in different places – or even play with or parody representations for sheer pleasure. So do the images and narra-tives of the body in the media matter? Perhaps not if they were neither per-ceived nor understood; not if they were dislocated, occasional and part of a huge variety of representations of femininity; not if women laughed at them and ignored the products for body-shaping and beauty-making. But what if women do absorb these narrow narratives of femininity and mea-sure their own femininity against them? Part Two considered the kind of research which, if valid, suggests these thin media body images and the narrative context they illustrate do matter because they affect audiences detrimentally.

- In a study among undergraduates, media consumption was positively associated with a strive for thinness among men and body dissatisfac-tion among women (Harrison and Cantor, 1997).
- Viewing commercials depicting women who modelled the unrealisti-cally thin-ideal type of beauty caused adolescent girls to feel less confident, more angry and more dissatisfied with their weight and appearance (Hargreaves, 2002).
- In a study on fifth graders, 10-year-old girls and boys told researchers they were dissatisfied with their own bodies after watching a music video by Britney Spears or a clip from the TV show *Friends* (Mundell, 2002).
- Another recent study on the media's impact on adolescent body dis-satisfaction, two researchers found that:

  1 Teens who watched soaps and TV shows that emphasized the ideal body type reported a higher sense of body dissatisfaction. This was also true for girls who watched music videos.
  2 Reading magazines for teen girls or women also correlated with body dissatisfaction for girls.

3   Identification with television stars (for girls and boys), and models
     (girls) or athletes (boys), positively correlated with body dissatis-
     faction (Hofschire and Greenberg, 2002).
                    (http://www.mediafamily.org/facts/facts_mediaeffect.shtml,
                                                accessed 12 November 2003)

Audience, interpretation and attitude

Such research suggests not only that the mass media significantly affect the
way audiences, particularly young audiences, think about themselves but
that representations of the body in particular have a resonance with self-
identity and self-worth. The analysis of media texts has shown the dominance of the thin aesthetic and positive correlation with sex, success and
happiness within a quite traditional heterosexual framework. The effect of
that could theoretically be the embracing of body-morphing activities to
conform to that thin aesthetic. The attractiveness of a slender female shape
was established by research in the 1970s and 1980s (Spillman and
Everington, 1989; Yates and Taylor, 1978) with women consistently esti-
mating that men preferred a thinner shape than they did (Fallon and
Rozin, 1985). Ironically, as women have preferred more slender shapes ide-
ally, so the actual size of women has increased (Wiseman et al., 1993),
except of course in the mediated world of fashion, beauty and fame. The
likelihood here is a correspondent increase in the sense of dissatisfaction
women feel about their bodies if the media are influencing self-perception,
which does seem to have been the case (Heinberg and Thompson, 1992a;
Heinberg et al., 1995) and a tendency for women to criticize others on the
basis of having unacceptable bulk (Beebe et al., 1996) or negate themselves
by comparison to more svelte friends or relatives (Rieves and Cash, 1996).
    The ideal self then becomes a measure against which the real self falls
short (or rather falls 'wide' of the preferred mark), a phenomenon evident
among both men and women suffering from eating disorders, as concluded by Jacobi and Cash (1994). As only a minority of real women are
slender, sexy and successful while most mediated women are, such
research implies that it may be mediated thinness that is the source of the
ideal. Repeated exposure to media stereotyping can create illusions that
representations are truth (Signorielli and Morgan, 1990) simply through
familiarity. These illusions then inform beliefs and experiences, making a
false basis for judgements and actions. The predominance of thin in the
context of sexiness and success in the media texts analysed in Chapters 4
and 5 may be operating in this way unconsciously to the extent that
some women function under illusionary models of normality where
size is the key to both misery and joy. Certainly, Cooper (1997) found that

self-starvers used food or weight to explain and evaluate many social situations unrelated to body size. Some one in five American young girls even, articulated a desire to emulate the skinny stars of the mass media world (Levine et al., 1994), accepting them as role models not because they were fit but because they were perceived as attractive (Shaw and Kemeny, 1989). Such work has established the importance of body image to self-identity and self-worth but theorized rather than tested that image as likely to be media-influenced.

However, the work in this book has established the prevalence of positive value 'skinny' stories and images in the millennial mass media whilst empirical studies have tested actual reported self-perception in relation to actual exposure to body images. Most of the survey-based studies of this type focused on young women audiences and drew on substantial evidence that girls, particularly in Westernized cultures, frequently self-reported as too fat (Button et al., 1997). Research on the relation between magazine reading and eating disorders has suggested correlations but these were found to be much stronger if young women were also conscious of broader socio-cultural thin ideals of femininity (Cusumano and Thompson, 1997). In other words, for magazine representations to resonate effectively with audiences they have to fit pre-existing concepts rather than offer new or different models. This was true for work with young men also. Magazine imagery appears not to be causal but perhaps to be reinforcing.

Studies of television viewing in relation to body dissatisfaction revealed that the amount of exposure was less significant than the nature of the programmes watched. Films, soap operas and music videos were found to correlate to the desire for thinness (Tiggemann and Pickering, 1996). Diet programmes also linked to dietary restraint (Polivy and Herman, 1985). Research by Harrison and Cantor (1997) found that the key influence on disordered eating among audiences, whether of television or print media, was attraction to thin 'stars'. This interpersonal comparison emerged as a strong variable in predicting self-starving behaviours in audiences, particularly when the respondent was already preoccupied with body image. Hence the quality, context and type of the mediated images were much more significant than the volume of exposure, with stars the most likely source of aspiration and low self-esteem. This process was marked among both white and black girls, but black girls were less likely to respond with body dissatisfaction and dieting and more likely to be satisfied with larger body size than white (Botta, 2000). Such surveys are indicative of rather than confirmative of effects and face the problem of effectively separating out the influences of media representations from other cultural influences. They also use self-reports to assess perceptions of size and shape and label shows/texts/characters as thin, average or heavy in sometimes unspecific ways.

These limitations have been partly addressed by experimental methodologies that have tended to show that glamorous body representations on television and in magazines can have short-term effects on self-image (Champion and Furnham, 1999; Heinberg and Thompson, 1995). This was more likely to be an effect on women audiences than on men (Kalodner, 1997). Two conditions ameliorated this effect on women in that it was less marked where the audience member was of a similar size and shape to the depicted model and/or where the audience member was self-confident in ways unrelated to their body image. The effect was also reduced when ordinary women rather than glamour models were used in the images (Posavac, 1998). Similar results were achieved in studies using televised advertising (Heinberg and Thompson, 1995), whilst Myers and Biocca (1992) found that as little as 30 minute's exposure to broadcast images could change young womens' perceptions of their own body size and shape but in an elastic manner in that perception fluctuated dependent on the type of 'ideal' images shown.

These studies go some way towards offering evidence of effect in relation to actual controlled viewing and reading but the methods of measuring both size and feelings about size remain a limitation and the experimental context is necessarily concerned with short-term effects according to researcher-defined and measurable variables whereas effects may be long-term and more subtle or insidious. Also, the focus on size/shape does not take into account other attractiveness features such as face, fashion sense or personality that might impact on evaluation and comparison. What appears to be most incontrovertible though is that already body-sensitive young women react most negatively towards themselves when presented with an abundance of thin beauty. The problem remains why some young women should develop such a body-sensitivity whilst others may have a more holistic sense of self-identity.

It is evident from media texts that they promulgate the current trend towards very slender female body types and evident from statistics that many people read or view these images on a regular basis. However, the research on the way audiences react to such imagery suggests the greatest impact may be on young women who already show a propensity towards eating disorders, but what is unclear is the source of that and why only some young women succumb to the thin aesthetic to the point of self-harm and even death. Research on anorexics indicates that some apparent causes of starving – hyperactive exercise, slow eating and obsession with food – are actually symptoms of the disease and parallel the reactions of other people in experimental or natural food-deprived situations (Epling et al., 1983). It may be that preference for and reactions to thin women in the media also result from self-starving rather than being causal, a phenomenon that may be exacerbated by the way anorexics overestimate their own body size, hence exaggerating their size in comparison to thin images (Freeman et al., 1983). Given these two effects of eating disorders, it would be surprising if exposure to a constant stream of slender beauty did not profoundly worsen already disturbed young women's sense of self.

The media representation of body images may at best therefore provide monotonously narrow, limited and rather conservative models of femininity and gender relations whilst concurrently exploiting the more liberated and ambitious attitudes of contemporary women while at worst it relentlessly confirms the lack of worth of already psychologically and physically disrupted girls. At best, media images of the feminine body are politically oppressive and commercially exploitative. At worst, they may justify a young woman's efforts at self-annihilation. At best, women may get some pleasure at purchasing pretty clothes and luxury treatments while they daydream about Prince Charming or they may parody and play with the 'looks' provided in subversive or creative ways. At worst, they will feel justified in trying to shrink because our culture writes sex and success on the body.

Culture, connotation and identity: concluding comments

Despite the plethora of constitutive images that bind sexual happiness and success to slenderness, not all women in media audiences diet to death – though arguably many, if not most, do diet in some way or exercise or use drugs such as nicotine or amphetamines or even surgery to reconstruct their bodies. Most women, we are told, are unhappy with their bodies and are many more times as likely to see themselves as overweight as are men (www.news.bbc.co.uk/1/hi/health/1320945.stm, accessed 10 November 2003). At the very least women try to display their best 'looks' and disguise or contain perceived worst aspects of shape or size. That thin-continuum places eating disorders in the pressurized context of sexual politics and commercial forces that characterize contemporary Western cultures and inform media messages, and may at least partly explain their apparent increase over the past three decades. On that continuum, where one in a hundred women may end up chronically damaged or dead, it becomes possible to at least make some sense of why they begin the route to self-reduction: it is all women's sensibility to be slender. Even those who claim pride in their fat can only know they are fat and seek to defend it because thin dominates the feminine.

Women 'read the slender body, and appropriate the messages they find there in different ways; those messages are enacted in the context of a personal situation and a personal history' (Woodward, 1997: 143). On top of already complex sets of choices and contradictions that constitute twenty-first-century womanhood, the extra burden, for many young women, of limited and demanding representations of women's selves and lives across the full range of the media is probably disappointing or diminishing or infuriating or daft or simply dull. For a few whose route to adult life is plagued by self-doubt their need to gain worth may contrive to make these illusory icons of sexual and financial success valid aspirational goals, particularly if they have internalized the idea that value and looks are commensurate and co-existent. Many others probably hover somewhere between the two positions sliding along a continuum of self-value judgements that are sometimes informed by feeling fat or thin and that sometimes lead to bouts of dieting or mad self-congratulatory shopping.

It would be amazing to be offered a mediated representation of the female world that shows women in their full variety, complexity and range of ability – amazing but unimaginable. But in many ways the limited way women are represented in the media is a salutory lesson not just on how that might effect the way they see themselves, but about how they are valued in life, in that for such images to resonate and be meaningful they must correspond with broader socio-cultural values and roles:

> How social groups are treated in cultural representation is part and parcel of how they are treated in life, ... poverty, harassment, self-hate and discrimination are shored up and instituted by representation. How we are seen determines in part how we are treated; how we treat others is based on how we see them; such seeing comes from representation. (Dyer, 1993: 1)

It is important to consider how media representation might impact not only on very vulnerable young women but on all women. More, it is important also to think what such representations say about our society and its attitudes towards women and how the media might be actively engaged in reproducing and legitimating ideas about femininity that neither comply with the reality of their experience and potential nor combat the ongoing inequities, abuses and self-violations which are the familiar everyday business of women's lives.

'By imposing a false standard of what is and what is not desirable' (Berger, 1972: 154), mass media representations of femininity and especially the female body not only set limits and controls on women's self-worth and the value assigned to them but nurture falsities by allying sexual and social success to size. However, those false standards serve powerful ideological and commercial interest groups which profit from encouraging the beauty aesthetic and are also only acceptable and attractive and pleasurable because they affirm for readers what is known and familiar about gender relations, revealing that less has changed since second-wave feminism than perhaps is indicated by legislation and the labour market. Girls are now expected to 'do it all' in competition with men, yet are immersed in a sex-saturated culture that seems only to measure feminine success according to looks – it is perhaps testimony to the strength and imagination of the great majority of women that they survive the onslaught, and an awful testimony to our culture that for some the thin aesthetic is a death sentence.

References

Abraham, S. and Llewellen-Jones, D. (1997) *Eating Disorders: The Facts*. Fourth edn. Oxford: Oxford University Press.

Abrams, K.K., Allen, L.R. and Gray, J.S. (1993) Disordered eating attitudes and behaviours, psychological adjustment, and ethnic activity: A comparison of Black and White female college students. *International Journal of Eating Disorders*, 14 (1), 49–57.

Altabe, M.N. and Thompson, J.K. (1992) Size estimation vs figural ratings of body image disturbance: relation to body dissatisfaction and eating dysfunction. *International Journal of Eating Disorders*, 11, 397–402.

Altabe, M.N. and Thompson, J.K. (1996) Body image: A cognitive self-schema? *Cognitive Therapy and Research*, 20, 171–193.

American Psychiatric Association (1987) *Diagnostic and Statistical Manual of Mental Disorders*. (DSM-III-R), 3rd edn, revised. Washington, DC: APA.

American Psychiatric Association (1994) Eating disorders, in *Diagnostic and Statistical Manual of Mental Disorders* (DSM-IV, 4th edn). Washington, DC: APA. pp. 539–550.

Anderson, A.E. and DiDomenico, L. (1992) Diet vs shape content of popular male and female magazines: A dose–response relationship to the incidence of eating disorders? *International Journal of Eating Disorders*, 11, 283–287.

Ang, I. (1985) *Watching Dallas: Soap Opera and the Melodramatic Imagination*. London: Methuen.

ANRED Anorexia Nervosa and Related Eating Disorders Inc. (http:www.anred. com/causes.html – 9.03.2003).

Arnett, J.J. (1995) Adolescents' use of media for self-socialisation, *Journal of Youth and Adolescence*, 24 (5), 511–518.

Arnold, R. (1999) Heroin chic, *Fashion Theory: The Journal of Dress, Body and Culture*, 3 September 1999, pp. 279–295.

Attie, I. and Brooks-Gunn, J. (1987) Development of eating problems in adolescent girls: A longitudinal study. *Developmental Psychology*, 25, 70–79.

Baker, P. (1997) 'The soft underbelly of the abdomen: Why men are obsessed with stomach muscles', in *Pictures of Lily: About Men by Men*. Exhibition catalogue, Underwood Gallery, London, September, pp. 18–23.

Bandura, A. (1977) *Social Learning Theory*. Englewood Cliffs, NJ: Prentice-Hall.

Banner, L. (1986) *American Beauty*. Chicago: University of Chicago Press.

Bardwell, M.D. and Choudry, I.Y. (2000) Body dissatisfaction and eating attitudes in slimming and fitness gyms in London and Lahore: A cross-cultural study. *European Eating Disorders Review*, 8 (3), 217–224.

Barker, M. and Petley, J. (eds) (1997) *Ill Effects*. London: Routledge.

Bar-Tel, D. and Saxe, L. (1976) Perceptions of similarly and dissimilarly attractive couples and individuals. *Journal of Personality and Social Psychology*, 33, 772–781.

Barthes, R. (1957) *Mythologies*. London: Paladin.

Barthes, R. (1977) *Image, Music, Text*. London: Fontana.

Baudrillard, J. (1983) *Simulations* (trans. Paul Foss et al.). New York: Semiotext(e).

Baudrillard, J. (1989) 'The anorexic ruins', in D. Kamper and C. Wulf (eds), translated by D. Antal. *Looking Back on the End of the World*. Semiotext(e) Foreign Agent Series: New York, pp. 29–45.

Beck, S.B., Ward-Hull, C.I. and McLear, P.M. (1976) Variables related to women's somatic preferences of the male and female body. *Journal of Personality and Social Psychology*, 34, 1200–1210.

Beebe, D.W., Hornbeck, G.N., Schober, A., Lane, M. and Rosa, K. (1996) Is body focus restricted to self-evaluation? Body focus in the evaluation of self and others. *International Journal of Eating Disorders*, 20, 415–422.

Beetham, M. and Boardman, K. (eds) (2001) *Victorian Women's Magazines*. Manchester: MUP.

Belch, G.E., Belch, M.A. and Villarreal, A. (1987) Effects of advertising communications: review of research. *Research in Marketing*, 9, 59–117.

Bell, R.M. (1985) *Holy Anorexia*. Chicago: University of Chicago Press.

Bem, S.L. (1977) On the utility of alternative procedures for assessing psychological androgyny. *Journal of Consulting and Clinical Psychology*, 45, 196–205.

Bemis, K.M. (1987) The present status of operant conditioning for the treatment of anorexia nervosa. *Behaviour Modification*, 11, 432–463.

Bennett, T. (1982): 'Theories of the media, theories of society', in M. Gurevitch, T. Bennett, J. Curran and J. Woollacott (eds), *Culture, Society and the Media*. Buckingham: Open University Press.

Benoy, W.J. (1982) The credibility of physically attractive communicators: A review. *Journal of Advertising*, 11 (3), 15–24.

Benson, S. (1999) 'The body, health and eating disorders', in K. Woodward (ed.) (1999) *Identity and Difference*. London: Sage.

Ben-Tovim, D.I., Whitehead, J. and Crisp, A.H. (1979) A controlled study of the perception of body width in anorexia nervosa. *Journal of Psychosomatic Research*, 23, 267–272.

Berger, J. (1972) *Ways of Seeing*. London: BBC and Penguin.

Berscheid, E., Walster, E. and Bohrnstedt, G. (1973) The happy American body: A survey report. *Psychology Today*, 7, 119–131.

Biocca, F.A. (1991) 'Viewer's mental models of political ads: Towards a theory of semantic processing of television', in F. Biocca (ed.), *Television and Political Advertising: Vol. 1. Psychological Processes*. Hillsdale, NJ: Lawrence Erlbaum Associates. pp. 27–91.

Birtchnell, S., Dolan, B. and Lacey, J. (1987) Body image distortion in non-eating disordered women. *International Journal of Eating Disorders*, 6 (3), 385–391.

Bivans, A.M. (1991) *Miss America: In Pursuit of the Crown*. Master Media: New York.

BMA (2000) *Eating Disorders, Body Image and the Media*. London: British Medical Association.

Bordo S. (1985) Anorexia nervosa: Psychopathology as the crystalization of culture. *The Philosophical Forum.* 17 (2), 73–105.

Bordo, S. (1993) *Unbearable Weight: Feminism, Western Culture, and the Body.* Berkeley, CA: University of California Press.

Borzekowski, D.L., Robinson, T.N. and Killen, J.D. (2000) Does the camera add 10 pounds? Media use, perceived importance of appearance and weight concerns among teenage girls. *Journal of Adolescent Health,* 26 (1), 36–41.

Boskind-Lodahl, M. (1976) Cinderella's stepsisters: A feminist perspective on anorexia nervosa and bulimia. *Signs: Journal of Women in Culture and Society,* 2, 342–356.

Boskind-Lodahl, M. and Sirlin, J. (1977) The gorging–purging syndrome. *Psychology Today,* March, pp. 50–52, 82, 85.

Boskind-White, M. and White, W. (1983) *Bulimarexia: The Binge/Purge Cycle.* New York: W.W. Norton.

Botta, R.A. (1999) Television images and adolescent girls' body image disturbance. *Journal of Communication,* 49, 22–41.

Botta, R.A. (2000) The mirror of television: A comparison of black and white adolescents' body image. *Journal of Communication,* 50 (3), 144–159.

Brodsky, C.M. (1954) A study of norms for body form–behaviour relationships. *Anthropological Quarterly,* 27, 91–101.

Brown, J.D., Novick, N.J., Lord, K.A. and Richards, J.M. (1992) When Gulliver travels: Social context, psychological closures, and self-appraisals. *Journal of Personality and Social Psychology,* 62, 717–727.

Brown, T.A., Johnson, W.G., Bergeron, K.C., Keeton, W.P. and Cash, T.F. (1988) *Assessment of Body-related Cognitions in Bulimia: The Body Image Automatic Thoughts Questionnaire.* Paper presented at the Association for the Advancement of Behaviour Therapy, New York.

Bruch, H. (1962) Perceptual and conceptual disturbances in anorexia nervosa. *Psychosomatic Medicine,* 24, 187–194.

Bruch, H. (1973) *Eating Disorders.* New York: Basic Books.

Bruch, H. (1978) *The Golden Cage.* Cambridge, MA: Harvard University Press.

Bruch, H. and Eurman, L. (1980) Social attitudes toward patients with anorexia. *American Journal of Psychiatry,* 137, 631–632.

Bryant J. and Zillmann D. (eds) (1991) *Responding to the Screen: Reception and Reaction Processes.* Hillsdale, NJ: Lawrence Erlbaum Associates, pp. 45–63.

Bryant, J. and Zillman, D. (1994) *Media Effects: Advances in Theory and Research.* Hillsdale, NJ: Lawrence Erlbaum.

Buchman, A.L., Ament, M.E., Weiner, M., Kodner, A. and Mayer, E.A. (1994) Reversal of megaduodenum and duodenal dysmotility associated with improvement in nutritional status in primary anorexia nervosa. *Digestive Diseases and Sciences,* 39 (2), 433–440.

Buss, D.M. (1989) Sex differences in human mate selection: Evolutionary hypotheses tested in 37 cultures. *Behavioural and Brain Sciences,* 12, 1–49.

Butcher, H. (1981) 'Images of women in the media', in S. Cohen and J. Young (eds) (1981) *The Manufacture of News: Deviance, Social Problems and the Mass Media.* London: Constable.

Butler, Judith (1990) *Gender Trouble – Feminism and the Subversion of Identity*. London: Routledge.

Button, E.J., Loan, P., Davies, J. and Sanuga-Burke, E.J. (1997) Self-esteem, eating problems and psychological well-being in a cohort of school girls aged 15–16: A questionnaire and interview study. *International Journal of Eating Disorders*, 21, 39–47.

Byely, L., Archibald, A.B., Graber, J. and Brooks-Gunn, J. (2000) A prospective study of familial and social influences on girls' body image and dieting. *International Journal of Eating Disorders*, 28 (2), 155–164.

Calden, G., Lundy, R. and Schlafer, R. (1959) Sex differences in body concepts. *Journal of Consulting Psychology*, 23, 378.

Cash, T.F. (1990) 'The psychology of physical appearance: Aesthetics, attributes and images', in T.F. Cash and T. Pruzinsky (eds), *Body Images: Development, Deviance and Change*. New York: Guilford Press.

Cash, T.F. (1997) *The Body Image Workbook: An 8–Step Program for Learning to Like Your Looks*. Oakland, CA: New Harburger.

Cash, T.F. and Brown, T.A. (1989) Gender and body images: Stereotypes and realities. *Sex Roles*, 21, 357–369.

Cash, T.F. and Green, G.K. (1986) Body weight and body image among college women: Perception, cognition and affect. *Journal of Personality Assessment*, 50 (2), 290–301.

Cash, T.F. and Henry, P.E. (1995) Women's body images: The results of a national survey in the USA. *Sex Roles*, 33, 19–28.

Cash, T.F. and Szymanski, M.L. (1995) The development and validation of the Body-Image Ideals Questionnaire. *Journal of Personality Assessment*, 64, 466–477.

Cash, T.F., Cash, D.W. and Butters, J.W. (1983) Mirror, mirror on the wall ...? Contrast effects and self-evaluations of physical attractiveness. *Personality and Social Psychology*, 9, 359–364.

Cash, T.F., Lewis, R.J. and Keeton, P. (1987) Development and Validation of the Body-Image Automatic Thoughts Questionnaire: A Measure of Body-related Cognitions. Paper presented at the meeting of the South Eastern Psychological Association, Atlanta, GA.

Cash, T.F., Winstead, B.A. and Janda, L.H. (1986) The great American shape-up. *Psychology Today*, 20, 30–37.

Cattanach, L. and Rodin, J. (1988) Psychosocial components of the stress process in bulimia. *International Journal of Eating Disorders*, 7, 75–88.

Cattarin, J., Thompson, J.K., Thomas, C.M. and Williams, R. (2000) Body image, mood and televised images of attractiveness: The role of social comparison. *Journal of Social and Clinical Psychology*, 19 (2), 220–239.

Champion, H. and Furnham, A. (1999) The effect of the media on body satisfaction in adolescent girls. *European Eating Disorders Review*, 7, 213–228.

Chandler, D. (2003) *Marxist Media Theory*. http://www.aber.ac.uk/media/Documents/marxism/marxism08.html. Accessed 12 march 2003.

Chapman, J. (2000) Alarm as steroid pushers muscle in on teenagers. *Daily Mail*, 6 September, p. 31.

Charles, N. and Kerr, M. (1986) Food for feminist thought. *The Sociological Review*, 34, 537–572.

Chernin, K. (1981) *The Obsession: Reflections on the Tyranny of Slenderness*. New York: Harper and Row.

Chernin, K. (1983) *Womansize*. London: The Women's Press.

Chibnall, S. (1977) *Law and Order News*. London: Tavistock.

Chipkevitch, E. (1994) Brain tumours and anorexia syndrome. *Brain and Development*, 16 (3): 175–182.

Chisholm, K. (2002) *Hungry Hell: What It's Really Like to be Anorexic – A Personal Story*. London: Short Books.

Christmas, L. (1997) *Chaps of Both Sexes*. Devizes: BT Forum.

Clark, K. (1980) *Feminine Beauty*. New York: Rizzoli.

Clark, K. (1992) 'The linguistics of blame: representations of women in the *Sun's* reporting of crimes of sexual violence', in M. Toolan (ed.), *Language, Text and Context: Essays in Stylistics*. London: Routledge.

Clifford, E. (1971) Body satisfaction in adolescence. *Perceptual and Motor Skills*, 33, 119–125.

Cohane and Pope (2001) *International Journal of Eating Disorders*, 29, 373–379. cited at http://www.doctorbob.com/2001k_04_11news05.html

Cohen, J., Mutz, D., Price, V. and Gunther, A. (1988) Perceived impact of defamation: An experiment on third-person effects. *Public Opinion Quarterly*, 52, 161–173.

Cohn, L.D. and Adler, N.E. (1992) Female and male perceptions of ideal body shapes. *Psychology of Women Quarterly*, 16, 69–79.

Colahan, M. and Senior, R. (1995) 'Family patterns in eating disorders: going round in circles, getting nowhere fasting', in G. Szmukler, C. Dare and J. Treasure (eds) *Handbook of Eating Disorders: Theory, Treatment and Research*. Chichester: Wiley. pp. 243–257.

Collins, M. (1991) Body figure perceptions and preferences among preadolescent children. *International Journal of Eating Disorders*, 10, 199–208.

Cooper, M. (1997) Do interpretive biases maintain eating disorders? *Behaviour Research and Therapy*, 35, 619–626.

Cooper, P.J., Taylor, M.J., Cooper, Z. and Fairburn, C.G. (1987) The development and validation of the Body Shape Questionnaire. *International Journal of Eating Disorders*, 6, 485–494.

Cooper, Z. and Fairburn, C.G. (1987) The Eating Disorder Examination: A semi-structured interview for the assessment of the specific psychopathology of eating disorders. *International Journal of Eating Disorders*, 6, 1–8.

Counihan, C. (1999) *The Anthropology of Food and Body: Gender, Meaning and Power*. London: Routledge.

Crandall, C. and Martinez, R. (1996) Culture, ideology, and anti-fat attitudes. *Personality and Social Psychology Bulletin*, 22, 1165–1176.

Crisp, A.H. (1965) Some aspects of the evolution, presentation and follow-up of anorexia nervosa. *Proceedings of the Royal Society of Medicine*, 58, 814–820.

Crisp, A.H. (1970) Anorexia nervosa: 'Feeding disorder,' nervous malnutrition or weight phobia?, *World Review of Nutrition*, 12, 452–504.

Crisp, A. (1992) *Anorexia Nervosa: Let Me Be*. Hove: Lawrence Erlbaum.

Crisp, A.H., Palmer, R.L. and Kalucy, R.S. (1976) How common is anorexia nervosa? A prevalence study. *British Journal of Psychiatry*, 218, 549–554.

Cusumano, D.L. and Thompson, K.J. (1997) Body image and body shape ideals in magazines: Exposure, awareness and internalization. *Sex Roles*, 37 (9/10), 701–721.

Dare, C. and Crowther, C. (1995) 'Psychodynamic models of eating disorders', in G. Szmuler, C. Dare and J. Treasure (eds), *Handbook of Eating Disorders: Theory, Treatment and Research*. Chichester: Wiley.

David, P. and Johnson, M.A. (1998) The role of self in third person effects about body image. *Journal of Communication*, 48 (4), 37–58.

Davis, C. and Katzman, M. (1997) Charting new territory: Body esteem, weight satisfaction, depression and self-esteem among Chinese males and females in Hong Kong. *Sex Roles*, 36, 449–459.

De Silva, P. (1995a) 'Cognitive-behavioural models of eating disorders', in G. Szmukler, C. Dare and J. Treasure (eds), *Handbook of Eating Disorders: Theory, Treatment and Research*. Chichester: Wiley.

De Silva, P. (1995b) 'Family models of eating disorders', in G. Szmukler, C. Dare and J. Treasure (eds), *Handbook of Eating Disorders: Theory, Treatment and Research*. Chichester: Wiley.

Demarest, J. and Allen, R. (2000) Body image: gender, ethnic and age differences. *Journal of Social Psychology*, 140 (4), 465–472.

Derrida, J. (1981) *Dissemination* (trans. Barbara Johnson). London: Athlone Press.

Derry, P.A. and Kuiper, N.A. (1981) Schematic processing and self-reference in clinical depression. *Journal of Abnormal Psychology*, 90, 286–297.

Dibiase, W.J. and Hjelle, L.A. (1968) Body-image stereotypes and body-type preferences among male college students. *Perceptual & Motor Skills*, 27, 1143–1146.

Dolan, B. (1989) Cross-cultural aspects of anorexia nervosa and bulimia: A review. *International Journal of Eating Disorders*, 10 (1), 67–78.

Dolan, B. and Gitzinger, I. (1991) *Why Women?: Gender Issues and Eating Disorders*. London: St Georges Hospital.

Dorer, D.J., Keel, P.K., Eddy K.T., Charat, V., Benn, R.C., Franko, D.L. and Herzog, D.B. (2002) Substance use disorders in women with eating disorders. Conference paper, International Eating Disorders Conference 2002, at http:www.hedc.org/whatwedo/abstracts.htm.

Douglas, S.J. (1994) *Where the Girls are: Growing up Female with the Mass Media*. New York: New York Times Books.

Downs, A.C. and Harrison, S.K. (1985) Embarrassing age spots or just plain ugly? Physical attractiveness stereotyping as an instrument of sexism on American television commercials. *Sex Roles*, 13 (1/2), 9–19.

Druss, R.G. and Silverman, J.A. (1979) Body image and perfectionism of ballerinas: Comparison and contrast with anorexia nervosa. *General Hospital Psychiatry*, 1, 115–121.

Duddle, M. (1973) An increase of anorexia nervosa in a university population. *British Journal of Psychiatry*, 123, 711–712.

Dworkin, A. (1981) *Pornography: Men Possessing Women*. London: Women's Press.

Dworkin, A. (1991) 'Against the male flood: censorship, pornography and equality', in R. Baird and S. Rosenbaum (eds), *Pornography*. Prometheus: New York.

Dwyer, J.T., Feldman, J.J. and Mayer, J. (1967) Adolescent dieters: Who are they? Physical characteristics, attitudes and dieting practices of adolescent girls. *American Journal of Clinical Nutrition*, 20, 1045–1056.

Dwyer, J.T., Feldman, J.J. and Mayer, J. (1970) The social psychology of dieting. *Journal of Health & Social Behaviour*, 11, 269–287.

Dwyer, J.T., Feldman, J.J., Sletzer, C.C. and Mayer, J. (1969) Adolescent attitudes toward weight and appearance. *Journal of Nutrition Education*, 1, 14–19.

Dyer, R. (1979/2000) 'Living stars', in J. Hollows, P. Hutchings and M. Jancovich, (eds), *The Film Studies Reader*. London: Edward Arnold. pp. 128–133.

Dyer R. (1993) *A Matter of Images*. London: Routledge.

Easthope, A. and McGowan K. (eds) (1992) *A Critical and Cultural Theory Reader*. Buckingham: Open University Press.

Ehrensing, R.H. and Weitzman, E.L. (1970) The mother–daughter relationship in anorexia nervosa. *Psychosomatic Medicine*, 32, 201–208.

El Badri, S.M. and Lewis M.A. (1991) Anorexia nervosa associated with Klinefelter's syndrome. *Comprehensive Psychiatry*, 32 (4), 317–319.

Epling, W.P., Pierce, W.D. and Stefan, L. (1983) A theory of activity-based anorexia. *International Journal of Eating Disorders*, 3, 22–46.

Evans, E.D., Rutberg, J., Sather, C. and Turner, C. (1991) Content analysis of contemporary teen magazines for adolescent females. *Youth and Society*, 23 (1), 99–120.

Fairclough, N. (1992) Discourse and text: Linguistic inter textual analysis within discourse analysis. *Discourse and Society*, 3 (2), 193–217.

Fairclough, N. (1995) *Media Discourse*. London: Edward Arnold.

Fallon, A. (1990) 'Culture in the mirror: Sociocultural determinants of body image', in T.F. Cash and T. Pruzinsky (eds), *Body Images: Development, Deviance and Change*. New York: Guilford Press. pp. 80–109.

Fallon, A. and Rozin, P. (1985) Sex differences in perceptions of desirable body shape. *Journal of Personality and Social Psychology*, 94, 102–105.

Faludi, S. (1992) *Backlash: The Undeclared War Against Women*. London: Chatto.

Felker, D.W. (1972) Social stereotyping of male and female body types with differing facial expressions by elementary age boys and girls. *Journal of Psychology*, 82, 151–154.

Festinger, L. (1954) A theory of social comparison processes. *Human Relations*, 7, 117–140.

Fischer, E. and Halpenny, K. (1993) 'The nature and influence of idealised images of men in advertising', in J.A. Costa (ed.), *Gender and Consumer Behaviour, Proceedings of the Second Conference*. Salt Lake City, UT: University of Utah Printing Service. p. 196.

Fisher, S. (1970) *Body Experience in Fantasy and Behaviour*. New York: Appleton–Century–Croft.

Ford, C.S. and Beach, F.A. (1952) *Patterns of Sexual Behaviour*. New York: Ace Books.

Forston, M.T. and Stanton, A.L. (1992) Self-discrepancy theory as a framework for understanding bulimic symptomatology and associated distress. *Journal of Social and Clinical Psychology*, 11, 103–118.

Foucault, M. (1970) *The Order of Things*. London: Tavistock.

Foucault, M. (1978/1992) 'From the history of sexuality', in A. Easthope and K. McGowan (eds), *A Critical and Cultural Theory Reader*. Buckingham: Open University Press.

Foucault, M. (1980) *Power/Knowledge*. Brighton: Harvester.

Foucault, M. (1981) *The History of Sexuality Volume One: An Introduction*. Harmondsworth: Penguin.

Fouts, G. and Vaughan, K. (2002) Television situation comedies: Male weight, negative references and audience reactions. *Sex Roles*, 45 (11/12), 439–442.

Fowler, R., Kress, G., Hodge, R. and Trew, T. (1979) *Language and Control*. London: Routledge Kegan Paul.

Franzoi, S.L. and Herzog, M.E. (1987) Judging physical attractiveness: What body aspects do we use? *Personality and Social Psychology Bulletin*, 13, 19–33.

Franzoi, S.L. and Shields, S.A. (1984) The Body Esteem Scale: Multidimensional structure and sex differences in a college population. *Journal of Personality Assessment*, 48, 173–178.

Freeman, R.J., Thomas, C.D., Solyom, L. and Miles, J.E. (1983) 'Body image disturbances in anorexia nervosa: A re-examination and a new technique', in P.C. Darby, P.E. Garfinkel, D.M. Garner and D.V. Cosana (eds), *Anorexia Nervosa: Recent Developments in Research*. New York: Liss. pp. 117–127.

Freud, S. (1905/1983) 'Case histories 1: Dora and little Hans', in J. Strachey (ed.), *Sigmund Freud 8: Case Histories 1*. Harmondsworth: Penguin.

Fries, H. (1977) 'Studies on secondary amenorrhoea, anorectic behaviour, and body image perception: Importance for the early recognition of anorexia nervosa', in R.A. Vigersky (ed.), *Anorexia Nervosa*. New York: Raven Press. pp. 163–176.

Furlong, A. (1977) *The Impact of Feelings of Subjective Deformity on Configurational Body-size Perception*. Unpublished doctoral dissertation, University of Montreal.

Furnham, A. and Alibhai, N. (1983) Cross cultural differences in the perception of female body shapes. *Psychological Medicine*, 13, 829–837.

Furnham, A., Hester, C. and Weir, C. (1990) Sex differences in the preferences for specific female body shapes. *Sex Roles*, 22 (11/12), 743–754.

Fursland, A. (1986) 'Eve was framed: Food and sex and women's shame', in M. Lawrence (ed.), *Fed Up and Hungry: Women, Oppression and Food*. London: Women's Press. pp. 8–15.

Gagnard, A. (1986) From feast to famine: Depiction of ideal body type in magazine advertising, 1950–1984. *Proceedings of the American Academy of Advertising, USA*, 41, 451–459.

Galtung J. and Ruge M. (1981) 'Structuring and selecting news', in S. Cohen and J. Young (eds) *The Manufacture of News: Deviance, Social Problems and the Mass Media*. London: Constable.

Garfinkel, P.E., Garner, D.M., Rose, J., Darby, P.L., Brandes, J.S., O'Hanlon, J. and
Walsh, N. (1983) A comparison of characteristics in the families of patients with
anorexia nervosa and normal controls. *Psychological Medicine*, 13, 821–828.

Garfinkel, P.E. and Garner, D.M. (1982) *Anorexia Nervosa: A Multidimensional
Perspective*. New York: Brunner/Mazel.

Garner, D.M. (1997) The Body Image Survey. *Psychology Today*, January/February,
32–84.

Garner, D.M. and Garfinkel, P.E. (1980) Socio-cultural factors in the development
of anorexia nervosa. *Psychological Medicine*, 10, 647–656.

Garner, D.M. and Garfinkel, P.E. (1981) Body image in anorexia nervosa:
Measurement, theory and clinical implications. *International Journal of Psychiatry
in Medicine*, 11, 283–284.

Garner, D.M., Garfinkel, P.E. and Olmsted, M. (1983) 'An overview of socio-
cultural factors in the development of anorexia nervosa', in P.L. Darby,
P.E. Garfinkel, D.M. Garner and D.V. Coscina (eds), *Anorexia Nervosa: Recent
Developments*. New York: Allan R. Liss. pp. 65–82.

Garner, D.M., Garfinkel, P.E., Schwartz, D. and Thompson, M. (1980) Cultural
expectations of thinness in women. *Psychological Reports*, 47, 483–491.

Garner, D.M., Garfinkel, P.E., Stancer, H.C. and Moldofsky, H. (1976) Body image
disturbances in anorexia nervosa and obesity. *Psychosomatic Medicine*, 38 (5),
227–336.

Geiselman, R.E., Haight, N.A. and Kimata, L.G. (1984) Context effects on the perceived physical attractiveness of faces. *Journal of Experimental Social Psychology*,
20, 409–424.

Gerbner, G., Gross, L., Morgan, M. and Signorielli, N. (1980) The 'mainstreaming'
of America: Violence profile No. 11. *Journal of Communication*, 30, 10–29.

Gerrard, N. (2003) *The Observer*, 13th May.

Gilroy, P. (1999) 'Diaspora and the detours of identity', in K. Woodward (ed.),
Identity and Difference. London: Sage.

Gitter, A., Lomranz, J. and Saxe, L. (1982) Factors affecting perceived attractiveness
of male physiques by American and Israeli students. *Journal of Social Psychology*,
118, 167–175.

Gitter, A., Lomranz, J., Saxe, L. and Bar-Tel, D. (1983) Cultural expectations of thinness in women. *Journal of Social Psychology*, 121, 7–13.

Glasgow University Media Group (1976) *Bad News*. London: Routledge.

Glasgow University Media Group (1980) *More Bad News*. London: Routledge
Kegan Paul.

Glasgow University Media Group (1982) *Really Bad News*. Glasgow: Readers and
Writers.

Glasgow University Media Group (1985) *War and Peace News*. Milton Keynes:
Open University Press.

Glassner, B. (1988) *Bodies: Why We Look the Way We Do and How We Feel About It*.
New York: Plenum.

Gledhill, C. (1997) 'Genre and gender: The case of soap opera', in S. Hall (ed.),
Representation: Cultural Representations and signifying Practices. Milton Keynes:
Open University Press. pp. 337–386.

Goethals, G.R. (1986) Social comparison theory: Psychology from the lost and found. *Personality and Social Psychology Bulletin*, 12 (3), 261–278.

Gonick, M. (1997) Reading selves: Refashioning identity – Teen magazines and their readers. *Curriculum Studies*, 5 (1), 69–86.

Gonzalez-Levin, A. and Smolak, L. (1995) Relationships between Television and Eating Problems in Middle School Girls. Paper presented at the meeting of the Society for Research in Child Development, Indianapolis, IN.

Goodman, W.C. (1995) *The Invisible Woman: Confronting Weight Prejudice in America*. Los Angeles, CA: Gurze.

Goodsitt, A. (1977) 'Narcissistic disturbances in anorexia nervosa', in S.C. Feinstein and P. Giovacchini, (eds), *Adolescent Psychiatry* Vol. V: Developmental and Clinical Studies. New York: Jason Aronson, Inc.

Griffiths, J.A. and McCabe, M.P. (2000) The influence of significant others on distorted eating and body dissatisfaction among early adolescent girls. *European Eating Disorders Review*, 8 (4), 301–314.

Grogan, S. (1999) *Body Image: Understanding Body Dissatisfaction in Men, Women and Children*. London: Routledge.

Grogan, S., Williams, Z. and Conner, M. (1996) The effects of viewing same-gender photographic models on body esteem. *Psychology of Women Quarterly*, 20, 569–575.

Guillan, E.O. and Barr, S.I. (1994) Nutrition, dieting and fitness messages in a magazine for adolescent women, 1970–1990. *Journal of Adolescent Health*, 15, 464–472.

Gull, W.W. (1874) Anorexia nervosa. *Transactions of the Clinical Society*, 7 (2), 22–28.

Gunter, B. (2000) *Media Research Methods*. London: Sage.

Gunter, B. (2002) *Media Sex: What Are the Issues?* London: Lawrence Erlbaum.

Gunter, B., Harrison, J. and Wykes, M. (2003) *Violence on Television: Distribution, Form, Context and Themes*. Hillsdale, NJ: Lawrence Erlbaum.

Gunther, A. (1991) What we think others think: Cause and consequence in the third-person effect. *Communication Research*, 18, 355–372.

Gunther, A. (1992) Biased press or biased public? Attitudes toward media coverage of social groups. *Public Opinion Quarterly*, 5, 147–167.

Gunther, A. (1995) Overrating the X-rating: The third-person perception and support for censorship of pornography. *Journal of Communication*, 45 (1), 27–38.

Gunther, A. and Mundy, P. (1993) Biased optimism and the third-person effect. *Journalism Quarterly*, 70, 58–67.

Gunther, A. and Thorsen, E. (1992) Perceived persuasive effects of product commercials and public service announcements: Third-person effects in new domains. *Communication Research*, 19, 574–596.

Haimes, A.L. and Katz, J.K. (1988) Sexual and social maturity versus social conformity in restraining anorectic, bulimia and borderline women. *International Journal of Eating Disorders*, 7, 331–341.

Hall, S. (1973/1980) 'Encoding/decoding', in S. Hall, D. Hobson, A. Lowe and P. Willis (eds), *Culture, Media, Language*. London: Hutchinson.

Hall, S. (ed.) (1997) *Representations: Cultural Representations and Signifying Practices*. London: Sage.

Halmi, K.A. (1974) Anorexia nervosa: Demographic and clinical features in 94 cases. *Psychosomatic Medicine*, 36, 18–25.

Halmi, K.A., Goldberg, S.C. and Cunningham, S. (1977) Perceptual distortion of body image in adolescent girls: Distortion of body image in adolescence. *Psychological Medicine*, 7, 253–257.

Hamilton, K. and Waller, G. (1993) Media influences on body size estimation in anorexia and bulimia: An experimental study. *British Journal of Psychiatry*, 162, 837–840.

Hamilton, L.H., Brooks-Gunn, J. and Warren, M.P. (1985) Sociocultural influences on eating disorders in professional female ballet dancers. *International Journal of Eating Disorders*, 4, 465–478.

Hargreaves, D. (2002) Idealized women in TV ads make girls feel bad. *Journal of Social and Clinical Psychology*, 21, 287–308.

Harmatz, M.G., Gronendyke, J. and Thomas, T. (1985) The underweight male: The unrecognised problem group in body image research. *Journal of Obesity and Weight Regulation*, 4, 258–267.

Harris, M., Harris, S. and Bochner, S. (1982) Fat, four-eyed and female: Stereotypes of obesity, glasses and gender. *Journal of Applied Social Psychology*, 10, 503–516.

Harrison, K. (1997) Does interpersonal attraction to thin media personalities promote eating disorders? *Journal of Broadcasting and Electronic Media*, 41, 478–500.

Harrison, K. (1999) Torn between Two Selves: Thin-ideal Media, Self-discrepancies and Eating Disorders in Adolescents. Paper presented at International Communication Association Conference, San Francisco, CA, May.

Harrison, K. (2000a) Television viewing, fat stereotyping, body shape standards, and eating disorder symptomatology in grade school children. *Communication Research*, 27 (5), 617–640.

Harrison, K. (2000b) The body electric: Thin-ideal media and eating disorders in adolescents. *Journal of Communication*, 50 (3), 119–143.

Harrison. K. and Cantor, J. (1997) The relationship between media consumption and eating disorders. *Journal of Communication*, 47 (1), 40–67.

Hart, A. (1991) *Understanding the Media*. London: Routledge.

Hartley, J. (1998) 'Juvenation: news, girls and power', in C. Carter, G. Branston and S. Allan, (eds), *News, Gender and Power*. London: Routledge.

Hawkes, T. (1977) *Structuralism and Semiotics*. London: Methuen.

Heatherton, T.F., Herman, C.P., Polivy, J., King, G.A. and Mcgee, S.T. (1988) The (mis)measurement of restraint: An analysis of conceptual and psychonomic issues. *Journal of Abnormal Psychology*, 97, 19–28.

Heidensohn F. (1985) *Women and Crime*. London: Macmillan.

Heinberg, L.J. (1996) 'Theories of body image: Perceptual, developmental, and sociocultural factors', in J.K. Thompson (ed.), *Body Image, Eating Disorders and Obesity: An Integrative Guide to Assessment and Treatment*. Washington, DC: American Psychological Association. pp. 27–48.

Heinberg, L.J. and Thompson, J.K. (1992a) The effects of figure size feedback (positive vs negative) and target comparison group (particularistic vs universalistic) on body image disturbance. *International Journal Eating Disorders*, 12, 441–448.

Heinberg, L.J. and Thompson, J.K. (1992b) Social comparison: Gender, target importance ratings and relation to body image disturbance. *Journal of Social Behaviour and Personality*, 7, 335–344.

Heinberg, L.J. and Thompson, J.K. (1995) Body image and televised images of thinness and attractiveness: A controlled laboratory investigation. *Journal of Social and Clinical Psychology*, 14 (4), 325–338.

Heinberg, L.J., Thompson, J.K., and Stormer, S. (1995) Sociocultural attitudes towards appearance scale (SATAQ). *International Journal of Eating Disorders*, 17, 81–89.

Heinberg, L.J., Wood, K.C. and Thompson, J.K. (1995) 'Body image', in V.L. Rickert (ed.), *Adolescent Nutrition: Assessment and Management*. New York: Chapman and Hall, pp. 136–156.

Henwood, K., Gill, R. and Mclean, C. (1999) Masculinities and the Body: Mapping Men's Psychologies. End of Grant report to Unilever Research, Norwich, University of East Anglia, School of Medicine, Health Policy and Practice.

Henwood, K., Gill, R. and Mclean, C. (2002) The changing man. *The Psychologist*, 15 (4), 182–186.

Herman, C.P. and Mack, D. (1975) Restrained and unrestrained eating. *Journal of Personality*, 43, 647–660.

Herman, C.P. and Polivy, J. (1975) Anxiety, restraint and eating behaviour. *Journal of Abnormal Psychology*, 84, 666–672.

Herman, C.P. and Polivy, J. (1980) 'Restrained eating', in A. Stunkard (ed.), *Obesity*. Philadelphia: W.B. Saunders, pp. 208–239.

Herman, E. and Chomsky, N. (1988) *Manufacturing Consent*. New York: Pantheon.

Hertzler, A.A. and Grun, I. (1990) Potential nutrition messages in magazines read by college students. *Adolescence*, 25, 717–724.

Heunemann, R.L., Shapiro, L.R., Hampton, M.C. and Mitchell, B.W. (1966) A longitudinal study of gross body composition and body conformation and their association with food and activity in a teenage population. *American Journal of Clinical Nutrition*, 18, 325–338.

Hibscher, J.A. and Herman, C.P. (1977) Obesity, dieting and the expression of obese characteristics. *Journal of Comparative and Physiological Psychology*, 91, 374–380.

Higgins, E.T. (1987) Self-discrepancy: A theory relating self and affect. *Psychological Review*, 94, 319–340.

Hofschire, L.J. and Greenberg, B.S. (2002) 'Media's impact on adolescents' body dissatisfaction', in J.D. Brown, J.R. Steele, and K. Walsh-Childers (eds), *Sexual Teens, Sexual Media*. Hillsdale, NJ: Lawrence Erlbaum.

Hoggart, R. (1972) *On Culture and Communication*. New York: Oxford University Press.

Hoggart, R. (1958) *The Uses of Literacy*. New York: Oxford University Press.

Holland, P. (1998) 'The politics of the smile: "Soft news" and the sexualisation of the popular press', in C. Carter, G. Branston and S. Allan (eds) *News, Gender and Power*. London: Routledge.

Hollows, J. (2000) *Feminism, Femininity and Popular Culture*. Manchester: Manchester University Press.

Hollows, J., Hutchings, P. and Jancovich, M. (eds) (2000) *The Film Studies Reader*. London: Edward Arnold.

Holway, W. (1989*) Subjectivity and Method in Psychology: Gender, Meaning and Science*. London: Sage.

Inglis, F. (1990) *Media Theory. An Introduction*. Oxford: Blackwell.

Irving, L. (1990) Mirror images: Effects of the standard of beauty on the self and body esteem of women exhibiting varying levels of bulimic symptoms. *Journal of Social and Clinical Psychology*, 9, 230–242.

Jackman, L.P., Williamson, D.A., Netemeyer, R.G. and Anderson, D.A. (1995) Do weight preoccupied women misinterpret ambiguous stimuli related to body size? *Cognitive Therapy and Research*, 19, 341–355.

Jacobi, L. and Cash, T.F. (1994) In pursuit of the perfect appearance: Discrepancies among self-ideal percepts of multiple physical attributes. *Journal of Applied Social Psychology*, 24, 379–396.

Jacobovits, C., Halstead, P., Kelley, L., Roe, D.A. and Young, C.M. (1977) Eating habits and nutrient intakes of college women over a thirty-year period. *Journal of the American Dietetic Association*, 71, 405–411.

Jewkes, Y. and Sharp, K. (2003) 'Crime, deviance and the disembodied self: Transcending the dangers of corporeality', in Y. Jewkes (ed.), *Dot-cons*. Cullompton: Willan.

Johnson, C. and Connors, M.E. (1987) *The Etiology and Treatment of Bulimia Nervosa: A Biopsychosocial Perspective*. New York: Basic Books.

Johnson, C.L., Stuckey, M.K., Lewis, L.D. and Schwartz, D.M. (1982) Bulimia: A descriptive survey of 316 cases. *International Journal of Eating Disorders*, 2, 3–15.

Kahneman, D. and Tversky, A. (1973) On the psychology of prediction. *Psychological Review*, 80, 237–257.

Kalodner, C.R. (1997) Media influences on male and female non-eating disordered college students: A significant issue. *Eating Disorders: The Journal of Treatment and Prevention*, 5, 47–57.

Kamal, N., Chami, T., Andersen, A. Rosell, F.A., Schuster, M.M. and Whitehead, W.E (1991) 'Delayed gastro-intestinal transit times in anorexia nervosa and bulimia nervosa', *Gastroenterology*, 101 (5), 1320–1324.

Katz, E. and Lazerfeld, J. (1955) *Personal Influence*. New York: Free Press.

Kaufman, L. (1980) Prime-time nutrition. *Journal of Communication*, 30 (3), 37–46.

Kaye, W.H. and Welstzin T.E. (1991) Serotonin activity in anorexia and bulimia nervosa: Relationship to the modulation of feeding and food. *Journal of Clinical Psychiatry*, 52 (Supplement), pp. 41–48.

Kenrick, D.T. (1989) 'Bridging social psychology and socio-biology: The case of sexual attraction', in R.W. Bell and N.J. Bell (eds), *Sociobiology and Social Sciences*. Lubbock, TX: Texas Technical University Press. pp. 5–23.

Kenrick, D.T. and Gutierres, S.E. (1980) Contrast effects and judgments of physical attractiveness: When beauty becomes a social problem. *Journal of Personality and Social Psychology*, 38, 131–140.

King, N., Touyz, C. and Charles, M. (2000) The effects of body dissatisfaction on women's perceptions of female celebrities. *International Journal of Eating Disorders*, 27 (3), 341–347.

Klassen, M.L., Wauer, S.M. and Cassel, S. (1990) Increases in health and weight loss claims in food advertising in the eighties. *Journal of Advertising Research*, 30 (6), 32–57.

Klein, J.D., Brown, J.D., Childers, K.W., Oliveri, J., Porter, C. and Dykers, C. (1993) Adolescents' risky behaviour and mass media use. *Pediatrics*, 92, 24–31.

Korner, J. and Leibel, R.L (2003) 'To Eat or Not to Eat – How the gut talks to the brain', in *NEJM* 4 September, PrespectiveVolume 349:926-928 http://www.medical-journals.com/r03049a.htm

Lacan, J. (1976) *The Language of Self* (trans. Anthony Willden). Baltimore: Johns Hopkins University Press.

Lacan, J. (1977) *Ecrits*. London: Tavistock.

Lamb, C.S., Jackson, L., Cassidy, P. and Priest, D. (1993) Body figure preferences of men and women: A comparison of two generations. *Sex Roles*, 28, 345–358.

Lasegue, C. (1873) On hysterical anorexia. *Medical Times and Gazette*, 2, 6/27 September, pp. 265–266, 367–369.

Lavine, H., Sweeney, D. and Wagner, S.H. (1999) Depicting women as sex objects in television advertising: Effects on body dissatisfaction. *Personality and Social Psychology Bulletin*, 25 (II), 1049–1058.

Lavrakas, P.J. (1975) Female preferences for male physiques. *Journal of Research in Personality*, 9, 324–334.

Lawson, M.C. (1980) Development of body build stereotypes, peer ratings and self-esteem in Australian children. *Journal of Psychology*, 104, 111–118.

Leibowitz, S.F. (1987) 'Hypothalamic neurotransmitters in relation to normal and disturbed eating patterns', in R.J. Wurtman and J.J. Wurtman (eds), *Human Obesity*. New York: New York Academy of Sciences.

Lerner, R.M. (1969a) The development of stereotyped expectancies of body build behaviour relations. *Child Development*, 40, 137–141.

Lerner, R.M. (1969b) Some female stereotypes of male body build-behaviour relations. *Perceptual and Motor Skills*, 28, 363–366.

Lerner, R.M. and Gellert, E. (1969) Body build identification, preference, and aversion in children. *Developmental Psychology*, 1, 456–462.

Lerner, R.M. and Karabenick, S.A. (1974) Physical attractiveness, body attitudes, and self-concept in late adolescents. *Journal of Youth and Adolescence*, 3, 307–316.

Lerner, R.M., Karabenick, S.A. and Stuart, J. L. (1973) Relations among physical attractiveness, body attitudes and self-concept in male and female college students. *Journal of Psychology*, 85, 119–129.

Lerner, R.M., Orlos, J.B. and Knapp, J.A. (1976) Physical attractiveness, physical effectiveness, and self-concept in late adolescents. *Adolescence*, 11, 313–326.

Levi-Strauss, C. (1958/1972) *Structural Anthropology*. Harmondsworth: Penguin.

Levine, M.P. and Smolak, L. (1996) Media as a context for the development of disordered eating, in L. Smolak, M.P. Levine and R. Striegel-Moore (eds), *The Developmental Psychopathology of Eating Disorders: Implications for Research, Prevention and Treatment*. Mahwah, NJ: Lawrence Erlbaum Associates. pp. 235–257.

Levine, M.P., Smolak, L. and Hayden, H. (1994) The relation of sociocultural factors to eating attitudes and behaviours among middle school girls. *Journal of Early Adolescence*, 14 (4), 471–490.

Lockett, J. (2002) Why women want to shape up like Kylie. *Daily Mail*, 24 April, p. 25.

Lynch, S.M. and Zellner D.A. (1999) Figure preferences in two generations of men: The use of figure drawings illustrating differences in muscle mass. *Sex Roles*, 40 (9/10), 833–843.

MacDonald, M. (1995) *Representing Women: Myths of Femininity in Popular Media*. London: Edward Arnold.

Mahoney, E.A. and Finch, M.D. (1976a) Body-cathexis and self-esteem: A reanalysis of the differential contribution of specific body aspects. *Journal of Social Psychology*, 99, 251–258.

Mahoney, E.R. and Finch, M.D. (1976b) The dimensionality of body-cathexis. *Journal of Psychology*, 92, 277–279.

Makkar, J.K. and Strube, M.J. (1995) Black women's self-perceptions of attractiveness following exposure to white versus black beauty standards: The moderating role of racial identity and self-esteem. *Journal of Applied Social Psychology*, 25 (17), 1547–1556.

Maloney, M.J., McGuire, J.B., Daniels, S.R. and Specker, B. (1989) Dieting behaviour and eating attitudes in children. *Paediatrics*, 84, 482–489.

Malson, H. (1998) *The Thin Woman*. London: Routledge.

Markus, H. (1977) Self-schema and processing information about the self. *Journal of Personality and Social Psychology*, 35, 63–78.

Markus, H. and Sentis, K. (1982) 'The self in information processing', in M. Cantor and J. Kihlstrom (eds), *Social Psychological Perspectives on the Self*. Hillsdale, NJ: Lawrence Erlbaum Associates. pp. 27–45.

Markus, H., Crane, M., Bernstein, S. and Siladi, M. (1982) Self-schemas and gender. *Journal of Personality and Social Psychology*, 42 (1), 38–50.

Markus, H., Hamill, R. and Sentis, K. (1987) Thinking fat: Self-schemas for body-weight and the processing of weight relevant information. *Journal of Applied Social Psychology*, 17 (1), 50–71.

Martin, M.C. and Gentry, J.W. (1997) Stuck in the model trap: The effects of beautiful models in ads on female pre-adolescents and adolescents. *Journal of Advertising*, 26, 19–33.

Martin, M.C. and Kennedy, P.F. (1993) Advertising and social comparison: Consequences for female preadolescents and adolescents. *Psychology and Marketing*, 10, 513–530.

Martin, M.C. and Kennedy, P.F. (1994) 'Social comparison and the beauty of advertising models: The role of motives for comparison', in C.T. Allen and D. Roedder John (eds), *Advances in Consumer Research*, Vol. 21. Provo, UT: Association for Consumer Research. pp. 365–371.

Martin, M.C., Gentry, J.W. and Hill, R.P. (1999) 'The beauty myth and the persuasiveness of advertising: A look at adolescent girls and boys', in M.C. Macklin and L. Carlson (eds), *Advertising to Children: Concepts and Controversies*. Thousand Oaks, CA: Sage. pp. 165–187.

Martinez, E.T. and Spinetti, M. (1997) Behaviour therapy in Argentina. *The Behaviourist Therapist*, 20, 171–174.

Masterson, J.F. (1977) 'Primary anorexia nervosa in the borderline adolescent – an object-relations view', in Hartocollis, P. (ed.), *Borderline Personality Disorders*. New York: International Universities Press.

Maude, D., Wertheim, E.H., Paxton, S., Gibbons, K. and Szmukler, C. (1993) Body dissatisfaction, weight loss behaviours, and bulimic tendencies in Australian adolescents with an estimate of female data representativeness. *Australian Psychologist*, 28, 128–132.

Mazur, A. (1986) US trends in feminine beauty and overadaption. *Journal of Sex Research*, 22, 281–303.

McCreary, D.A. and Sasse, D.K. (2000) An exploration of the drive for muscularity in adolescent boys and girls. *Journal of the American College of Health*, 48 (6), 297–304.

McLoughlin, Linda (2000) *The Language of Magazines*. London: Routledge.

McRobbie, Angela (1995) *Feminism and Youth Culture*, 2nd edn. London: Macmillan.

McRobbie, Angela (1996) 'More!: New sexualities in girls' and women's magazines', in James Curran et al. (eds), *Cultural Studies and Communications*. London: Arnold.

Mecklenburg, R.S., Loriaux, D.L., Thompson, R.H., Anderson, A.E. and Lipsett, M.B. (1974) Hypothalamic dysfunction in patients with anorexia nervosa. *Medicine*, 53, 147–157.

Mendelson, D.K. and White, D.A. (1982) Relation between body-esteem and self-esteem of obese and normal children. *Perceptual and Motor Skills*, 54, 899–905.

Miller, T.M., Coffman, J.G. and Linke, R.A. (1980) Survey on body-image, weight, and diet of college students. *Journal of the American Dietetic Association*, 77, 561–566.

Millman, M. (1981) *Such a Pretty Face: Being Fat in America*. New York: W.W. Norton.

Mintz, L.B. and Betz, N.E. (1986) Sex differences in the nature, realism, and correlates of body image. *Sex Roles*, 15, 185–195.

Mintz, L.B. and Betz, N.E. (1988) Prevalence and correlates of eating disordered behaviours among undergraduate women. *Journal of Counseling Psychology*, 35, 463–471.

Mizes, J.S. (1988) Personality characteristic bulimia and non-eating-disordered female controls: A cognitive-behavioural perspective. *International Journal of Eating Disorders*, 7, 541–550.

Morley, D. (1992) *Television Audiences and Cultural Studies*. London: Comedia.

Morris, A., Cooper, T. and Cooper, P.J. (1989) The changing shape of female fashion models. *International Journal of Eating Disorders*, 8, 593–596.

Mort, F. (1987) *Dangerous Sexualities: Medico-moral Politics in England since 1830*. London: Routledge.

Mort, F. (1988) 'Boys own? Masculinity, style and popular culture', in R. Chapman and J. Rutherford (eds), *Male Order: Unwrapping Masculinity*. London: Lawrence and Wishart.

Motz, A. (2001) *The Psychology of Female Violence: Crimes against the Body*. Hove: Brunner–Routledge.

Mundell, E.J. (2002) Sitcoms, Videos Make Even Fifth-Graders Feel Fat. Reuters Health http://story.news.yahoo.com/news?tmpl=story2&cid=594&ncid=594&e= 2&u=/nm/20020826/hl_nm/obesity_television_dc_1

Myers, P.N. and Biocca, F.A. (1992) The elastic body image: The effect of television advertising and programming on body image distortion in young women. *Journal of Communication*, 42 (3), 108–133.

Ndangam, L. (2003) British Newspapers' Coverage of Child Sexual Abuse: Relating News to Policy and Social Discourses. PhD thesis, University of Sheffield.

Nemeroff, C.J. (1995) Bodies in the Media: Emerging Trends as Reflected in Magazine Article Content. Paper presented at the annual meeting of the Eastern Psychological Association, Boston, MA.

Nemeroff, C.J., Stein, R.I., Diehl, N.S. and Smilak, K.M. (1994) From the Cleavers to the Clintons: Role choices and body orientation as reflected in magazine article content. *International Journal of Eating Disorders*, 16 (2), 167–176.

Newman, J.P., Wallace, J.F., Strauman, T.J., Skolaski, R.L., Oreland, K.M., Mattek, P.W., Elder, K.B. and McNeely, J. (1993) Effects of motivational significant stimuli on the regulation of dominant responses. *Journal of Personality and Social Psychology*, 1, 165–175.

Nichter, M. and Nichter, M. (1991) Hype and weight. *Medical Anthropology*, 13, 249–284.

Nixon, S. (1996) *Hard Looks: Masculinities, Spectatorship and Contemporary Consumption*. London: UCL Press.

Nixon, S. (1997) 'Exhibiting masculinity', in S. Hall (ed.) *Representation: Cultural Representation and Signifying Practices*. London: Sage.

Norris, P. (1987) *Politics and Sexual Equality: The Comparative Position of Women in Western Democracies*. Brighton: Wheatsheaf.

Nylander, I. (1971) The feeling of being fat and dieting in a school population. *Acta Socio-Medica Scandinavia*, 1, 17–26.

O'Sullivan, T. Dutton, B. and Rayner, P. (1994) *Studying the Media*. London: Edward Arnold.

O'Dea, J.A. and Abraham, S. (2000) Improving the body image, eating attitudes and behaviours of young male and female adolescents: A new educational approach that focuses on self-esteem. *International Journal of Eating Disorders*, 28 (1), 43–57.

Ogden, J. (1992) *Fat Chance! The Myth of Dieting Explained*. London: Routledge.

Ogden, J. and Mundray, K. (1996) The effect of the media on body satisfaction: The role of gender and size. *European Eating Disorders Review*, 4, 171–181.

Ogletree, S.M., Williams, W.W., Raffield, P., Mason, B. and Fricke, K. (1990) Female attractiveness and eating disorders: Do children's television commercials play a role? *Sex Roles*, 22, 791–797.

Orbach, S. (1978) *Fat is a Feminist Issue*. Feltham: Hamlyn.

Orbach, S. (1993) *Hunger Strike*, London: Penguin.

Palazzoli, M.S. (1978) *Self-Starvation*. New York: Jason Aronson.

Palmer, R.L. (1979) The dietary chaos syndrome: A useful new term? *British Journal of Medical Psychology*, 52, 187–190.

Palmer, R.L., Oppenheimer, R., Dignon, A., Chaloner, D. and Howells, K. (1990) Childhood sexual experience with adults reported by women with eating disorders: An extended series. *British Journal of Psychiatry*, 156, 699–703.

Parham, E.S., Frigo, V.L. and Perkins, A.H. (1982) Weight control as portrayed in popular magazines. *Journal of Nutritional Education*, 14, 153–156.

Pierce, K. (1990) A feminist theoretical perspective on the socialisation of teenage girls through *Seventeen* magazine. *Sex Roles*, 23, 491–500.

Pirk, K.M. and Ploog, D. (1986) 'Psychobiology of anorexia nervosa', in R.J. Wurtman and J.J. Wurtman (eds), *Nutrition and the Brain*, Vol. 7. New York: Raven Press.

Pierloot, R.A. and Houben, M.E. (1978) Estimation on body dimensions in anorexia nervosa. *Psychological Medicine*, 8, 317–324.

Polivy, J. (1976) Perception of calories and regulation of intake in restrained and unrestrained subjects. *Addictive Behaviours*, 1, 237–243.

Polivy, J. and Herman, C.P. (1985) Dieting and binging: A causal analysis. *American Psychologist*, 40, 193–201.

Polivy, J. and Herman, C.P. (1987) Diagnosis and treatment of normal eating. *Journal of Consulting and Clinical Psychology*, 55, 635–644.

Polivy, J., Garner, D.M. and Garfinkel, P.E. (1986) 'Causes and consequences of the current preference for thin female physiques', in C.P. Herman, M.P. Zanna and E.T. Higgins (eds), *Physical Appearance, Stigma and Social Behaviour: The Ontario Symposium*, Vol. 3. Hillsdale, NJ: Lawrence Erlbaum Associates. pp. 89–112.

Pope, H.G. Jr, Gruber, A.J., Mangweth, B. and Bureau, B. (2000) Body image perception among men in three countries. *American Journal of Psychiatry*, 157 (8), 1297–1301.

Posavac, N.D., Posavac, S.S. and Posavac, E.J. (1993) Exposure to media images of female attractiveness and concern with body weight among young women. *Sex Roles*, 38, 187–209.

Porter, R. and Porter, D. (1988) *In Sickness and in Health: The British Experience, 1650–1850*. London: Fourth Estate.

Propp, V. (1968) *Morphology of a Folk Tale* (trans. L. Scott). Bloomington, IN: Indiana University Press.

Pyle, R.L., Neuman, P.A. Halvorson, P.A. and Mitchell, J.E. (1990) An ongoing cross-sectional study of the prevalence of eating disorders in freshman college students. *International Journal of Eating Disorders*, 10 (6), 667–677.

Radner, H. (1989) 'This time's for me: making up and feminine practice', *Cultural Studies*, 3 (3), 301–322.

Ravelli, A.M., Helps, B.A., Devane, S.P., Lask, B.D. and Milla, P.J. (1993) Normal gastric antral myoelectrical activity in early onset anorexia nervosa. *Archives of Disease in Childhood*, 69 (3), 342–346.

Richins, M. (1991) Social comparison and the idealised images of advertising. *Journal of Consumer Research*, 18, 71–83.

Rieves, L. and Cash, T.F. (1996) Social developmental factors and women's body image attitudes. *Journal of Social Behaviour and Personality*, 11, 63–78.

Ritenbaugh, C. (1982) Obesity as a culture-bound syndrome. *Culture, Medicine and Psychiatry*, 6, 347–361.

Roberts, J.V. and Herman, C.P. (1980) Physique Stereotyping: An Integrated Analysis. Paper presented at the Canadian Psychology Association Convention, Calgary.

Rogers, T.B., Kuiper, R.A. and Kirker, W.S. (1977) Self-reference and the encoding of personal information. *Journal of Personality and Social Psychology*, 35, 677–688.

Rolland, K., Farnill, D. and Griffiths, R.A. (1997) Body figure perceptions and eating attitudes among Australian schoolchildren aged 8 to 12 years. *International Journal of Eating Disorders*, 21, 273–278.

Rosen, G.M. and Ross, A.O. (1968) Relationship of body image to self-concept. *Journal of Consulting and Clinical Psychology*, 32, 100.

Rosin, J.C., Saltzberg, E. and Srebnik, D. (1989) Cognitive behaviour therapy for negative body image. *Behaviour Therapy*, 20, 293–404.

Rothblum, E. (1990) Women and weight: Fad and fiction. *Journal of Psychology*, 124, 5–24.

Ruderman, A. and Wilson, G.T. (1979) Weight, restraint, cognitions and counter-regulation. *Behaviour Research and Therapy*, 17, 581–590.

Rudofsky, B. (1972) *The Unfashionable Human Body*. New York: Doubleday.

Sanbonmatsu, D. and Fazio, R. (1991) 'Construct accessibility: Determinants, consequences, and implications for the media', in J. Bryant and D. Zillmann (eds), *Responding to the Screen: Reception and Reaction Processes*. Hillsdale, NJ: Lawrence Erlbaum Associates. pp. 45–63.

Santomastaso, P., Favaro, A., Ferraro, S., Sala, A. and Zanetti, T. (1995) Prevalence of body image disturbance in a female adolescent sample: A longitudinal study. *Eating Disorders: The Journal of Treatment and Prevention*, 3, 342–350.

Sassatelli, R. (2000) 'Interaction, order and beyond: A field analysis of Body Culture within fitness gyms', in M. Featherstone (ed.), *Body Modification*. London: Sage.

Schwartz, D.M., Thompson, M.G. and Johnson, C.L. (1982) Anorexia nervosa and bulimia: The sociocultural context. *International Journal of Eating Disorders*, 1 (3), 20–36.

Scott, D.W. (1987) The involvement of psychosexual factors in the causation of eating disorders: Time for a reappraisal. *International Journal of Eating Disorders*, 36, 199–213.

Seddon, L. and Berry, N. (1996) Media-induced disinihibition of dietary restraint. *British Journal of Health Psychology*, 1, 27–33.

Segal, L. (1990) *Slow Motion: Changing Men, Changing Masculinities*. London: Virago.

Seid, R.P. (1989) *Never Too Thin: Why Women Are at War with Their Bodies*. New York: Prentice-Hall.

Selvini-Palazzoli, M. (1974) *Self-Starvation – From the Intrapsychic to the Transpersonal Approach to Anorexia Nervosa*. London: Chaucer Publishing.

Serdulla, M.K., Collins, M.E., Williamson, D.F., Anda, R.F., Pamuk, E. and Buyers, T.E. (1993) Weight control practices of US adolescents and adults. *Annals of Internal Medicine*, 119, 667–671.

Shaw, S.M. and Kemeny, L. (1989) Fitness promotion for adolescent girls: The impact and effectiveness of promotional material which emphasizes the slim ideal. *Adolescence*, 24 (95), 677–687.

Sheldon, W.H. and Stevens, S.S. (1942) *The Varieties of Temperament: A Psychology of Constitutional Differences*. New York: Harper.

Shilling, C. (2003) *The Body and Social Theory*, 2nd edn. London: Sage.

Shontz, S. (1969) *Perceptual and Cognitive Aspects of Body Experience*. New York: Academic Press.

Signorelli, N. and Morgan, M. (1990) *Cultivation Analysis: New Directions in Media Effects Research*. Newbury Park, CA: Sage.

Silverstein, B., Perdue, L., Peterson, B. and Kelly, E. (1986) The role of mass media in promoting a thin standard of bodily attractiveness for women. *Sex Roles*, 14 (9/10), 519–532.

Silverstein, B., Peterson, B. and Perdue, L. (1986) Some correlates of the thin standard of physical attractiveness of women. *International Journal of Eating Disorders*, 5, 898–905.

Silverstein, L., Streigel-Moore, R.H., Timko, C. and Rodin, J. (1988) Behavioural and psychological implications of the thin standard of bodily attractiveness for women. *International Journal of Eating Disorders*, 5, 907–916.

Singh, D. (1993) Body shape and female attractiveness: The critical role of waist-to-hip ratio (WHR). *Human Nature*, 4, 297–321.

Slade, P.D. (1977) Awareness of body dimensions during pregnancy: An analogue study. *Psychological Medicine*, 3, 245–252.

Slade, P.D. and Russell, G. (1973) Awareness of body dimensions in anorexia nervosa: Cross sectional and longitudinal studies. *Psychological Medicine*, 3, 188–199.

Sleet, D.A. (1969) Physique and social image. *Perceptual and Motor Skills*, 28, 295–299.

Smith, M.C. and Thelen, M.T. (1984) Development and validation of a test for bulimia. *Journal of Consulting and Clinical Psychology*, 52, 863–872.

Smolak, L., Levine, M.P. and Gralen, S. (1993) The impact of puberty and dating on eating problems among middle school girls. *Journal of Youth and Adolescence*, 22, 355–368.

Sobal, J. and Stunckard, A. (1989) Socio-economic status and obesity: A review of the literature. *Psychological Bulletin*, 105, 260–275.

Sours, J.A. (1974) The anorexia nervosa syndrome. *International Journal of Psychoanalysis*, 55, 567–576.

Spence, J.T., Helmreich, R. and Stapp, J. (1975) Ratings of self and peers on sex-role attributes and their relation to self-esteem and conceptions of masculinity and femininity. *Journal of Personality and Social Psychology*, 32, 29–39.

Spillman, D.M. and Everington, C. (1989) Somatotype revisited: Have the media changed our perception of the female body image? *Psychological Reports*, 64, 887–890.

Spitzack, C. (1990) *Confessing Excess*. Albany, NY: State University of New York Press.

Staffieri, J.R. (1967) A study of social stereotype of body image in children. *Journal of Personality and Social Psychology*, 7, 101–104.

Staffieri, J.R. (1972a) A study of social stereotypes of body image in children. *Journal of Personality and Social Psychology*, 7, 101–104.

Staffieri, J.R. (1972b) Body build and behavioural expectancies in young females. *Developmental Psychology*, 6, 125–127.

Steiner, H., Smith, C., Rosenkrantz, R.T. and Litt, L. (1991) The early care and feeding of anorexics, *Child Psychiatry and Human Development*, 21 (3) 163–167.

Stephens, D.L., Hill, R.P. and Hanson, C. (1994) The beauty myth of female consumers: The controversial role of advertising. *Journal of Consumer Affairs*, 28, 137–153.

Stern, S., Whittaker, C.A., Hagerman, N.J. and Bargman, C.J. (1981) Anorexia nervosa: The hospital's role in family treatment', *Family Process*, 20, 395–408.

Stevenson, S. (2000) Big 'is not beautiful', *Daily Mail*, 12 October, p. 10.

Stice, E. and Shaw, H.E. (1994) Adverse effects of the media portrayed thin-ideal on women and linkages to bulimic symptoms. *Journal of Social and Clinical Psychology*, 13, 288–308.

Stice, E., Schupak-Neuberg, E., Shaw, H.E. and Stein, R. (1994) Relation of media exposure to eating disorder symptomatology: An examination of mediating mechanisms. *Journal of Abnormal Psychology*, 103, 836–840.

Stormer, S.M. and Thompson, J.K. (1995) Explanations of body image disturbance: A test of maturational status, negative verbal commentary, social comparison, and sociocultural hypotheses. *International Journal of Eating Disorders*, 19, 193–202.

Story, L. (1976) Caricature and impersonating the other: Observations from psychotherapy of anorexia nervosa. *Psychiatry*, 39, 176–188.

Stoutjesdyk, D. and Jevne, R. (1993) Eating disorders among high performance athletes. *Journal of Youth and Adolescence*, 22 (3), 271–282.

Strauman, T.J. and Higgins, E.T. (1987) Automatic activation of self-discrepancies and emotional syndromes: When cognitive structures influence affect. *Journal of Personality and Social Psychology*, 53, 1004–1014.

Strauman, T.J., Vookles, J., Berenstein, V., Chaiken, S. and Higgins, E.T. (1991) Self-discrepancies and vulnerablility to body dissatisfaction and disordered eating. *Journal of Personality and Social Psychology*, 61, 946–956.

Strauss, J., Doyle, A.E. and Kriepe, R.E. (1994) The paradoxical effect of diet commercials on reinhibition of dietary restraint. *Journal of Abnormal Psychology*, 103, 441–444.

Streigel-Moore, R.H., Wilfley, D.E., Caldwell, M.B., Needham, M.L. and Brownell, K.D. (1996) Weight-related attitudes and behaviours of women who diet to lose weight: A comparison of black dieters and white dieters. *Obesity Research*, 4, 109–116.

Streigel-Moore, R., McAvoy, G. and Rodin, J. (1986) Psychological and behavioural correlates of feeling fat in women. *International Journal of Eating Disorders*, 5, 935–947.

Striegel-Moore, R.H., Silverstein, L.R. and Rodin, J. (1986) Toward an understanding of risk factors for bulimia. *American Psychologists*, 41, 246–263.

Strober, M., Goldenberg, I., Green, J. and Saxon, J. (1979) Body image disturbance in anorexia nervosa during the acute and recuperative phase. *Psychological Medicine*, 9, 695–701.

Stropp, B. (1984) Bulimia: A review of the literature. *Psychological Bulletin*, 91, 247–257.

Sullivan, P.F. (1995) Mortality in anorexia nervosa. *American Journal of Psychiatry,* 152 (7), 1073–1074.

Szyrynski, V. (1973) Anorexia nervosa and psychotherapy. *American Journal of Psychotherapy,* 27, 492–505.

Tantleff-Dunn, S. and Thompson, J.K. (1998) Body image and appearance-related feedback: Recall, judgement, and affective response. *Journal of Social and Clinical Psychology,* 17, 319–340.

Theander, S. (1985) Outcome and prognosis in anorexia nervosa and bulimia: Some results of previous investigations, compared with those of a Swedish long-term study. *Journal of Psychiatric Research* 19 (2/3), 493–508.

Then, D. (1992) *Women's Magazines: Messages They Convey about Looks, Men and Careers.* Paper presented at the 100th annual convention of the American Psychological Association, Washington, DC.

Thompson, C.J. and Hirschmann, E.C. (1995) Understanding the socialised body: A poststructuralist analysis of consumer's self-conceptions, body images, and self-care practices. *Journal of Consumer Research,* 22, 139–153.

Thompson, J.K. (1990) *Body Image Disturbance: Assessment and Treatment.* Elsmford, NY: Pergamon Press.

Thompson, J.K. (1992) 'Body image: Extent of disturbance, associated features, theoretical models, assessment methodologies, intervention strategies and a proposal for a new DSM-IV diagnostic category – Body image disorder', in M. Heren, R.M. Eisler and P.M. Miller (eds), *Progress in Behaviour Modification.* Sycamore, IL: Sycamore. Vol. 28, pp. 3–54.

Thompson, J.K. and Psaltis, K. (1988) Multiple aspects and correlates of body figure ratings: A replication and extension of Fallon and Rozin (1985). *International Journal of Eating Disorders,* 7, 813–818.

Thompson, J.K., Heinberg, L.J. and Tantleff, F. (1991) The Physical Appearance Comparison Scale (PACS). *The Behaviour Therapist,* 14, 174.

Thompson, J.K. (1986) Many women see themselves as roundfaced and pudgy, even when no one else does. *Psychology Today,* 39–44.

Thompson, M.G. and Schwartz, D.M. (1982) Life adjustment of women with anorexia nervosa and anorexic-like behaviour. *International Journal of Eating Disorders,* 1 (2), 47–60.

Thomsen, S.R., McCoy, J.K. and Williams, M. (2000) Reconstructing the world of the anorectic outpatient: Procedures for enhancing trustworthiness and credibility. *The Quantitative Report,* 5 (1–2). Available at http://www.nova.edu/ssss/QR/QR5-1/thomsen.html

Thomsen, S.R., McCoy, J.K. and Williams, M. (2001) Internalizing the impossible: Anorexic outpatients' experiences with women's beauty and fashion magazines. *Eating Disorders,* 9, 49–64.

Thornton, B. and Maurice, J. (1997) Physique contrast effects: Adverse impact of idealised body images for women. *Sex Roles,* 37, 433–439.

Thornton, B. and Moore, S. (1993) Physical attractiveness contrast effect: Implications for self-esteem and evaluations of the social self. *Personality and Social Psychology Bulletin,* 19, 474–480.

Tiggemann, M. and Pickering, A.S. (1996) Role of television in adolescent women's body dissatisfaction and drive for thinness. *International Journal of Eating Disorders*, 20, 199–203.

Tiggemann, M. and Wilson-Barrett, E. (1998) Children's figure ratings: Relationship to self-esteem and negative stereotyping. *International Journal of Eating Disorders*, 23, 83–88.

Tincknell, E., Chambers, T., Van Loon, J. and Hudson, N. (2003) Begging for it: 'New femininities', social agency and moral discourse in contemporary and men's magazines. *Feminist Media Studies*, 3 (1), 47–63.

Toro, J., Cervera, M. and Perez, P. (1988) Body shape, publicity and anorexia nervosa. *Social Psychiatry Epidemiology*, 23, 132–136.

Touyz, S.W., Beumont, P.J., Collins, J.K., McCabe, M. and Jupp, J. (1984) Body shape perception and its disturbance in anorexia nervosa. *British Journal of Psychiatry*, 144, 167–171.

Touyz, S.W., Beumont, P.J., Collins, J.K. and Cowle, I. (1985) Body shape perception in bulimia and anorexia nervosa. *International Journal of Eating Disorders*, 4, 259–265.

Tuchman, G. (1981) 'The symbolic annihilation of women by the mass media', in S. Cohen and J. Young (eds), *The Manufacture of News: Deviance, Social Problems and the Mass Media*. London: Constable.

Tunstall, J. (1996) *Newspaper Power*. Oxford: Clarendon Press.

Van den Bulck, J. (2000) Is television bad for your health? Behaviour and body image of the adolescent 'couch potato'. *Journal of Youth and Adolescence*, 29 (3), 273–288.

Van Dijk, T. (1987) *Communicating Racism: Ethnic Prejudice in Thought and Talk*. London: Sage.

Van Zoonen, L. (1994) *Feminist Media Studies*. London: Sage.

Van Zoonen, L. (1998) 'One of the girls: The changing gender of journalism', in C. Carter, G. Branston and S. Allan (eds) *News, Gender and Power*. London: Routledge.

Vandereycken, W. and Van Deth, R. (1994) *From Fasting Saints to Anorexic Girls*. London: Athlone Press.

Vigersky, R.A. (ed.) (1977) *Anorexic Nervosa*. New York: Raven Press.

Vincent, L.M. (1979) *Competing with the Sylph: Dancers and the Pursuit of the Ideal Body Form*. New York: Andrews and McMeel.

Vincent, M.A. and McCabe, M.P. (2000) Gender differences among adolescents in family and peer influences on body dissatisfaction, weight loss, and binge eating behaviours. *Journal of Youth and Adolescence*, 29 (2), 205–211.

Waddington, D., Wykes, M. and Critcher, C. (1991) *Split at the Seams*. Buckingham: Open University Press.

Wagner, B.S., Hartmann, A.M. and Geist, C.R. (2000) Effect of exposure to photographs of thin models on self-consciousness in female college students. *Psychological Reports*, 86 (3) (Pt 2), 1149–1154.

Walker, R.N. (1962) Body build and behaviour in young children: I. Body and nursery school teacher's ratings. *Monographs of the Society for Research in Child Development*, 27, No. 3.

Waller, G., Hamilton, K. and Shaw, J. (1992) Media influences on body size estimation in eating disordered and comparison subjects. *British Review of Bulimia and Anorexia Nervosa*, 6, 81–87.

Warner, M. (1985) *Monuments and Maidens: The Allegory of the Female Form*. London: Picador.

Wassenaar, D., Le Grange, D. and Winship, J. (2000) The prevalence of eating disorder pathology in a cross-ethnic population of female students in South Africa. *European Eating Disorders Review*, 8 (3), 225–236.

Weedon, C. (1987) *Feminist Practice and Post Structural Theory*. Oxford: Blackwell.

Wells, W.D. and Siegel, B. (1961) Stereotyped somatotypes. *Psychological Reports*, 8, 73–78.

Werlinger, K., King, T., Clark, M., Pera, V. and Wincze, J. (1997) Perceived changes in sexual functioning and body image following weight loss in an obese female population: A pilot study. *Journal of Sex and Marital Therapy*, 23, 74–78.

Wertheim, E.H., Paxton, S.J., Schutz, H.K. and Muir, S.L. (1997) Why do adolescent girls watch their weight? An interview study examining sociocultural pressures to be thin. *Journal of Psychosomatic Research*, 42, 345–355.

Weston, L.C. and Ruggiero, J.A. (1985/86) The popular approach to women's health issues: A content analysis of women's magazines in the 1970s. *Women and Health*, 19 (4), 47–62.

White, J.H. (1992) Women and eating disorders, Part 1: Significance and sociocultural risk factors. *Health Care for Women International*, 13, 351–362.

Whittaker, A., Davis, M., Shaffer, D. and Johnson, J. (1989) The struggle to be thin: A survey of anorexic and bulimic symptoms in a non-referred adolescent population. *Psychological Medicine*, 19, 143–163.

Wichstrom, L. (1995) Social, psychological and physical correlates of eating problems: A study of the general adolescent population in Norway. *Psychological Medicine*, 25, 567–579.

Wiggins, J., Wiggins, N. and Conger, J. (1968) Correlates of heterosexual somatic preference. *Journal of Personality and Social Psychology*, 10, 82–90.

Wilcox, K. and Laird, J.D. (2000) The impact of media images of super-slender women on women's self-esteem: Identification, social comparison and self-perception. *Journal of Research in Personality*, 34, 278–286.

Williams, J.M. and Currie, C. (2000) Self-esteem and physical development in early adolescence: Pubertal timing and body image. *Journal of Early Adolescence*, 20 (2), 129–149.

Williams, R. (1958) *Culture and Society, 1780–1950*. London: Chatto and Windus.

Williams, R. (1961) *The Long Revolution*. Harmondsworth: Penguin.

Williams, R. (1981) *Culture*. London: Fontana.

Wilson, G.T. and Smith, D. (1989) Assessment of bulimia nervosa: An evaluation of the eating disorders examination. *International Journal of Eating Disorders*, 8, 173–179.

Wingate, B.A. and Christie, M.J. (1978) Ego strength and body image in anorexia nervosa. *Journal of Psychosomatic Research*, 22, 201–204.

Wiseman, C.V., Gray, J.J., Mosimann, J.E. and Ahrens, A.H. (1990) Cultural expectations of thinness in women: An update. *International Journal of Eating Disorders*, 11, 85–89.

Wiseman, C.V., Gunning, F.M. and Gray, J.J. (1993) Increasing pressure to be thin: Nineteen years of diet products in television commercials. *Eating Disorders: The Journal of Treatment and Prevention*, 1, 52–61.

Wolf, N. (1992) *The Beauty Myth: How Images of Beauty Are Used Against Women*. NY: Anchor Books.

Wood, J.V. (1989) Theory and research concerning social comparisons of personal attributes. *Psychological Bulletin*, 106, 231–248.

Wood, J.V. and Taylor, K.L. (1991) 'Serving self-relevant goals through social comparison', in J. Suls and T.A. Wills (eds), *Social Comparison: Contemporary Theory and Research*. Hillsdale, NJ: Lawrence Erlbaum Associates. pp. 23–50.

Wood, K.C., Altabe, M. and Thompson, J.K. (1998) *The Commentary Interpretation Scale: A Measure of Judgement of Neutral Appearance Commentary*. Unpublished manuscript, University of South Florida.

Woodward, K. (ed.) (1999) *Identity and Difference*. London: Sage.

Woody, E.Z., Constanzo, P.R., Leifer, H. and Conger, J. (1980) *The Effects of Taste and Caloric Perceptions on the Eating Behaviour of Restrained and Unrestrained Subjects*. Unpublished manuscript, Duke University, NC.

Worsley, A. (1981) In the eye of the beholder: Social and personal characteristics of teenagers, and their impressions of themselves and fat/slim people. *British Journal of Medical Psychology*, 54, 231–242.

Wyden, P. (1965) *The Overweight Society*. New York: Morrow.

Wykes, M. (1995) 'Passion, marriage and murder: Analysing the press discourse', in R. Dobash, R. Dobash and L. Noaks (eds), *Gender and Crime*. Cardiff: University of Wales Press. pp. 49–77.

Wykes, M. (1998) 'A family affair: Sex, the press and the Wests', in C. Carter, et al. (eds), *News, Gender and Power*. London: Routledge. pp. 233–247.

Wykes, M. (1999) 'The Burrowers: News about tunnellers, tree-dwellers and green guerrillas', in S. Allan, B. Adam and C. Carter (eds) *Environmental Risks and the Media*. London: Routledge.

Wykes, M. (2001) *News, Crime and Culture*. London: Pluto Press.

Wykes, M. (2003) 'September 11th 2002: Reporting, remembering, reconstructing 9/11/2001', in S. Chermak, F. Bailey and M. Brown *Media Representations of 9/11*. Praeger Publishing.

Yates, J. and Taylor, J. (1978) Stereotypes for somatotypes: Shared beliefs about Sheldon's physiques. *Psychological Reports*, 43, 777–778.

Young, A. (1988) Wild women: The censure of the suffragette movement. *International Journal of the Sociology of the Law*, 16, 179–293.

Young, A. (1990) *Femininity in Dissent*. London: Routledge.

Young, A. (1996) *Imagining Crime*. London: Sage.

Young, J.K. (1991) Estrogen and the aetiology of anorexia nervosa. *Neuroscience and Biobehavioral Reviews*, 15 (3) 327–331.

Index

654032